The Shell Book of
BRITISH
WALKS

General Editor
JOHN WHATMORE

The Shell Book of
BRITISH
WALKS

DAVID & CHARLES
Newton Abbot   London

CONTENTS

INTRODUCTION 7

HOW TO USE THIS BOOK 24

MAPS 25

MOUNTAIN WALKS 32

RIVERS AND VALLEYS 61

COASTS 93

MOORLANDS AND HILLS 114

CITY HERITAGE 146

CANAL WALKS 178

WRITERS AND ARTISTS 210

LOWLANDS 239

DOWNLANDS 268

OLD RAILWAY LINES 294

WOODS AND FORESTS 318

MYTHS AND LEGENDS 345

THE CONTRIBUTORS 367

(title page) *Wolds harvest, near Great Driffield, North Humberside* (Geoffrey N. Wright)
(pp 4–5) *Gradient post near Padstow* (John Gibberd) (*see* page 316)

Triple-span iron bridge over Little Petherick Creek (*see* page 316)

Line illustrations by Gill Hayles

British Library Cataloguing in Publication Data
The Shell book of British walks.
1. Great Britain——Description and travel
——1971– ——Guide-books
914.1'04858   DA650

ISBN 0–7153–8810–X

Typeset by ABM Typographics Limited, Hull
and printed in Great Britain
by Butler & Tanner Limited, Frome and London
for David & Charles Publishers plc
Brunel House   Newton Abbot   Devon

INTRODUCTION

Anyone who has known the solid thump of a boot meeting turf in some wild place, and the feeling of satisfaction that flows from it, will be aware of the special relationship which exists between the walker and his environment. In this life so bounded by restrictions and frustrations, there is something special about escaping into our last true freedom – the freedom to wander. To do so is to open up the mind, to let a windy upland or some quiet bridleway help to clear out the accumulation of stale convention and to return, hopefully, better able to deal with the problems that society imposes upon us.

 In a place where the only company is a bootmark of some previous walker still visible in the peaty soil, one is best able to consider not only what the world is all about but also what one's own place in it should be. Life for most of us is a pretty routine affair, for man by his nature is a creature of habit. But built into that nature is a spark, a desire to break away if only for a short time. Man has always been a wanderer. From the first time that some primitive being felt the need to see what was over the horizon, and walked away from what was safe and familiar, the spirit of adventure was born. Indeed, the history of man is entwined with the steady migration of populations across the globe. It is true that such mass movements were essentially undertaken for practical reasons; man moved because circumstances such as drought or the presence of a strong enemy forced him to do so. But are we so sterile in our view of early man that we cannot credit him with deep-seated satisfaction when he tied his few belongings onto his back, or that of his pack animals, and moved onto a new phase in life? Mountain ranges, rivers, deserts; none of these provided any permanent obstacle to early man. Whatever the specific reasons, man was a peripatetic animal; he was also, as we know from the magnificent artefacts that so many cultures produced, capable of appreciating beauty. Would he have been unmoved by the wonders he must have seen?

How important it is that we should not lose that primitive urge to journey always a little further, to want to know what is around the next corner; and if experience teaches us that it is not necessarily something better, at least it will be something different. I recall that when at school in Birmingham, the classroom in which the French lessons were held was on an upper floor, and from my desk, if I squinted to one side, I could see a distant green hill far beyond the rooftops. It had a copse on the southern slope which caught the afternoon sun. That hill was probably responsible for my never learning to speak French very well, but it did instil in me a love of England and a desire always to stand on the next hill.

It is not long before any serious walker is asked by his friends, 'How many miles can you walk in a day?' The answer is rarely very satisfactory or revealing. Twenty? Perhaps but it could be rather more – or much less. It is not the answer which is inadequate but the question; for it implies that the sheer covering of distance is in some way the goal, the elusive something which walking is all about, whereas clearly it is not. 'To travel hopefully is better than to arrive', goes the oft-quoted saying, and any walker will tell you that for him this is true. It might make more sense if one's friends asked, 'How many hours of the day do you actually spend walking?' At least the question would then focus on one reason for our pastime – to travel leisurely through countryside that we love, respect and feel a bond with. Anyone setting out to write down just why he walks is facing a near-impossible task; the reasons are too elusive, too rooted in our deepest selves. Scenery, freedom to wander, companionship or the need to be alone, perhaps all these are important, but they never add up to the full reason that so many people go out of their way to cast off the trappings of civilisation they have struggled so hard to acquire.

Why does the backpacker delight in using the flimsiest nylon tent when he has so recently left behind him a house that he works so hard to afford? Why do so many people, especially later in life, take country walks without any specific commitment to being part of that community called 'ramblers'? Just what is it that is so satisfying? I know of no answers to these questions and perhaps it is better not to ask them. Reading the travels of Robert Louis Stevenson in Spain, George Borrow in Wales or the letters of Tobias Smollett as he huffed and puffed his way through eighteenth-century Europe, tells us much of the delights and hardships that were met along the way, but anyone insisting 'Yes, but why do we do it?' will have to seek the answer deep within himself.

How pleasant it would be, then, if one were able to go on to describe a situation where the delights of these islands were unfettered, where the countryside was protected from urban and industrial development, where the woodlands were free from the roar of the bulldozer and where we could be sure of passing on the wild moorlands and forests to our grandchildren and their descendants – surely their rightful inheritance. These are great days for the rambler, but he should be aware that a battle is raging, and will continue to rage, over the future of the countryside and our access to it; and a bitter battle it will have to be if the land we now enjoy is to continue to be open to us. On the one side are ranged the rambling clubs, conservation groups and many, many individuals who are determined to retain that access. On the other are industrial concerns, builders and developers and, unfortunately, too many of the landowners and farmers who both live in the countryside and live off it; though of course it would be quite wrong to see all farmers and landowners as

The Pennine Way near Horton-in-Ribblesdale (Geoffrey N. Wright)

Track of the Corridor route up Scafell Pike, near the head of Piers Gill. Great Gable is on the right (Geoffrey N. Wright) (*see* page 49)

grasping people, or all ramblers as saints. In a perfect world the conflicting needs would be reconciled in compromise; in fact little of the sort is happening. There is a conflict, however many pious speeches are made in public. But the very large tracts of wild country that have been opened up to walkers by agreement, as in the Peak District, pay tribute to the way in which agreement can be reached. What a pity it is not always like that!

There are an estimated 120,000 miles (over 193,000km) of rural footpaths in England and Wales, yet there is still a huge and unfulfilled demand for access to the countryside. Any new long-distance path that is created – and thereby publicised – is soon pounced upon by eager walkers to the point where a legitimate criticism is that at weekends it is too busy. Footpaths in the Lake District and North Wales are in places literally becoming worn out, and the national parks authorities have to divert them to allow them to be restored. Surveys show that 20 per cent of the people of Britain go for walks of at least 2 miles (3km) once a month. That puts rambling among the most popular outdoor activities in the country, yet the number of footpaths and open spaces is diminishing.

Sometimes footpaths are closed legally, but more often they are ploughed up and not restored, blocked by barbed wire or stiles are knocked down and bridges destroyed. A few hundred yards from the room where I am writing, there is a delightful footpath winding through woodlands and over a favourite hillside from where I can see from Surrey downland across to the Kentish hills. Along that path, which is fortunately well used, are huge notices warning that the land off the path is private and that anyone causing damage will be dealt with 'with the utmost rigour of the law'. These threatening signs have advanced to within a foot of the path; they will be kept at bay only by the concerted action of all who enjoy the countryside.

At the root of the problem is the fact that footpaths, when originally created, were used by country people who had to travel between places of importance to them – from cottage to farm, to church, to a road where a carrier's cart could take them to market, to a village pump and so on. These people were accustomed to handling farm animals and were closely involved in the rural work scene. They were almost entirely local people, well known to the farmers and landowners and so no conflict arose. Now those same paths are used for recreation purposes by people from outside the farming community, often coming from cities, people with very different attitudes to the owners of the land and not always, it must be admitted, behaving correctly. The toll of hedges, stiles and crops which have been damaged has done much to build up a case against the rambler as has the greatest of all sins in the countryside, the allowing of dogs to harass sheep and cattle.

In areas where footpaths are most heavily used, the problem seems to be less marked. Where paths are signposted, where stiles are well maintained and where there is clear direction, little damage is likely to be done. It is where a footpath is indicated at the point where it meets the road, and then the line becomes indistinct, that trouble arises. Every rambler knows the frustration of walking only a few hundred yards along a path to find it disappearing into a ploughed field. If he takes what seems the most sensible course and avoids walking on the newly planted land, he may find himself well off the true right of way and in no position to complete the walk. Regretfully he retraces his steps to the road and so another pathway is under threat through not being used. It is difficult in law to get a widely used path made the subject of an extinguishment order: much easier if it can be shown to be unused. The scores of rambling guides that have been published in recent years show how great is the desire of so many people to get off the beaten track. Let us don a pair of boots or stout shoes and do just that.

NECESSARY·EQUIPMENT

Compared to most pastimes, the walker is fortunate in that the equipment he needs is simple and long lasting; note, that which he *needs*, not what some manufacturer is prepared to sell him. Catalogues from equipment suppliers get fatter and more glossy each year, but a rambler really requires only a relatively small number of items unless he is tackling very high country and/or continually bad weather, such as winter walking in the mountains. The essentials are that he must be able to walk in comfort and remain warm and dry. The first requirement, then, is to be well shod.

Whatever else is economised on, it must not be footwear. This is the walker's single most expensive item of equipment and certainly the most important. First, are boots really essential? It depends on what you are going to do; if your walking is to be restricted to pleasant lowland rambles when the weather is good, no doubt you can get away with merely a strong pair of *well-fitting* shoes. Manufacturers of walking boots also produce shoes which have some of the character of boots, but are lighter. On a summer day they are a pleasure to wear and they even cope well with a small amount of mud, slippery grass and the odd bit of rocky ground. But the pathways of Britain and Ireland do not stay in this ideal condition for long. It wants only a couple of days of rain to turn a footpath into a sea of mud, especially if it is also used by horses. Your rambling will be severely curtailed if you have to stay at home every time the woodlands get a bit soggy. For my money, boots are essential, and you can always leave them behind in preference for a stout pair of shoes if you are undertaking only a local walk.

It is now some years since we saw the revolution in footwear construction which resulted in the truly lightweight boot. Previously ramblers managed with boots that were designed on the lines of those used by the army – a leather boot that was almost indestructible and which supported the ankle well, but which was infernally heavy and took a long time to break in. Advances in technology plus a demand for something better resulted in a boot which was much lighter, and we are now well into the second generation of these boots. Basically, there is a choice between two types: those made with the traditional, though now much lighter, leather uppers, and those constructed from a variety of synthetic fabric materials. There is little doubt that these 'fabric boots' as they are known, though actually they are built up with a combination of fabric and leather, are the lighter of the two; and as weight saved on the feet is traditionally equivalent to five times that carried on the back, this is something to be considered. On the other hand, fabric

Morning clouds from the summit of Cribin, Brecon Beacons (Geoffrey N. Wright) (*see* page 52)

boots do let in some water under very wet conditions, even after following the manufacturer's instructions and spraying them with a proprietary water-proofing solution. Manufacturers are also seeking to overcome the problem that fabric uppers tend to hold water and take some time to dry out. This heightens the danger that the stitching will eventually rot and the metal shanks that hold the laces will corrode. Spraying with a waterproofing solution goes a long way towards easing these problems. Leather boots, however, are not only more waterproof, they also last longer provided they are regularly waxed.

Getting a perfect fit, however, is more important than deciding on the merits of one design of boot against another. When going to the shop, wear the type of stocking that you usually use for walking, and if you are in the habit of using a pair of rag socks as well, take them with you. Unlace the boots in the shop and push your foot forward into the boot until the toes touch its front. There should be enough space between your heel and the inside of the rear of the boot for you to insert your finger. Now push your foot firmly to the back of the boot and lace it up. There should be adequate space in front of your toes so that they are not forced forward against the toe of the boot when you are walking down steep hills. If all is correct, there will be very little movement of your heel inside the boot. The laces do not need to be tightened evenly along the whole length of the boot; try slackening them near the toes and tightening them at the ankle, or the other way round, until the boots feel really comfortable.

Having got a pair of boots that are just right, they will need looking after. Leather boots should be waxed before use or treated with whatever proofing the manufacturer recommends, as this varies according to the method used in the preparation of the leather. Fabric-top footwear needs to be sprayed to improve its water-resistant qualities. Both types should be cleaned thoroughly after use, and be particularly careful to wash away any acidic peaty soil as this can play havoc with even the best boots. They should then be allowed to dry out at room temperature and never be dried before a fire, radiator or other heat source, nor even in the drying room of a mountain hotel or youth hostel. The drying process can be speeded up by stuffing the boots with newspapers, which should be replaced as soon as they have absorbed an appreciable amount of moisture.

'Keep warm, keep dry, and not much harm will come to you' – the old saying is as true today as it ever was. We are fortunate in our choice of rambling as a pastime, that it is as good a sport in the winter as it is during the warmer time of year; indeed, with the right clothes there never need be an 'off season'. The body burns up calories at a great rate while one is walking, ensuring that, provided we are well fed and dry, we remain warm and enjoy that healthy glowing feeling.

The body loses the heat it produces by radiating it to the outside air, so by careful choice of clothing we can reduce the heat loss to an acceptable level. The insulation quality of our clothing depends largely on the amount of air that is trapped in the fabric because air is a poor conductor of heat, which is why two thin sweaters are better than one thick one – an extra layer of air is trapped between the two garments. It follows, then, that clothes such as wool which contains many tiny pockets of air, are warmer than synthetic materials which do not. Wool also has the advantage that it is still a good insulator when wet. At cooler times of year it is difficult to beat woollen shirts and trousers for rambling. Those long colourful shirts can be just the thing, and woollen breeches with a toughened seat are available from specialist walking shops. They are worn with woollen stockings – colourful if you like, more muted if you do not. In really cold conditions it is worth wearing wool next to the skin; a light sweater worn under the shirt gives a feeling of real luxury on a cold morning. At warmer times of year cotton underwear is to be preferred, if only because it is easier to launder. String vests are warm in winter and cool in summer, again because they trap many pockets of air.

Unlike air, water is a good conductor of heat, so once your clothing becomes damp it feels cold. If we walk briskly in clothing totally sealed by an outer garment which will not permit water to pass in or out, it will not be long before we are soaked by our own perspiration however cold it may be outside. To combat this we need a system of ventilation. The usual method is to wear a jacket which, while waterproof, opens down the front, usually fastening with a zip which allows us to vary the amount of ventilation at will. The sort of waterproof anorak which pulls over the head of the walker and has no ventilation, is not suitable for lengthy walks. Such materials as Goretex allow perspiration to evaporate while remaining waterproof, and are becoming popular despite their much higher price. The body loses a surprising amount of its heat through the head so in cold conditions a hat can be a necessity. The headgear need not be elaborate, just a simple woollen cap will work wonders in keeping the body warm. If the weather is wet, the hood of the walker's jacket can be pulled up over it. For mountain walking, woollen balaclava helmets can be bought cheaply which go a long way towards keeping out even a blizzard, and they double well for cleaning the snow off the windscreen of your car when returning from the walk!

When out for a half-day ramble, the rucksack carried need be no more than a container in which to carry lunch, map, an extra sweater and whatever odds and ends the wearer wishes. Heavy loads, however, can only be carried with any degree of comfort when either the rucksack embodies an external frame to distribute the load or is of the anatomic design, where an internal frame is moulded to the shape of the wearer's back and fits him snugly. In either case the sack will embody a padded hip-belt so that the load is not suspended from the walker's shoulders, as is the case with a day-sack, but is largely borne by the hips. Some rucksacks are referred to as 'size tolerant', being made only in one size. These are invariably meant for carrying light loads only; for heavier loads – say anything much more than 10lb (4.5kg) – it is preferable to have a frame sack and, as with everything else that is worn, it must be a good fit.

One last word on rucksacks: whatever type you choose, and whatever the manufacturers claim, do not assume that it is totally waterproof. Belongings should be packed inside plastic bags before putting them in the sack; this not only keeps them clean and dry but helps to give order to the packing of the rucksack. I well remember walking through North Wales on one particularly wet day, and pausing at the top of the Llanberis Pass to open the map compartment. There was so much water in it that the map almost floated out – so be warned.

Further reading:
Sharp, David. *Walking in the Countryside* (David & Charles, 1978)
Wickers, David and Pedersen, Art. *Britain at Your Feet* (Hamlyn, 1981)

Rights·of·Way

ENGLAND AND WALES

A public path in the countryside may either be a footpath, in which case the public has a right of way along it, or a bridleway, where there is a right to walk, ride a horse or a pedal cycle. Let us be quite clear that we have a legal right to use these paths, and in law they are part of the queen's highway just as is any main road and they cannot be closed by the landowner. In fact, the paths can only be closed or diverted after certain legal and public processes.

The safest way to decide whether a path is in fact a right of way is to consult the definitive maps of rights of way prepared by county councils under the Wild Life and Countryside Act of 1981. These maps, which have been produced for all rural areas, are held at the offices of county and district councils and must by law be available for public inspection. Most ramblers, of course, will consult their Ordnance Survey sheets when out walking, which is normally a safe action as the rights of way shown on these were derived from the definitive maps and updated by later amendments. The OS sheet shows the exact date when the information was extracted. The danger is that rights of way change: the course of a path can be diverted, or it can be closed by what is called an extinguishment order, so before getting into any legal arguments it is necessary to check against the council's definitive map.

All land in England and Wales beongs to someone, and under the Highways Act of 1980 the surface of a public path is considered for most purposes to belong to the county council, though the land itself over which the path passes remains the property of the owner of the land on either side. A right of way, as its name implies, merely give a right to pass and repass over the land; it does not follow, therefore, that there is a right, for example, to camp without permission. Nevertheless, there is no need to hurry along the path; the law protects your right to make a *bona fide* journey and to do so without hindrance. There is also the right to take with you what the law calls a 'natural accompaniment', for example a pram or push-chair, and this could also include a dog, though clearly it would have to be kept under proper control.

Public Footpath »

Few public paths became rights of way through the conscious intention of the landowner to make them so, although a landowner may dedicate a path for that purpose. Most came about because they had been used in this way for more than twenty years, so the law assumes that the landowner intends them to be for the use of the public. It is a very important point, however, that the reverse does not apply: a right of way unused for twenty years does not cease to be a public path. As the old legal maxim has it, 'once a highway, always a highway'.

Problems for walkers most frequently arise when a path is found to be obstructed. If the path has merely become overgrown, it should be reported to the highway authority which is responsible for its maintenance – probably the county council, though this task may have been delegated to the local district council. The greater problem arises where a path has been deliberately blocked by a farmer or landowner to prevent the path being used by the public. The immediate question arises: what can the walker do about it before resorting to legal action? Provided that you are a *bona fide* traveller along the path (ie, you have not gone out with the specific intention of moving the obstruction), you can safely move it but only as far as is necessary for you to pass by. If it is possible to go around the obstruction, even if this means stepping off the path, that is what you should do. The point is that the action you take to ensure that you can pass along the footpath should be reasonable. If there is a barbed-wire strand across a path, clamber over or under it and write to the owner of the land and to the local council, but do not cut it or tear it down. Similarly, do not remove any notices that you believe to be illegal. If a sign is placed on a footpath saying 'no right of way' when there is, this is a misleading notice and illegal. Nevertheless, keep your anger in check and report the matter to the council, which has considerable powers to see that such notices are removed.

There are specific rules for farmers wishing to plough up a field across which runs a public path. It is not illegal for the farmer to plough up the path, but he must generally make good the surface of the path to make it reasonable for the public to use it and he must do this within two weeks of starting to plough. If exceptional weather prevents him from doing this within the stipulated time, there are provisions allowing him to delay. But note that the right to plough field-paths relates only to those crossing fields; there is no right for a landowner to plough up a path which runs along the edge of a field or one over which the public has vehicular rights. It is legal and proper for a walker to continue to follow the line of a path which has been ploughed up, even if crops are growing on it, but it is necessary to avoid unnecessary damage and to stick rigidly to the line of the path. It is tempting to walk instead around the edge of the field, and while this might seem to be good sense, in fact it would be trespassing as there is no legal right to be along the edge of the field, and once the true line of the path has been walked, others can follow more easily.

Another vexed question concerns bulls kept in fields across which run public paths. The former local bylaws have been replaced with national legislation under the Wildlife and Countryside Act of 1981. This act bans bulls of a 'recognised dairy breed' from fields crossed by public paths under all circumstances and bans all other bulls unless with cows and heifers. If such bulls act in a way which endangers the public, an offence may have been committed under the Health and Safety at Work Act 1974. Incidentally, the recognised dairy breeds are Ayrshire, British Friesian, British Holstein, Dairy Shorthorn, Guernsey, Jersey and Kerry. However, all breeds of bull can be dangerous and any walker entering a field with a bull in it is taking a risk.

There is another type of thoroughfare frequented by ramblers, namely what appears on the OS maps as 'a road used as a public path'. These are usually unsurfaced, broad trackways which often carry some motor traffic, frequently to farm buildings. The classification came about under the National Parks Act of 1949 when it was intended to ensure that the roads were recorded on the definitive maps and so not lost completely. Gradually, all these ways are being reclassified, and they will become either footpaths, bridleways or byways open to all traffic. The rights of the walker on roads used as public paths are at least as great as over bridleways.

On uncultivated land, such as moorland or mountainous areas, there is no general legal right to walk, although some progress is being made in obtaining access agreements under which the owners of the land are normally compensated by the government for the inconvenience. This has been particularly successful in the Peak District, though it has yet to be copied on a large scale elsewhere. Frequently there is no objection to walkers crossing wild areas of country, but this is a custom and not a right. It may also vary depending on the time of year. On grouse moors, for example, walkers will be unpopular in the breeding season or when shooting is under way, but there may be no objection at other times.

Further reading:
The Ramblers' Association is extremely active in working to reduce the number of footpaths lost each year and publishes various helpful leaflets. Their address is 1–5 Wandsworth Road, London SW8 2LJ.

British Trust for Conservation Volunteers. *Footpaths, a Practical Handbook* (36 St Mary's Street, Wallingford, Oxfordshire, 1983)
Clayden, Paul and Trevelyan, John. *Rights of Way: A Guide to Law and Practice*, Open Spaces Society and Ramblers' Association (see address above, 1983)

SCOTLAND

Unlike England, Scotland has no general procedure for registering public rights of way, and so these are not shown on the Ordnance Survey maps of Scotland, although local planning authorities in many areas are now preparing maps showing rights of way within their areas. This absence of clearly defined paths may at first seem confusing, but in practice the walker north of the Border is in a happy position and in the hills is likely to meet only courtesy and friendliness from tenants, keepers and shepherds if he shows thought for the sporting and agricultural interests of the countryside. Indeed, as that excellent organisation, the Scottish Rights of Way Society, points out, the access to the mountains problem, which has been such a troublesome issue in England and Wales, has scarcely arisen in Scotland.

Nevertheless, there are from time to time disputes in Scotland over whether a particular path is a right of way, and the rules concerning these are fairly straightforward. There are four elements if a public right of way is to exist at law: the path must have been used by the general public for a continuous period of at least twenty years; the use must be a matter of right and not attributable to mere tolerance on the part of the landowner; it must connect two public places or places to which the public habitually and legitimately resort; and it must follow a route which is more or less defined. Let us take each of these points in turn.

First, the twenty-year 'prescriptive period' as this is known. It is not necessary that this be the last twenty years; it is sufficient that the route has been used at any time within the past twenty years and for a period of twenty uninterrupted years before that time. When it comes to the second question, use as a matter of right, the law recognises that if a landowner has allowed the use of the path by the public for twenty years, it would be unjust if his generosity were used as grounds for his being prevented from closing it. Whether the public use is a matter of right or due only to the tolerance of the owner is a matter to be decided in the circumstances of each case. Where, however, the landowner *has* allowed uninterrupted use of a route, there is a strong presumption of the existence of a right of way. The question of the route beginning and ending in a public place is fairly straightforward, though where a path to the coast is involved it is worth remembering that the seashore is public only where the public are in the habit of resorting, eg for swimming. However, the public does have the inalienable right to walk anywhere on the foreshore, ie the area below highwater mark. Finally there is the question of a 'reasonably defined route'. It is not necessary that there be a visible track or that the route be marked in any way, but it must be shown that the public have followed a more or less consistent and generally defined route. Minor deviations are of no importance.

Further reading:
Scottish Rights of Way Society. *Rights of Way: A Guide to the Law in Scotland* (1 Lutton Place Edinburgh, EH8 9OD, 1986)

SAFETY·IN·HIGH·COUNTRY

The hills and mountains of Britain and Ireland are small by the standards of the huge ranges of mainland Europe, a fact which all too often leads people to underestimate the severity of the weather that can be experienced there even in summer. The proximity of much high ground to the west of Britain and the frequency of westerly winds off the sea mean that a mixture of rain, wind and snow will be all too frequent. There are not many greater delights to the serious walker than to tramp the wild ridge of a mountain with the country falling away on both sides, but the tragic number of deaths which occur in our hills each year warns us all to take precautions when in high country.

Perhaps the greatest asset one can take into the hills is a healthy respect for the dangers they hold. To venture into the mountains is to match one's skills against the dangers; it is when caution and common sense are sacrificed to achieve a predetermined aim that the dangers both to oneself and to those who may have to try a rescue make the situation a foolhardy one.

First, then, take the right equipment and know how to use it. It ought to be unnecessary to say that no one should go into the mountains without suitable boots, but among those who find themselves in trouble each year are sure to be some wearing only training shoes or other totally unsuitable footwear. Second, it is no use taking a map and compass unless one knows how to use them, so learn and practise the techniques again and again – don't wait for the mist to come down. Once you feel confident in your ability to use a compass, trust it; it is far more accurate than your sense of direction.

Cold is a killer in the hills. For every thousand feet of height you gain, the temperature will fall by between 3 and 5 degrees Fahrenheit, depending on the humidity. The winds will also be stronger higher up, making the summits seem even colder than one would expect. Add to this the effect created by rain or mist wetting the skin of the walker and it does not take much imagination to see how quickly life can be put in danger. Clearly, a hill walker needs really good woollen clothing and an outer shell garment which must be windproof and waterproof; he must also have a hat, adequate supplies of extra warm clothing, emergency food and a first-aid kit. He must have something more, a feeling for the hills and a knowledge of how the weather can behave in wild places – something that comes only from experience and being willing to learn from others who have spent much of their lives in our lonely uplands.

Mindful of the need for instruction, the British Mountaineering Council has produced an excellent booklet called *Safety on Mountains* which sets out the basics of looking after yourself in the hills. I cannot do better than quote from its summary on safety precautions:

BEFORE YOU SET OUT

- Carry a map of a least 1:50 000 scale.
- Have spare warm clothing, especially gloves, balaclava and spare sweater as well as windproof and waterproof outer garments.
- Carry emergency rations (and don't eat them en route!)
- Carry a whistle, torch and small first-aid kit in case of accident.
- Leave information of your route at, for example, your youth hostel, hotel or guest house; or at a police station, information centre or mountain rescue post or, best, on day trips, at home. Then keep to this route.
- Until you have a great deal of experience, never go out on mountains alone – the safest number is four or more.
- Know where your local mountain rescue posts and nearest telephones are situated.

PLANNING YOUR ROUTE

- Estimate the time that it will take and make sure that you have sufficient hours of daylight, leaving a wide safety margin for any miscalculation or delay.
- Remember that the weather can change very quickly; if conditions are bad in the valley they will be considerably worse higher up, and a walk that you found easy in summer may be very different in winter. Always plan your route in relation to the prevailing conditions and be very cautious about what you attempt in bad weather.
- Do not overestimate your own stamina or ability.
- Treat hills with very great respect in snow conditions and do not go up snow-covered mountains unless you are familiar with the techniques of snow and ice climbing and the use of an ice axe. Plan your day accordingly.

OUT ON THE HILLS

- Never let anyone get left behind. A party should always stay together moving at the pace of the slowest.
- Never be afraid of turning back if the weather worsens or you realise that the route is too long or too hard for you.
- If you wear boots soled with composition rubber, be sure that you are aware of their limitations – slippery on wet grass; lichened, mossy or greasy rock; ice or hard snow.
- On a steep slope be very careful not to dislodge loose rocks onto those below. When rock scrambling, a party should keep close together so that if a stone is dislodged it will not have had much time to gather momentum should it hit one of the party below. On a scree slope it is better to zigzag or adopt an arrowhead formation.

ON THE DESCENT

Most mountain accidents occur on the descent from a peak when, once the climb is over, there is a tendency to become hasty and careless. Particular points to note are,

- Don't take a short cut; invariably the path takes the safest, easiest and quickest way.
- Always descend the longer, more gradual side of a mountain; scrambling down steep rocky ground can be very dangerous.
- Never run or glissade down a slope unless you can see a clear way to the bottom.
- Do not follow streams downhill, they may end in a waterfall.

IF YOU GET LOST

Stay together, sit down and keep calm. Carefully work out from your map your approximate position and consider whether to stop or continue. If the latter, decide which way to go and then trust your compass. If a member of the group is exhausted or if you find that darkness is descending and you are still on the mountain, it is better not to try to get down in the dark unless the whole group can move on and you are on a path or quite certain of the route. Map reading at night is extremely difficult and one cannot tell the difference between a boulder and a precipice. Accept the fact that you are out for the night, look around for some shelter from the wind and make yourself as comfortable as possible. You should, of course, be carrying spare clothing and emergency rations.

If the weather and visibility are good you will be able to descend next morning to another valley, then get word to your original destination before a search party is sent out. If at dawn the weather and visibility are poor so that you feel it is dangerous to try to move, give the international distress signal in case a rescue party is searching for you. The signal is six blasts on a whistle (or six shouts or flashes of a torch) followed by a pause of a minute and then a repetition of the six blasts. If your signals are eventually heard you should hear an answering whistle – three blasts followed by a pause of a minute repeated several times. If your whistle or torch is missing and your voice does not carry because of the wind, you can wave a white or coloured cloth.

Further reading: British Mountaineering Council. *Safety on Mountains* (Crawford House, Booth St, Manchester, M13 9RZ, 1975)

Northern·Ireland· and·the·Republic

The sheer logistical problems of compiling this book have meant that the routes have had to be confined to England, Wales and Scotland; but that is not the sum total of these islands of ours. Northern Ireland and the Republic of Ireland have mountains, moors, peat bogs, rivers and valleys which will match any country in the world as a walker's heaven. But Ireland, both sides of the border, consists not only of geographical features: it is the people of the land that makes it what it is. These delightful folk are so often parodies of themselves, stage Irishmen with blue twinkling eyes, tousled hair and a way of looking at life that turns it upside down. They will walk far out of their way to put a stranger on the right track, make him a pot of tea in some remote cottage, or just give him a cheery word to help him on his way.

Do not always expect them to be strictly truthful, for sure; that would be unkind. Why tell a man it is five miles to the next town when he would be happier believing it is only two? Long ago, the author sat in the bar of a pub in Kerry and listened to the conversation about a new signpost erected in the village. ' 'Tis a fine signpost', said one man. His companion nodded silently, then the first man added, 'But 'tis pointing the wrong way'. Perhaps it still is.

How·to·Use·this·Book

Unlike many walking books, this Shell Guide is arranged on a thematic basis, ie each chapter groups walks with a common theme and includes rambles on that theme in many parts of the country. There are mountain walks, strolls through gentle lowlands, studies of our most beautiful cities; there are walks through wild places where the mists drift over the moors and where the only sound is the mournful cry of the curlew; there are rambles along old canals, disused railway lines; there is a chapter of walks in the realm of myths and legends, and one on walks associated with a writer or artist.

Much discussion went into how best to present a book that is essentially practical yet which it is hoped will be uplifting in its enthusiastic approach and inspire walkers to try new experiences – or just give them a taste of another sort of walking while relaxing in an armchair on a dark night. We decided against printing sketch maps for each ramble as, because of the problems of scale, these can never match the detail available on the 1:50 000 Ordnance Survey sheets which we presume any walker is likely to carry. Where there may be some difficulty in finding the starting point to a walk, grid references have been included, otherwise they have been omitted, but always the relevant OS sheet numbers are included. A map of Britain, and more detailed regional maps, are provided as a key to indicate the position of each walk. North American readers should be reassured that the detailed Ordnance Survey sheet (approximately 1¼ mile to 1 inch) is always available locally and contains so much more and varied information than could have been possible even in detailed maps prepared especially for the book. The regional maps in the book will allow for advance planning of itineraries, but should you wish to obtain the OS maps in advance, they are available by mail from Edward Stanford Ltd, 12 Long Acre, London WC2.

The majority of walks begin and end at the same point and, as most of us today use cars, some indication of parking space has been given. In the case of walking old railway lines and canals, it was often not possible to make the walks circular. Where appropriate, indications have been given of bus and train services for the return journey.

In some walks, the type of footwear needed is indicated. This is usually given in walks where the rambler may be unsure of the degree of difficulty of the terrain, though such advice can only be a very general guide for what can be an easy ramble in good weather may, of course, be something very different after heavy rain. In the mountain and moorland chapters, it should be assumed that boots and appropriate clothing are always essential.

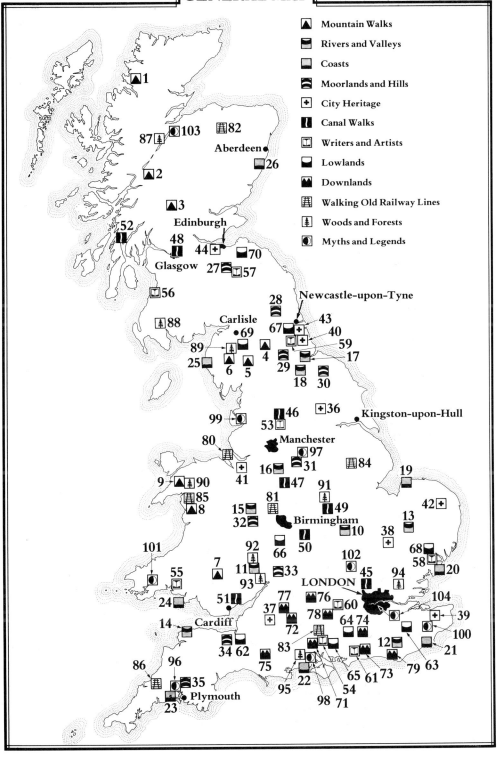

GENERAL MAP

Legend:
- ▲ Mountain Walks
- ▦ Rivers and Valleys
- ▢ Coasts
- ◗ Moorlands and Hills
- ⊞ City Heritage
- ▮ Canal Walks
- ▢ Writers and Artists
- ▭ Lowlands
- ▩ Downlands
- ⊞ Walking Old Railway Lines
- ⸙ Woods and Forests
- ◐ Myths and Legends

▲1

87 ⸙ ◐103   ⊞82
Aberdeen ●
              ▭26

▲2

▲3
Edinburgh
52 ▮   48 ⊞
        44 ⊞   ▭70
Glasgow 27 ◗ ▢57

▢56

⸙88   Carlisle
        ●69   Newcastle-upon-Tyne
89   ◗28   43
25   ⸙   67▭ ⊞   40
  6 5 ▲4   59   17
        29
        18 30

99 → ◐   ⊞46   ⊞36
        53▢   Kingston-upon-Hull
80   Manchester
⊞   ◐97
9 ▲⸙90   16▮ 31   ⊞84   19
85   ▮47   91   ▭
▲8   81   ⸙   42⊞
15   ⸙   ▮49
32   Birmingham   13
        ◗   10   38
101   66   ▮50   ⊞   68▭
7   92   102   58▢
55   11   ◐   45   94   20
24   93 ⸙   ◐   LONDON▮   104
    51▮   77   ▩76   39
14 Cardiff   37⊞ 78▩ 60   64 74   ◐   100
34 62   72   ⸙   ◐ 63   21
86 96   83   65 61 73   79
    35   75   22 95 98 54 71
23 ● Plymouth

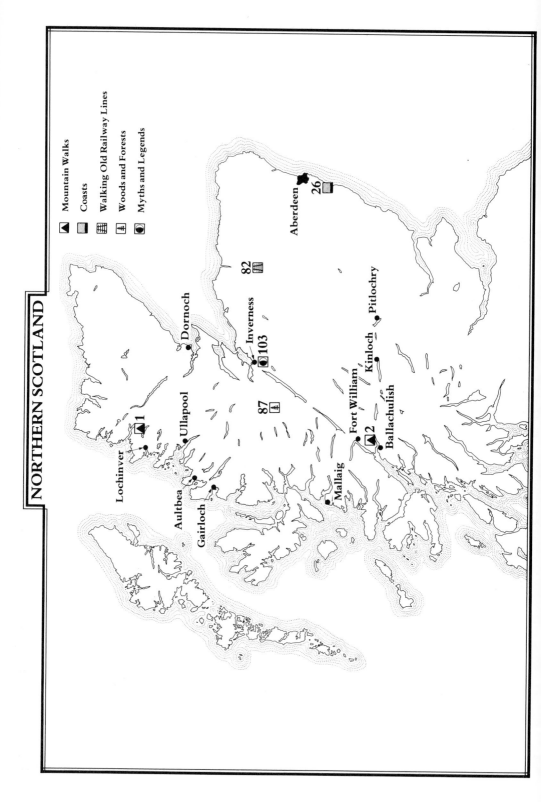

NORTHERN SCOTLAND

Mountain Walks
Coasts
Walking Old Railway Lines
Woods and Forests
Myths and Legends

Aberdeen
26

82

Dornoch

Inverness
103

87

Kinloch
Pitlochry

Fort William
2
Ballachulish

Lochinver
1

Ullapool

Aultbea

Gairloch

Mallaig

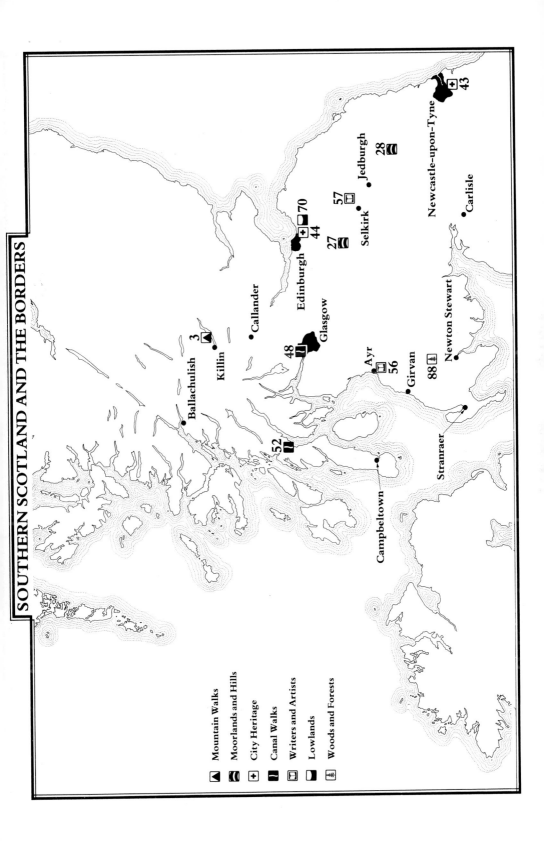

SOUTHERN SCOTLAND AND THE BORDERS

Newcastle-upon-Tyne

Jedburgh

Selkirk

Carlisle

Edinburgh

Callander

Glasgow

Killin

Ballachulish

Newton Stewart

Ayr

Girvan

Stranraer

Campbeltown

43

28

70

57

44

27

3

48

52

56

88

- ◣ Mountain Walks
- ◖◖ Moorlands and Hills
- ⊞ City Heritage
- ▬ Canal Walks
- ▤ Writers and Artists
- ◗ Lowlands
- ⊞ Woods and Forests

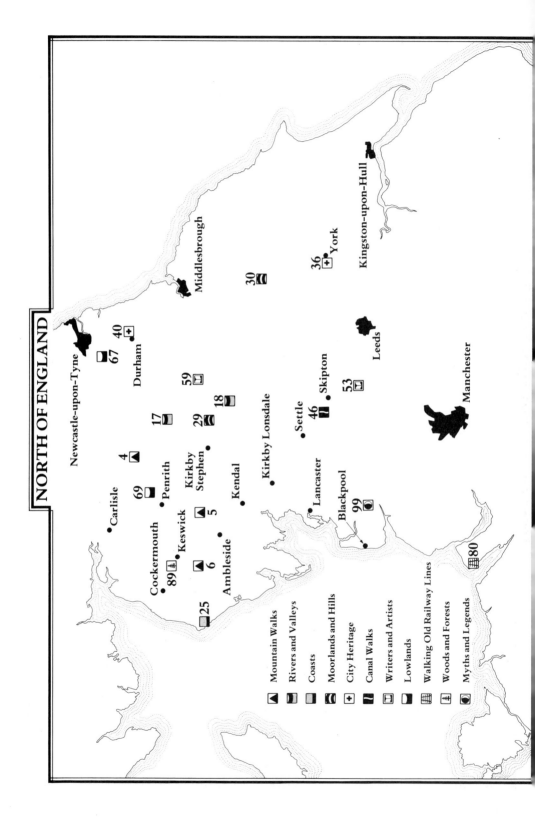

NORTH OF ENGLAND

Newcastle-upon-Tyne

Middlesbrough

Kingston-upon-Hull

York

Durham

Leeds

Skipton

Settle

Manchester

Carlisle

Penrith

Kirkby
Stephen

Kirkby Lonsdale

Kendal

Lancaster

Blackpool

Cockermouth

Keswick

Ambleside

Mountain Walks
Rivers and Valleys
Coasts
Moorlands and Hills
City Heritage
Canal Walks
Writers and Artists
Lowlands
Walking Old Railway Lines
Woods and Forests
Myths and Legends

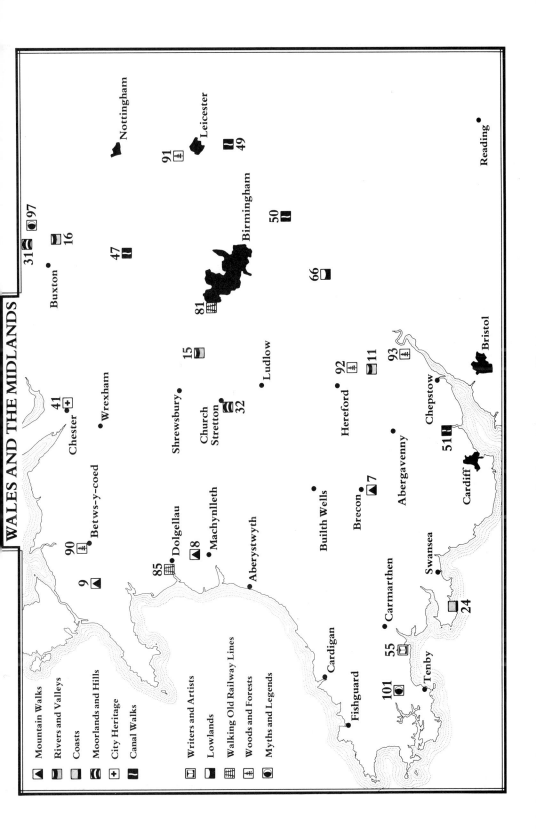

WALES AND THE MIDLANDS

Mountain Walks
Rivers and Valleys
Coasts
Moorlands and Hills
City Heritage
Canal Walks

Writers and Artists
Lowlands
Walking Old Railway Lines
Woods and Forests
Myths and Legends

Nottingham

Leicester

91
49

Birmingham

31 97
16

Buxton

47

50

Reading

66

Chester

41

Wrexham

Ludlow

Shrewsbury

15

Church
Stretton
32

Bristol

92
11

93

Hereford

51

Chepstow

Betws-y-coed

90

Dolgellau

Machynlleth

85

Abergavenny

Cardiff

9

Aberystwyth

8

Builth Wells

Brecon
7

Cardigan

Carmarthen

Swansea

Fishguard

101
55

Tenby

24

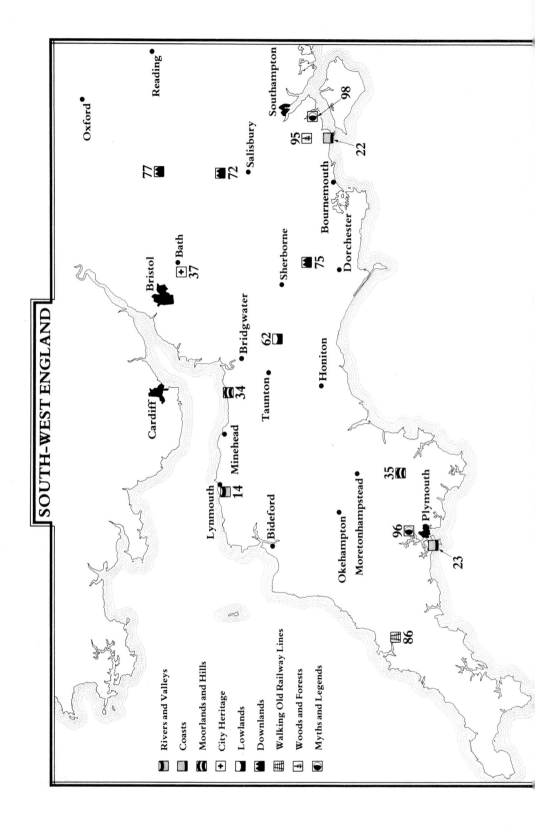

SOUTH-WEST ENGLAND

Rivers and Valleys
Coasts
Moorlands and Hills
City Heritage
Lowlands
Downlands
Walking Old Railway Lines
Woods and Forests
Myths and Legends

Oxford
Reading
Bristol
Bath 37
Cardiff
Minehead
14
Lynmouth
Bideford
Okehampton
Moretonhampstead
Plymouth
96
35
23
86
Taunton
Bridgwater
62
34
Honiton
Sherborne
75
Dorchester
Bournemouth
Salisbury
77
72
95
98
22
Southampton

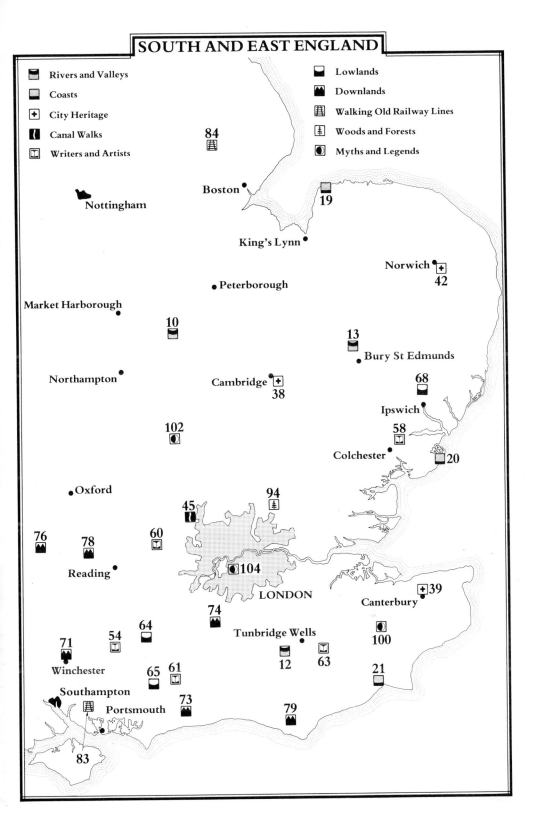

SOUTH AND EAST ENGLAND

Rivers and Valleys
Coasts
City Heritage
Canal Walks
Writers and Artists

Lowlands
Downlands
Walking Old Railway Lines
Woods and Forests
Myths and Legends

Nottingham

Boston

84

19

King's Lynn

Norwich
42

Peterborough

Market Harborough

10

13
Bury St Edmunds

Northampton

Cambridge
38

68

Ipswich

102

58

Colchester

20

Oxford

94

45

76   78

60

104

LONDON

39
Canterbury

74

64

Tunbridge Wells

100

71   54

Winchester

12   63

65   61

21

Southampton

Portsmouth

73

79

83

MOUNTAIN·WALKS

To start with two definitions: in this context a mountain is regarded as land above the 2,000ft contour, or 600m to the nearest round metric number; walking is placing one foot in front of the other while progressing forwards, as well as upwards or downwards. It does not involve using hands, except perhaps to steady oneself; it does not involve gymnastics or the use of ropes or specialised equipment. Indeed, it may be more accurate to describe it as fell-walking, an activity which, be it measured merely in mileage covered or height climbed, presents a physical challenge to be conquered. I prefer to regard it as a superb recreation amid the natural and inspiring beauty of high places.

Perhaps in early youth the attractions of mountain walking are largely physical, with the joy of tautened muscles, stretched limbs and an exhilarating sense of freedom. But later other aspects come into play – factors of an aesthetic, even sensual nature involving a keen awareness of the surroundings. For this deeper joy, all that is needed is modest physical effort, sensible equipment and, in Wordsworth's words, 'an eye to perceive, and a heart to enjoy'.

Three factors contribute to the joys of mountain walking: lightness of foot, rhythm of movement, and common sense. When climbing a slope, be it steep or gentle, use the toes and ball of the foot, not the flat of it, still less the heel. Vary the length of stride to the gradient – the steeper the slope the shorter the step, like changing down a gear on a bicycle or in a car. Similarly with breathing – like engine revs, try to keep it even. Breathe in rhythm with the steps: on level ground, or in descent, take so many strides to a breath; on steep gradients this may even be reduced to one or two strides! Again, in descent, avoid the frame-jarring habit of clumping down on the heels; instead, walk with knees slightly bent, acting as shock-absorbers.

The common-sense factor is harder to explain. An instinct for mountains develops from going among them, familiarising oneself with their sizes, shapes and even their names. This way the mountains become friends, not monsters to be dreaded. Challenging and demanding they may be, and always to be respected, but our British mountains are rarely to be feared, and then only in severe or hostile conditions of weather. Common sense then tells one not to go on them; it is only a foolhardy person who takes risks. Common sense also dictates when to turn back. Weather is fickle among our British hills, and even the most promising day can change for the worse, with lower-

Crib-y-Ddysgl from Crib Goch, Snowdon (Geoffrey N. Wright) (*see* page 58)

ing cloud or mist restricting visibility. Unless confident of your navigational ability to press ahead with your intended walk, don't be afraid to turn back. If you go on, you certainly won't be rewarded with fine views! Incidentally, summits are not usually the best viewpoints, being too remote from valleys. Photographers will find part-way up is better, with land above and below.

I admit to enjoying solitary mountain walking. I can choose my own speed, stop when and where I like, listen to the bird song, and I do not have to talk. Climbing and conversation are poor bedfellows, the one detracting from the other. To talk while on a steep slope is both to waste breath and lose rhythm, and you may not be so careful where you place your feet. Even the best-defined mountain path has its pitfalls and little hazards – an outcrop of rock, scree or loose stones, worn grass or a bog. Following such a track demands care and concentration, pushing to the back of the mind most of the other pressing problems of life. Being among the mountains restores perspective.

As to safety, much has already been written about this and it all boils down to common sense. Mountain walking is for enjoyment; it is not an attempt to prove something. Know where you intend to go, take the appropriate 1:50 000 OS sheet and a compass, and know how to use both. Carry a whistle if there is a possibility of getting lost, and have plenty of food with you. Wear too many clothes rather than too few; it is several degrees colder at 2,000ft (610m) than in the valley. Some form of waterproof and windproof jacket or anorak is desirable. Carry a comfortable, but not unduly heavy, rucksack, and wear comfortable boots with Commando or Vibram soles. Boots are much safer than shoes, trainers, or wellingtons for they support the ankles, an important consideration in descent, where most accidents happen.

No mountain walk here described is dangerous, though foolhardiness can make it so. All walks are over public rights of way, although in Scotland there may be access restrictions in the lambing season (April–May) and while deer-stalking is in progress (August–October). They have been chosen to include different mountain characteristics in various parts of Britain, and represent a tiny cross-section of what is available. In the words of that great climber, F. S. Smythe, whose exploits took him from the Surrey hills to Everest: 'These hills of ours may be low in stature, yet they reach very nearly to heaven.'

1	Quinag, Highland	10 miles (16km)
2	Beinn a Bheithir, Highland	12 miles (19km)
3	Ben Lawers, Tayside	10 miles (16km)
4	Cross Fell, Cumbria	11 miles (17.5km)
5	High Street, Cumbria	6 miles (9.6km)
6	Scafell Pike, Cumbria	10 miles (16km)
7	Brecon Beacons, Powys	7½ miles (12km)
8	Cader Idris, Gwynedd	5 miles (8km)
9	Snowdon (Yr Wyddfa), Gwynedd	7½ miles (12km)

The old railway line in the Derwent Valley (Geoffrey N. Wright) (*see* page 257)

1 QUINAG

Time: As this walk involves a gain of height of 3,300ft (1,006m) it would be unwise to allow less than 6 hours, though more time would be ideal for this really grand scramble.

Start and finish: Park your car on the large area of hard ground just south of the highest point of the road (A894) between Skiag Bridge AA box and Kylesku Bridge (grid reference 232273).

Approach: The A837 from Lochinver runs along the north shore of Loch Assynt giving access to the A894 at Skiag Bridge.

Attractions: Quinag is the most extensive of that extraordinary succession of peaks that rise in individual isolation from the intricate hummocks and hollows of Assynt, like a row of monsters from the deep. From the north, the mountain displays two massive brooding buttresses which seem to threaten the safety of the new Kylesku Bridge, while the western aspect is of a great mountain wall, dragon-backed. The most photogenic view is from the head of Loch Assynt, where the elegant cone of Spidean Coinich draws the eye. One of the many factors which make Quinag an ideal mountain to climb is that, not only can you avoid the long trek across bogland that is so often necessary in the northern Highlands, you can also start from 800ft (244m) by parking your car at the spot mentioned above.

OS sheet: 15

Follow a clear track which leads at right angles from the road some way up a low ridge, then turn left to make your way along the areas of bare rock to achieve the main ridge dry shod. Your task now is to climb this broad stony ridge, easy underfoot and made interesting by the lovely mountain plants and mosses. Before long a shallow col is reached, where there are little sandstone crags ideal for teaching children the basics of rock climbing. A short, steep climb sees you safely to the top of Spidean Coinich, 2,508ft (765m). This is a superb top, with crags to the north, and steep slopes everywhere. There are lovely views of Loch Assynt and of the unique, loch-dappled surrounding area.

Ahead, north-west, the wonderful ridge swoops, broad enough for safety, narrow enough for vivid experience. Two rounded rocky lumps are the first features after descending carefully from Spidean Coinich; after the second lump a steep descent of 250ft (76m) or so down grass and rock, brings you to the Bealach a Charnaidh. This is the great notch visible from the road, and seems a good spot to rest and have lunch.

On and up, out from the bealach (col), past small but steep crags, fetches you to the bifurcation of the ridge. The broad top, paved with rounded stones

Loch Assynt from Spidean Coinich (Geoffrey N. Wright)

carpeted with moss, leads east to Sail Gharbh, at 2,653ft (809m) the highest point on Quinag. After admiring the suberb views from here, return to the north-tending ridge, which surfs along in fine style with a great wall of crags on the left, overlooking Gleann Leireag. One super little hump on the ridge can be bypassed on the east, but it is more fun to go over it; and on the long rise to Sail Ghorm there is a really exciting gully swooping down a precipitous notch in the maroon blocks of Torridon sandstone, a perfect foreground for the vista over Assynt to the sea outside Lochinver. There is something indefinably elevating about these high ridges, some quality that pervades through the bootsoles from the scrunching clean rock or the springy moss, or maybe some buoyant element in the upper air; the ancients were right in postulating that heaven is upwards.

At last you reach the northern spur, Sail Ghorm, which name strictly applies to the great crags invisible below. The panorama is wild and fantastic; as the eyes rove from the reefs offshore northwards the tortuous coastline towards Kinlochbervie and further, to the little lump of Handa of the birds, can be seen. Inland, are the great grey hills of Foinaven and the Reay Forest; nearer at hand, the hills drop precipitously into the lochs of Kylesku – waterfall land. To the east, the highest waterfall in Britain is just hidden among the spectacular scenery, and a little further round you can admire the serried crags of dark red sandstone of Sail Gharbh. Between you and those crags is a great green soggy corrie full of peat hags.

With some reluctance it is time to leave, and for most of 2 miles (3km) return by the outward route, as far as the bealach. This is no drawback, as the ridge presents itself in a wholly different aspect – the shapes and forms on Quinag would inspire a sculptor for years.

On reaching the bealach, head down to the loch, to keep the left side. In hot weather, this loch has all that could be required for mountain refreshment; it is a fine place to cool the feet and admire the way Spidean Coinich's crags hurl themselves down. The orange sand, with so few footprints, is particularly beautiful.

Now follow 1½ miles (2km) of rough walking over heather, rock and burn, keeping Spidean Coinich ridge on the right, tending south of east. Presently the car can be seen ahead, and at last you attain it, having walked and climbed a route of extraordinary beauty.

2 BEINN·A·BHEITHIR

Time: At least 8 or 9 hours. Some 4,500ft (1,372m) of climbing is involved.
Start and finish: Park in the Forestry Commission car park near the church
1½ miles (2km) east of Ballachulish Bridge on the way to Glencoe village
(grid reference 067585).
Approach: The A82 running around both the north and south shores of Loch
Leven gives access to the start of this walk.
Attractions: This steep and splendid mountain looms large to the south of
Ballachulish Bridge, and is underclimbed. It is an unsurpassed viewpoint,
never likely to be crowded; there are all the things looked for in a fine mountain – airy ridges, sharp tops, crags, scree. All that is needed is energy and a
fine day.
OS sheet: 41

Walk into Laroch and head south up the glen for a short distance. Make your
way up the burn that comes down from Beinn Bhan towering above to the
west. This part of the climb onto the first ridge is hard work, use lots of zigzags
to break the slope, not haphazardly but making the best use of every little
ledge. The interest of creating your own route ameliorates the labour
involved. There are tracks on the slope, but they don't seem continuous.

Once on the broad ridge of Beinn Bhan, life becomes easier; the heather is left
behind, it is all rock and shaven hill turf and moss from now on. There is now
a good track up the rock and grit, and the lovely rockiness of the ridge to the
right keeps the spirits high. This is good climbing. In due course persistence
and hard work leads to the first top, a neat little cone, at 3,104ft (946m).
Ahead rises a beautiful ridge, curved as a scythe blade, which fairly pulls the
feet onward to the main height of the day. Ten minutes sees arrival at this
point, Sgorr Dearg, 3,362ft (1,025m). The Ordnance Survey triangulation
station here is rather unusual, being a cylinder. What a superb panorama
there is! Due north is the now-tiny bridge at Ballachulish, and behind, across
Loch Linnhe are the vast rumpled miles of Lochaber and beyond; the great
hill Garbh Bheinn of Ardgour lies to the west; swinging round, there is
Ardnamurchan, Morvern and the great Isle of Mull; look down the length of
Loch Linnhe to the rich islands of Seil and Luing, with wild Jura behind; now
southwards to the glorious array of mountains and glens that is Lorn, but not
forlorn – this is great, inspiring stuff. Nearer to hand, and breathtakingly
grand, is the great steep solidity of Bidean nam Bian guarding the south side
of Glencoe, with Aonach Eagach holding the north; a little nearer you can
make out the long scar of Clachaig Gully; then towards the north, Loch
Leven's hills, the dragon crest of the Mamores and, finally, the square dome

of Ben Nevis. Truly a noble view, to absorb fully; to pull from the memory in times of boredom or futility back in that silly world far below, and know that there really is beauty in the world, grandeur, wilderness and meaning.

The next stage is descent to the bealach (col) westward, the legs enjoying the downhill motion. As you climb from the col, note the tremendous stony slopes to the left; no sensible route here, just a steep rocky desert. More easily than expected, you gain height. The path at times veers very close to the northern edge, and affords better appreciation of the rocks dropping steeply – be careful in a high wind. Because of the interest, this sort of climbing seems much easier than plodding up steady slopes. The top of Sgurr Dhonuill, 3,284ft (1,001m), is quite expansive, and there are plenty of boulders and patches of grass where it is possible to lie out of the wind to recover, and listen to the rich silence.

Up here you may well see ptarmigan, ravens, perhaps an eagle. When time calls, descend south-west for a while, being careful crossing the boulders. The first sensible descent is down a short gully of red scree; not, alas, a good scree run, but it gets you through the rim of crags. It is apparent that many people ascend this gully; climbing scree is masochistic, unimaginative and dangerous; there are several alternative routes.

Head downhill towards the forest. A fairly good track down the left bank of the main burn eventually brings you to the forestry road. The way ahead is a steady tramp down Gleann a Caolas (the Glen of the Narrows), at junctions tend downhill and west of the burn. Shortly after passing a small car park, the road bears left by a cottage; go straight on down a rough track swinging right and left, cross an old railway bridge, and just before some farm buildings, cross a stile by a gate on the right, to follow an obvious hard path alongside a sparse wood. After two more gates the main road, the A82, is reached. Turn right, and walk the last mile or so back to your vehicle. The passing traffic will do little to dent your satisfaction at having climbed such a superb mountain, and covered so many steep miles.

3 BEN·LAWERS

Time: Allow 6 to 7 hours. Why hurry a good thing?

Start and finish: The Mountain Visitor Centre on the hill road between Loch Tay and Glen Lyon, well signposted some 5 miles (8km) east of Killin (grid reference 603383).

Approach: Killin, on the A827 is reached from the west by the A85 (Oban road). Those approaching from the east will find a variety of routes converging on Dunkeld.

Attractions: Ben Lawers is Perthshire's highest mountain at 3,984ft (1,214m) – a big, chunky massif which prevents Loch Tay from spreading northward. Enjoyment of the day will be much enhanced by a look around the Centre, which will indicate the unique importance of this mountain mass in terms of natural history, notably alpine and arctic flora.

OS sheet: 51

Start the walk along a wooden causeway across a peat moor, and very soon there is a choice, to follow the nature trail or the Ben Lawers track. Follow the nature trail. After winding hither and yon up a burnside with little forays to see this and that, the main path is regained; and after some meandering across a sheep-grazed grassy hill, the collar-work begins.

It is always interesting to know a little of what lies beneath your feet, for that largely determines what you see. Ben Lawers is a lump of metamorphic rock called schist, this particular form of which rapidly decomposes to form instant soil, which is why the slope up which you are determinedly plodding is more earth than scree. This schist contains quite a high proportion of base elements, which encourage the growth of lime-hungry alpine plants. The relatively fruitful soil also fosters the growth of over 200 different kinds of moss, and afforded me the unusual sight of an earthworm crossing the path above the 3,000ft (914m) contour; maybe the highest worm in the land.

After some toil, the side of the ridge is climbed and you are more able to enjoy the unfolding views and the lovely wavy bedding of the little rock outcrops. The track is impossible to miss, there are no route-finding problems at all. People with superabundant energy have erected large cairns on the way, but the only one to matter just now is that atop Beinn Ghlas, the first summit, about 3,700ft (1,128m).

Here is a good spot to draw breath and savour the splendid view. Far below is Coire Odhar with its ski-hut, and coming up from the glen to the north is a beautifully graded zigzag track – possibly a stalkers' path, or a route for pack-horses. It leads the mind back to when people set off through the hills on business, raiding or pleasure bent, with not an orange anorak to be seen.

Probably the hills saw more folk then, but they would have kept to the glens and passes, not the ridges and summits as we do today.

Rested, refreshed, with one Munro under your belt already, march with delight down the bonny ridge towards the main target. There are impressive views of the great, even, southern slopes down to Loch Tay, also some craggy bits up to the right. Now, once more, it is a steady, even plod that gets you up the fairly steep but perfectly safe slope to the top of the mountain.

Some tops are a disappointment, vast, flat and boring; this summit is rocky, small and interesting. It deserves to be 16ft (5m) higher, to attain 4,000ft (1,219m). It feels good to prowl along the south-east ridge among the jutting rocks, and to sense the swoop of the unseen ground below. The ridge northwards offers a delightful up-and-down stride above Lochan na Cat to Meall Garbh, which could become a fine horseshoe walk if someone were to wait with a car – at Lawers village, for example.

Having enjoyed the great views that a good day allows, from coast to coast over a multitude of mountains, there's but one direction – downwards. Everything seems very different as you retrace your steps, and always there is the possibility of something delightful to catch the eye. My abiding memory of this mountain is that when I was climbing the last few score feet, eight white quartz rocks suddenly took flight and scythed across in front of me – they were ptarmigan. To me, these delightful birds contain the very spirit of the high, clean mountains and the free places.

From Beinn Ghlas, it is possible to take a different route back. A quick and safe descent can be made to the col north-west of the mountain, where you should be able to find the previously mentioned path going down into Coire Odhar; you will inevitably find the main path again further down. This route avoids the press of folk if the mountain is busy, and there is a better chance of seeing wildlife in consequence.

Otherwise, carry on down the way you climbed up, but not by the nature trail. As you return to your car, I'm sure you will agree that Ben Lawers was well worth climbing.

4 CROSS·FELL

Time: At least 6 hours should be allowed.

Start and finish: Garrigill in the South Tyne valley (grid reference 745415); see Attractions for details of finish.

Approach: Garrigill is 4 miles (6km) south of Alston, and lies just off the B6277 Middleton-in-Teesdale road.

Attractions: At 2,930ft (893m) the highest summit in the Pennines, Cross Fell is a remote, bleak, upland wilderness, a giant of a mountain difficult to incorporate into a circular walk. The shortest route is from Kirkland, beneath the western flanks; the easiest is to cheat, driving from Knock, north of Appleby, on Britain's highest surfaced road towards the radar station on Great Dun Fell, reaching 2,480ft (756m) and walking north from there. But for a true mountain walk start from Garrigill near Alston, using the Pennine Way to the summit, and descending to Kirkland, having arranged for transport to await there (co-operation with wife, friend, relative or lover, being necessary).

OS sheets: 86 and 91

Watering trough for packhorses on the miners' track up Cross Fell from Garrigill (Geoffrey N. Wright)

Garrigill has cottages of grey stone, some rendered and whitewashed, bordering a pleasant village green embowered with trees, so that it is hard to realise that it is 1,100ft (343m) above sea level. Much of the village dates from the early decades of last century when the Quaker London Lead Company developed it as a community for lead miners and their families. The northern slopes of Cross Fell were a rich mining ground, and there is much of industrial archaeological interest along the 7½ mile (12km) way to the summit.

The track leaves the southern end of Garrigill, west of the river, and immediately starts climbing as a walled lane. About a mile (1.6km) from the village, where the lane makes a second kink to the right (west), a 'short cut' across heather and rough grass is best avoided. Stick to the lane, which soon swings back onto a southerly course, and leaves the enclosed fields. Beyond a gate it retains only a single wall, crosses the 2,000ft (610m) contour on Pikeman Hill, and for the next mile (1.6km) contours the western slopes of Long Man Hill. When I first climbed this way there was a small iron water-trough by the side of the track, a welcome sight for packhorses; but on a more recent visit it seemed to have vanished.

Small blue crystals of fluorspar bejewel the path, and nearby spoil heaps indicate the melancholy devastation of old workings, as well as being roughly the halfway point between Garrigill and Cross Fell, whose broad bulk looms ahead. Beyond the workings the track crosses Cash Burn and passes the ruins of a former mine shop, where a small number of lead miners lived during each working week at these lonely mines among the high fells, returning home to Garrigill on a Saturday evening. Two miles (3km) further on is Greg's Hut, a cottage which has been restored as a mountain bothy to provide a welcome shelter for stormbound Pennine Wayfarers. At about 2,300ft (701m) this must surely, on such occasions, be the highest occupied house in England.

Nearby are many mining relics, including the arched entrances to various levels, taller ones giving access to where veins of lead ore were worked, smaller ones representing drainage adits. The masonry shows high-quality craftsmanship characteristic of lead-mining buildings throughout the northern Pennines. Near one level I saw the wheel-less remains of a horse-drawn truck.

The cairned path continues westwards, climbing on Cross Fell's northern shoulder. As well as being a miners' track it was also a corpse road, used in times long past to carry the dead of Garrigill for interment in the burial ground at Kirkland on the opposite side of the mountain. Why a graveyard at Alston was not used remains a mystery. Soon after passing a line of sinkholes to the left of the path, turn sharp left and strike southwards up the shoulder, penetrate Cross Fell's girdle of stones and scree, and emerge onto the vast summit plateau. Apart from the official OS triangulation station, numerous cairns together with 'stone men' and a far more useful wall-shelter, provide an assorted display on the thin turf – a mere fleabite of man-made structures compared with the sprouting ironmongery of Great Dun Fell's radar equipment to the south.

The view west from the summit of Cross Fell (Geoffrey N. Wright)

Given good visibility, the panorama is enormous, especially westwards to the Lakeland skyline. Since this is ahead throughout the descent, enjoy to the full the eastwards prospect embracing the main watershed of the South Tyne and Tees, and including in its wildscape the vast Upper Teesdale Nature Reserve. Here is the very essence of Pennine wilderness – austere, awesome, often sullen, sometimes savage, but scarcely beautiful. Nowhere in England is there anything quite like Cross Fell, nowhere quite so lonely.

Leave the summit by the same route, going northwards along the shoulder as far as the corpse road, turning left (westwards) and descending gradually for a mile (1.6km). The gradient increases and the path becomes very steep, passing shallow depressions and small mounds marking former coal pits. Route-finding presents no problem, for the track becomes increasingly distinct as it winds across the steeper contours with the woods and hedgerows of the Vale of Eden below presenting their friendly sylvan pattern. Gradually the track swings southwards, easing across rough pasture towards the pleasant, intimate valley of Kirkland Beck and, following the river's left bank opposite a small wood soon reaches Kirkland hamlet. After the wild, majestic grandeur of Cross Fell, once known as 'Fiend's Fell', the fields and trees of Eden are indeed a paradise.

5 High·Street

Time: Allow at least 5 hours.

Start and finish: Mardale Head at the end of the surfaced road down the east side of Haweswater, 14 miles (22km) south of Penrith (grid reference 469107).

Approach: Mardale Head, where the road ends, is about 2½ miles (4km) beyond the Haweswater Hotel. Midway along this stretch, near the small island of Wood Howe, a particularly good viewpoint across the head of the lake to the jutting promontory of the Rigg allows you to appraise, in morning sunlight, the route of ascent which looks pleasantly challenging without any obvious hazards. Given the right conditions, this is indeed what it is. Even in mist or low cloud the very direct ridge route up Rough Crag may be safely attempted, for it is impossible to go astray.

Attractions: As the Lakeland ravens fly, High Street's summit is only about 8 miles (13km) from M6 motorway at Shap, yet its lonely beauty has characteristics both of the Cumbrian mountains and of the northern Pennines. Unlike most high places, which until relatively recently were regarded with awe and seldom visited, High Street has been humanised by 2,000 years of use since Roman times. Historically it linked the important Roman fort at Brougham, near Penrith, with a lesser one at Ambleside, 19 miles (30km) to the south, and for 6 of these miles (9.6km) it crosses a succession of hills well over 2,000ft (610m) in height, an unlikely and impracticable route for an engineered highway, but one of proven course and construction. High Street represents its climax, a worthy objective for any mountain walk.

OS sheet: 90

From the end of the road, where there is adequate parking – early arrivals in a small car-parking area, later ones by the roadside – go through the gate, turn right along a wall, cross Mardale Beck by a new footbridge and turn right again, with the head of the lake still on your right. The next ½ mile (.8km) is sheer delight on a sunny morning, with the path gentling along to the end of the wooded spur. Resist the temptation to linger and, before reaching a wall, turn sharply left, almost back on yourself, and really start climbing.

Ahead and above lies 1,800ft (549km) of climbing, in just over 2 miles (3km), an average gradient of 1 in 6 – relatively easy by Lake District standards. The character alternates between short steep sections and gentler grassy ones, always with the steep flanks down to Riggindale on the right where circling buzzards mew like kittens, while on the left Blea Water reflects the steel-blue tints of the frowning crags beyond. Immediately above this tarn the path crosses a grassy depression called Gospel Gate, but there is neither

Small Water (below) and Hawes Water (distant) from Mardale Ill Bell (Geoffrey N. Wright)

gate nor gospel, although a silent benediction would not be amiss for the sheer glory of the surrounding beauty. In every respect this is a classic little climb to be savoured both in the accomplishing and in subsequent recollection. Its last section up the rocky stairway of Long Stile seems wholly appropriate, a climax by which to reach a summit so deep-rooted in history.

The OS triangulation station is to the south, near the drystone wall which snakes along the thinly grassed crest of a broad, ice-smoothed plateau quite remarkably devoid of scenic interest. Skylark song breaks the quietness; here, so remote from valley heads, the sounds of tumbling becks fail to penetrate. My old Baddeley guide to the Lake District refers to High Street as 'a vast sheepwalk'. Indeed, until 1835 an annual fair and shepherds' meet was held on its broad back, with horse-racing and various other sports; hence the name Racecourse Hill for an area immediately south of the summit, 2,719ft (829m). To enjoy the best views you need to stroll to the edges of the plateau and look down on a swirl of chasms between exciting ridges on the east, with a long, though less dramatic line of cliffs falling on the west to Hayeswater.

The Pennines are a misty blue away to the north-east, Morecambe Bay a silvery gleam on the opposite horizon.

From the summit the way is southwards, soon swinging south-east above Blea Water Crag, losing height only very gently, and aiming for Mardale Ill Bell, 2,496ft (761m). At one point, near a small cairn, there is a dramatic view down to Blea Water, while a short detour to the north-east along a shoulder of the mountain reveals in a neighbouring corrie, Small Water, also occupying a former volcanic crater. These tarns and their assorted streams are known as Mardale Waters, eyes of the mountains reflecting both the hills and the heavens above.

Two cairns crown the summit of Mardale Ill Bell, breaking an undulating mass of soft, thin turf. Down to the south-east, ½ mile (.8km) away, the wall-shelter on the crest of Nan Bield Pass is distinctly visible. Keep to the right of the direct line to it, when a cairned track soon becomes apparent. At the wall-shelter turn left (north) and follow the easy gradient down the Nan Bield Pass by the northern shore of Small Water, from where the head of Haweswater and the surfaced road is but a mile (1.6km) away. Three stone shelters by Small Water's boulder-strewn shore, low-roofed but just access- ible, were for wayfarers using Nan Bield Pass when it was an important route for traders and travellers between Kentmere and Mardale.

6 SCAFELL·PIKE

Time: With the summit 5 miles (8km) from Seathwaite, involving about 3,000ft (914m) of climbing, allow at least 3 hours for the ascent, and don't be ashamed of taking 4 or even more, with 2½ to 3½ for the descent. Scafell Pike is too good a mountain to be rushed at, too rugged and stony to be tackled lightly.

Start and finish: Seathwaite. Although there is a National Park car park at Seatoller, at the foot of Honister Pass, most walkers prefer to take their vehicles towards Seathwaite, thus saving a mile (1.6km) road walk at the beginning and end of the climb. Early arrivals park closest to the hamlet, later ones progressively farther down the road. There are convenient grass verges (grid reference 236123).

Approach: Borrowdale is easily reached by car from Keswick or Buttermere on the B5289. Seathwaite is about a mile (1.6km) to the south of that road.

Attractions: To climb Scafell Pike is the ambition of many, probably most, walkers who visit the Lake District. Not only is it the highest summit in England, but it has all the attributes of a mountain – ruggedness and steepness, a commanding appearance and, given good weather, a superb view. Ascents can be made from four valleys which, if only remotely, radiate from the mountain – Borrowdale, Eskdale, Langdale and Wasdale. The route from Wasdale is the shortest and steepest, the various routes from Borrowdale probably the most popular because this valley is handiest to Keswick, the centre for northern Lakeland. Starting from Borrowdale gives also a choice of routes, thus enabling a different return. The chosen route is by Styhead Tarn and the Corridor, broadly in a south or south-west direction, returning along the high plateau by Broad Crag eastwards to Esk Hause, northwards down towards Sprinkling Tarn, then diverting by Ruddy Gill to Grains Gill and Stockley Bridge.

OS sheet: 90

In Seathwaite turn right below a barn, cross the beck, and follow a well-defined track up the north side of the valley – very marshy and boggy in wet weather – towards Taylor Gill Force. The route up the right-hand side of this is rocky and involves using hands, knees and everything, but is scenically magnificent. Beyond the top of the waterfall the gradient eases and the track follows the sparkling beck to Styhead Tarn, gloriously situated in an amphitheatre of mountains. Ahead are the great rocky western slopes of Great End and Broad Crag, and the Corridor Route is the only 'easy' track along this ravaged flank, providing an exciting route to the distant Lingmell col.

From the top of Styhead, near the mountain rescue post, a good short cut south-eastwards leads directly to Skew Gill, descending slightly. Climb steeply out of Skew Gill, and keep climbing diagonally, eventually reaching a more grassy section. The next ravine to be crossed is Greta Gill, with the scenery becoming wilder and grander all the time. The route is distinct, marked by small cairns at irregular intervals, and the track is now stony and rough, continuing steadily upwards. Lingmell is the mountain ahead, slightly right, with Scafell Pike to the left, and the next aiming-point, Lingmell col, is a saddle between the two.

About 2,200ft (671m) some tiny tarns are passed on the right before the route swings round the head of Piers Gill, one of the most dramatic ravines in the Lake District. Beyond, across Wasdale Head, Great Gable's majestic west flank, with rocky buttresses above, commands the view. All this is mountain scenery of the highest quality.

At Lingmell col, given good weather, the westwards view is to the coast and the Isle of Man far distant. Continue across the col for 150yd (137m) to join the track coming up from Wasdale, swinging left (south-east) to toil the final 750ft (229m) up an increasingly stony, boulder-strewn, well-cairned track to the summit, easily identified by the huge cairn and, by comparison, small triangulation column. This is it, the top of England – a wilderness of stones and boulders in pink, buff and grey, and all of volcanic origin. It is a place of grandeur but not of beauty, and it is rarely warm enough to linger long. In any case the descent is long, and for the first mile (1.6km), demanding.

Leave the summit eastwards, then north-eastwards, over stones, descending very steeply to Broad Crag col, then climbing across the southern shoulder of Broad Crag. More boulders, then a slight drop to Ill Crag col, another short climb to a gravelly plateau followed by a section of boulder-hopping leading to an easier track beyond Calf Cove, giving way to more grass and a gentle slope down to Esk Hause. This is the most famous of Lakeland's mountain crossroads, with tracks coming up from Langdale and Eskdale. A cross-walled shelter identifies the place, and the Borrowdale route swings down left (north-north-east) from Esk Hause, continuing to drop at an easy gradient. In ½ mile (.8km), where the track becomes markedly red and the Styhead route continues ahead, turn off right across the head of Ruddy Gill, an impressive ravine initially on the right but subsequently always to the left of the steeply dropping well-defined path which takes a direct line down to the main valley of Grains Gill. Several grassy swards near the beck offer enticing places to rest tiring legs, and the beck's clear waters can be a benediction on a hot day.

After crossing a wooden footbridge the way ahead to Stockley Bridge is easy and straightforward. This packhorse bridge is, for thousands of walkers and climbers, the real beginning and end of so many great days on the hills, the last stop before Seathwaite another mile (1.6km) away; and Stockley Beck itself soothes many aching feet. Shadows lengthen in the valley; there is a great sense of satisfaction on the completion of a memorable day on Scafell Pike.

Eskdale and Scafell range from Harter Fell, Cumbria (Geoffrey N. Wright)

7 BRECON·BEACONS

Time: Allow at least 4 hours as the views on this walk are much too good to rush through.

Start and finish: The route goes from Bailea, south of Brecon, to the three main summits of the Beacons, returning by a different route, part of which is along a Roman road. There are two steep ascents, otherwise easy gradients on grass or stony tracks. The descent is very gradual (grid reference 039241).

Approach: Although the easiest ascent is from Storey Arms on the crest of the pass on the A470 Brecon–Merthyr road, the route chosen, though longer and in places steeper, is far more rewarding. Take a minor road from Brecon, turning south off the A40/470 ½ mile (.8km) west of the town centre (signposted Cantref). After 3 miles (5km) this narrowing lane ends near Bailea Farm, where a widening allows space for a few cars to park.

Attractions: Twelve summits over 2,000ft (610m) form the complete Brecon Beacons range, but this mountain walk embraces only the top three: Cribin, 2,608ft, Pen-y-fan, 2,907ft, and Corn Dû, 2,863ft (794, 886 and 872m) taken in that order. Not only are the Beacons the highest land in south Wales but they represent the highest point of the Old Red Sandstone south of Scotland and, when seen from the north near Brecon, the three rounded summits of this climb form impressive sentinels above steep scarp faces. Most mountain country is of particular appeal to anyone with even a slight interest in geology, and the Beacons are no exception.

OS sheet: 160

Walk along the stony track immediately past the parking space, through a gate, and climb the grassy ridge ahead. If the weather is clear, Cribin's crown, 2 miles (3km) away, seems dauntingly high, while the striated structure of the Beacons' eastern slopes reveals the very bones of upland landscape. Ahead, the long grassy ridge of Bryn-teg presents no problems, although the track itself is rarely more than a sketchy route over rough pasture. Progress is marked by occasional steeper sections, and small cairns suggest obvious pausing points. On one crest are a few tiny pools, non-existent in dry weather, and beyond them the rib of Bryn-teg becomes steeper.

Before the really hard work begins you pass an enticing track contouring off to the right. This represents an easier route to the broad col between Cribin and Pen-y-fan and is a way of avoiding Cribin's summit, although it is an exposed traverse with awkward sections across scree, and particularly hazardous under snow. Determined walkers will ignore it, and gather breath for the last 300ft (91m), up a sharp arête of eroded grass and loose stone. The going is hard, on no account to be rushed, but it is nowhere dangerous. You will wisely stop every few minutes – to admire the view, of course – but eventually will reach the summit of the 'snout' and flop down by its cairn to recover. When I climbed this in October, cloud was pillowed in the cwm to the north, stretching in an unbroken blanket over the Brecon landscape. Only the tops of the Black Mountains rose above it, but close at hand Pen-y-fan's north-east cliffs caught the morning sunlight, which gleamed on its fractured strata. From late morning onwards this seamed and gullied scarp face becomes increasingly shadowed – photographers take note!

From Cribin's summit a grassy track northwards descends steeply to a broad col above the 'short cut' route, with an unremittingly steep climb of about 600ft (183m) up a badly eroded broad highway to the top of Pen-y-fan. Approaching the summit plateau, notice, to the right, how it is supported by upended blocks of red sandstone lying on alternate layers of banded sandstone and red soil. The triangulation station is distinguished by a National Trust plaque, a satisfying reminder that the Brecon Beacons are in safe keeping, to be enjoyed by unnumbered future generations of climbers tempted to its windy ridges and broad summits. The panoramic view is ample reward. If the weather is right, enjoy it to the full before continuing the easy track westwards for ½ mile (.8km) to the cairn on Corn Dû, along the summit ridge rimmed with splendid crags to its north.

Far below to the north-west is the glacial pool of Llyn-cwm-llwch, but the way back lies in the opposite direction. This can be by way of Pen-y-fan, but

a pleasant variation cuts across its southern shoulder, the path easily identified from Corn Dû, its start being 110yd (100m) east from the summit cairn.
From here it contours towards the col between Pen-y-fan and Cribin, then
takes a more southerly course across Cribin's flanks, on a well-trodden track
catching all the afternoon sunshine. Neuadd Reservoirs gleam silvery in the
valley ahead, as the path swings eastwards to join the Roman road at the
'Gap', the top of the pass on an ancient route between Merthyr and Brecon.
Turn left and follow an excellent track, stony in places, above Cwm Cynwyn
to Bailea, a good 2½ miles (4km) to the north. Above, to the left, Bryn-teg's
ridge recalls the first part of the climb, while the gentler scene in the valley
ahead beckons onwards, descending all the time, along a track used for 2,000
years – a satisfying finish to a great day on the Beacons.

Summit of Pen-y-fan

8 CADER·IDRIS

Time: Allow 4 to 5 hours as, although this is a relatively easy walk, the going can be rough.

Start and finish: Minffordd near the northern end of Tal-y-llyn lake. There is very limited roadside car parking near the iron gates of the old Idris Estate at Minffordd (grid reference 730113).

Approach: Minffordd is on the A487 about 9 miles (14km) north of Machynlleth, or can easily be reached from Dolgellau.

Attractions: Although at 2,928ft (893m) this is not one of the highest Welsh mountains, its ice-gouged cwms and great line of cliffs guarding the northern side of its long east-west ridge dominating Dolgellau to the north, make it particularly impressive. The Mawddach estuary and the nearness of the sea give to Cader a wonderful impression of height and isolation. Its popularity is partly due to its easy accessibility, partly to the superb northern view from anywhere along its airy crest.

OS sheet: 124

Cader Idris is not only a walker's mountain. Almost all of its southern face from the summit ridge down to the Idris Gate near the road was designated a national nature reserve in 1976, because of its geological and botanical interest. Within its area of about one mile (1.6km) square, occur fine examples of various rock strata formed during the Ordovician Period. Different strata yield different soils and habitats from the oakwoods of Idris to the arctic-alpine plants on bare summits, for many of which Cader Idris is roughly the southern limit in Britain.

Go through the gates into a conifer avenue where rhododendrons add spring colours, cross a bridge and enter the nature reserve through a small gate. A well-defined but eroded path climbs steeply through oak-birch woodland, noisy with the sounds of Nant Cader on the right cascading and tumbling over grey boulders, with conifers on the far bank. The path winds upwards, crosses a small stream, the gradient easing as the end of the woodland is reached at a metal gate, with a Nature Reserve sign nearby. At this point the mountain straight ahead to the north, and a mile (1.6km) distant, is Mynydd Moel, from which the return descent will be made. Study the lie of the land, seeking landmarks which may be useful, for there is no obvious path between Mynydd Moel and the Idris woods.

The ascent now continues over open rough pasture, sheep grazed, climbing gently and swinging left, away from the stream. Passing two small nature conservancy experimental enclosures the yellow, stony track crosses a wet grassy plateau, becomes a slaty-blue path and reaches a cairn. You sense rather than

View south towards Corris from the Minffordd path (Geoffrey N. Wright)

see Llyn Cau, and it is worth a short detour ahead for a closer view. If you are there before about 11am, you will appreciate the splendid modelling effect of morning sunlight on the shattered eastern face of Cym Cau. Llyn Cau's water reflects back to the crags an enhanced glow of sombre blues and greys, and a lone gull emphasises the solitude.

Returning to the main path, which slants steeply up to the ridge on the left, once this is reached you are rewarded with superb views – south-east-wards to Corris with its woods and quarries, south-westwards across Tal-y-llyn Lake to the Tarren Hills. The Minffordd Path climbs steadily across the 2,000ft (610m) contour, past strata striated and speckled with veins of white quartz, the strata's own colours alternating from yellow to slate, with tormentil and bell heather adding to the spectrum. Swinging north-westwards the track reaches a fine ridge between Cwm Cau on the right and Cwm Amarch on the left before reaching the incongruity of a remarkably elegant ladder-stile on Craig Cau, at 2,617ft (798m) the crest of the long Mynydd Pencoed ridge. When I was there in October a polecat ran across the track. Who was the more surprised I don't know!

All this time Cader Idris's shapely summit and sweeping southern face have been beautifully revealed, and the way ahead easily identifiable. After a short descent from Craig Cau to the grassy col of Bwlch Cau, the track gradually climbs past a number of small cairns to the OS point on the summit of Pen y Gadair. Nearby is a boulder-built refuge, successor to the refreshment hut of Victorian times erected for the benefit of the many visitors who climbed the mountain then, probably led by a guide from Dolgellau. Good shelter and expansive views embracing almost all the mountains of north and central Wales merit a long stay here – a place for lunch sandwiches after three hours of climbing.

From the summit the ridge route to Mynydd Moel, a mile (1.6km) distant, starts in a north-easterly direction, first descending a short spur, followed by a grassy plateau, before making for a broad col with the savage cliffs of Twr Du falling steeply away to the left. Small cairns indicate the path, which heads for the gentle slopes of Mynydd Moel, crosses the nature reserve boundary fence by a ladder-stile, and soon reaches the cairn and large, walled shelter at the summit, 2,804ft (855m). It was here I saw my second polecat of the day, perched on the cairn, vigilant against a sombre sky.

The most direct descent is to follow the boundary fence southwards from the ladder-stile, crossing and recrossing it by more stiles, to avoid awkward patches of ground, either crags or bogs. After about 2/3 mile (1.2km), where the fence meets a stone boundary wall coming in from the north-east, turn south-westwards away from the fence and descend rough ground diagonally towards lower Cwm Cau and the familiar path of the earlier ascent. If the wall is missed, it doesn't matter – merely continue down by the reserve's boundary fence, eventually swinging right along the upper edge of the Idris woodlands to the Nant Cader. If there are difficulties in crossing this, move upstream to a suitable place. Minffordd is only 1/2 mile (.8km) away!

9 SNOWDON
YR WYDDFA

Time: Allow at least 7 hours, but be prepared to take 8!
Start and finish: Pen-y-Pas on the A4086 (grid reference 647557).
Approach: Being on a main road, Pen-y-Pas is easily reached by car through Capel Curig if coming from the east, or from the Caernarvon direction if approaching from any of the North Wales coastal resorts.
Attractions: Rightly regarded as the finest ridge walk south of the Black Cuillin of Skye, this walk involves steep scrambling on rock, an exposed traverse along a sensationally airy knife-edge, steep descents on rocky and scree-strewn slopes, followed by an easy finishing stretch. You need a good head for heights, and the promise of a fine day, so that poor visibility inhibits neither the views of stunning mountain scenery, nor adds to any problems of route finding. Unless you are an expert in conditions of snow and ice, this route should be avoided in severe winter weather.
OS sheet: 115

Start in the car park at Pen-y-Pas with the useful platform of 1,170ft (375m) already below you, and with your back to the hostel take the track in the far north-west corner (signposted 'Pyg Track'). For about ¾ mile (1.2km) this is a rough, well-marked track slanting diagonally up the hillside, its surface stabilised with huge boulders of slate. After passing among gigantic boulders littering the rough hillside, the track steepens and swings left by an old sheep-fold near the foot of crags. Small cairns mark its course as it emerges onto the small col on Bwlch y Moch, astride the 1,750ft (533m) contour. After an hour's steady climbing this small grassy area is an inviting spot to pause, admire the newly revealed view to the south and indulge in loin-girding for the hard work ahead as represented by the soaring pyramid of Crib Goch. When I climbed this route in late October streams of brilliantly lit vapour swirled across the mountains, parting only occasionally to allow glimpses of the summit, yet never obscuring the track immediately ahead, creating their own mystery and magic.

From Bwlch y Moch the Pyg Track contours round the southern flanks of Crib Goch, while the Horseshoe route, forking right, makes a frontal assault on the great buttress, slowly at first, then with increasing steepness, rising about 1,000ft (305m) from the col to the crest. Grass soon vanishes, rock rules, and raven's croak echoes from the cliffs. The track winds in and out between successive outcrops so numerous that it is both difficult and unnecessary to describe it in detail; bootmarks of thousands of climbers are the guide. In places you will need to use hands as well as feet, but eventually, after negotiating a rocky stairway, the cairn on the first summit is reached.

The Crib Goch Ridge from Crib-y-Ddysgl (Geoffrey N. Wright)

Ahead is the classic view of the Snowdon Horseshoe, with the narrow rocky ridge leading to the Pinnacles framing between their jagged peaks the elegant cone of Yr Wyddfa. To its left the skyline falls to Bwlch y Saethau, rising again to Y Lliwedd's massive, shadowed cone. Steep rock slopes fall sharply away from both sides of the Crib Goch ridge, left to Llyn Lldaw, right into Cwm Glas. About 400yd (366m) of knife-edge arête leads to the Pinnacles. In calm, clear weather, if you have a good head for heights, you can accept the challenge of the crest; in cross-winds, or merely because you prefer it, you can follow it more easily by keeping below on its left-hand (southern) side, continuing past the Pinnacles too. With care and confidence, but not foolhardiness, the Pinnacles can be traversed, using the ample hand- and foot-holds. Eventually you reach the grassy col of Bwlch Coch, another good place to rest and draw breath, before tackling Crib-y-Ddysgl. The track rises along the crest of another ridge, and, at a rocky wall, although there is a scramble through rocks to the left, a bolder approach up a chimney to the right is more rewarding in the magnificent views it eventually reveals. In any event the white concrete OS pillar at the summit is a beckoning beacon. The hard work for the morning is now over and the track, descending slightly to Bwlch Glas, encounters the Snowdon Mountain Railway and follows its more gentle gradients to the summit of Yr Wyddfa.

Given the right conditions the panorama from here is vast; but while it may be interesting to identify distant Scafell Pike or the Isle of Man it is more satisfying to appraise, with wonder, the way you have come, marvelling that Crib Goch, almost puny from this angle and with the green waters of Glaslyn in its embrace, is a mere 600ft (183m) lower. The Summit station and hotel are incongruous interlopers in this majestic, elemental landscape of shattered rocks; the summit cairn is east of the station. The Horseshoe route to Y Lliwedd descends from the walled enclosure at the far (southern) end of the hotel, soon swinging left and dropping very steeply across loose scree, continually slanting eastwards to the col at Bwlch y Saethau. Level ground for about ½ mile (.8km) comes as a great relief, although Y Lliwedd looks increasingly daunting. A large cairn marks where the Watkin Path leaves (or joins) the Horseshoe. Our way keeps left, soon climbing steeply to Y Lliwedd's twin peaks, where the track is sensationally close to the edge of the highest precipice in Wales, where great cliffs plunge darkly into the shadowed depths of Cwm Dyli.

The summit of West Peak, and that of Crib Goch, are the most dramatic highlights of this magnificent mountain walk; and as the track continues, after a short descent and climb, over East Peak, muscles ache, inviting more frequent stops to enjoy the retrospective view. After reaching a prominent cairn on some welcoming grass, the path drops down left, steeply but not presenting any difficulty, eventually joining the well-used Miners' Track near the waters of Llyn Llydaw. Follow it to the right, relieved that the hard work is over, and Pen-y-Pas is a mere 1¼ level miles (2km) away. Look back at the mountains you have climbed – Lliwedd and Yr Wyddfa in proud dark profile, Crib Goch catching the westering sun, the entire Horseshoe revealed in splendour, the whole a mountaineering memory of rock and wind and high places etched into experience.

Rivers·and·Valleys

Walking by rivers and through their valleys introduces you to the widest variety of scene and landscape. There is, however, a marked difference between the rivers with towing paths – the navigations past or present – and those without. The Lee, for example, has a firm towing path from Hertford to London, and the navigable reaches of the Wey, Great Ouse and Medway have similar paths alongside. A long-distance path is being established by the Thames, with a descriptive guide, *The Thames Walk*, obtainable from the Ramblers' Association. By the Severn a succession of riverside paths now forms the Severn Valley Way, a 31 mile (49.5km) walk from Stourport to Ironbridge. The splendid 52 mile (83km) Wye Valley walk connects Hereford with Chepstow through rolling countryside and the wooded gorges of the lower valley. There is also a 36 mile (57.5km) path between Hay-on-Wye and Rhayader; this beautiful river is now far more accessible than it used to be.

Two other old navigations with good footpaths are the Itchen, 11 miles (17.5km) from Winchester to Woodmill, and the Gipping, 17 miles (27km) from Ipswich to Stowmarket. There are paths alongside much of the Warwickshire Avon, the Witham and the Trent, and some of the more attractive reaches of the Nene are accessible by rights of way. In Yorkshire there is a right of way along the once navigable Derwent from Malton to Howsham, and lengths of towing path are still intact by some of the Sussex rivers once used for commerce – Ouse, Arun, Adur and Rother.

On these walks there are locks – or the remains of locks – weirs, sites of wharves and docks and other evidences of navigation to be seen. Occasionally there is a pub that once served the working boatmen but now has been turned round to face a road. To visualise these rivers as one-time commercial highways, or byways, may take some imagination, and an idea of the river's history should add interest to your walk.

Rivers that were never navigable, and navigable rivers in their higher reaches, are often less easy of access and you need to check in advance that rights of way exist. One of the finest areas for this type of walking is the Peak District National Park. Avoid the popular Dovedale walk in summer; try instead the Upper Dove north of Hartington, the Manifold, or the Wye through Miller's Dale and Chee Dale. There is good walking in the Churnet Valley in Staffordshire, in Lancashire's Ribblesdale and by Lune and Kent further north. The north-east has many fine rivers: the upper Wear and upper Tees, the Greta from Sleightholme to Greta Bridge, the Swale above Rich-

mond, the Dee through Dentdale, the Nidd above Knaresborough – these are just samples of the richness you can find. The slow-flowing rivers of East Anglia have less to offer, but much of Constable's Stour is delightful (though crowded in summer) and there is pleasant walking through Thetford Forest by the Little Ouse, in the higher reaches of the Waveney and the Lark and, more famously, from Cambridge to Grantchester beside the Cam.

Welsh river walking is usually more rugged; among the many choices, the Usk, Towy, Teifi, and in North Wales the Dee, Clwyd and Glaslyn in Snowdonia give many opportunities. Apart from the Wye Valley Walk in Powys, Wales has no long-distance riverside paths. There is one, however, in Scotland, the Speyside Way, a 30 mile (48km) walk from Spey Bay to Ballindalloch, much of it through the whisky country. A shorter path is the 7½ mile (12km) Water of Leith Walkway from Balerno to Leith, and the Scottish Tourist Board has compiled a booklet, *Walks and Trails*, which includes details of several short and easily accessible riverside rambles suitable for all ages, some with facilities for disabled people. Good, energetic walking can be enjoyed by the Tay, and in the Border country by the Tweed and its many tributaries.

Ireland's rivers are better known by anglers than by walkers and you may meet few people as you explore them. The Barrow in the south-east, with 40 miles (64km) of navigation, is delightful, especially in the lower reaches. The Suir, which flows into the Barrow estuary is at its best near the town of Cahir. Equally beautiful are the Lee and the Blackwater in the south-west.

Riverside and valley walking is often muddy, even in dry weather, and can lead into wild and isolated regions. Don't follow a river if you want to get from A to B as quickly as possible. This is walking to take your time over, often with ducks, herons or even kingfishers as your companions. Always take a map and study it carefully before setting off to ensure that you can cross any tributaries or side streams on the route. And make sure you know beforehand in which direction the river is flowing. It's very frustrating to find that for some time past you've been heading the wrong way!

10	Middle Nene, Northamptonshire	8½ miles (14km)
11	River Wye, Herefordshire	8½ miles (14km)
12	Upper Medway, East Sussex	6½ miles (10km)
13	River Lark, East Suffolk	4½ miles (7km)
14	East Lyn and Hoar Oak rivers, Devon	7 miles (11km)
15	Severn at Ironbridge, Shropshire	5 or 10 miles (8 or 16km)
16	Derbyshire Wye	5½ miles (9km)
17	River Tees, County Durham	6 miles (9.6km)
18	River Swale, North Yorkshire	5 or 11 miles (8 or 17.5km)

Further reading: Scottish Tourist Board. *Walks and Trails* (PO Box 15, Edinburgh EH1 1UY, 1983)

Sharp, David. *The Thames Walk*, Ramblers' Association (1–5 Wandsworth Road, London SW8 2LJ, 1985)

Low Force, Upper Teesdale (Geoffrey N. Wright) (*see* page 87)

10 MIDDLE·NENE

Time: 4 hours.
Start and finish: Thrapston. Turn into De Vere Road, west off A605, 300yd from the junction with the A604; continue onto a rough road alongside playing fields. There is space for parking near a lake on the right. Boots are recommended; there are plenty of nettles en route.
Approach: Thrapston is a small town on the A604/A605 crossing, between Huntingdon and Kettering.
Attractions: A quiet river and lakeside walk with a short but lovely wooded stretch and two interesting villages and several good churches either on the walk or within easy reach. The first stretch, repeated on the return, is past gravel workings; but reclamation is rapid and is resulting in a chain of lakes which soon become acclimatised. There is a pleasant pub in Wadenhoe.
OS sheet: 141

The Nene (pronounced neen or nen) is one of England's quietest major rivers. It rises near Daventry and flows through Northampton, Peterborough and Wisbech, and thence into the Wash. It has a wide flood plain; then the Northamptonshire hills rise gently on either side. No county seems to have more church spires and towers visible as you walk.

Walk along the track bordering the lake until you come to a footbridge below a lock; the Nene locks have guillotine type lower gates and conventional upper ones. Across the footbridge there is an old mill; there used to be a mill by every lock. Don't cross the bridge, but turn northwards alongside the river and past the gravel workings. Cross by the middle of three Meccano-like bridges and follow the course of the river as it curves east and then northeast. The path is just discernible through a rough meadow with a variety of wild flowers. Signs indicate that the lake on the left and its surroundings are a nature reserve administered by the Northampton Trust for Nature Conservation, and you may meet an ardent bird-watcher hurrying to or from the small hide, open to the public, which is shortly passed.

The path continues between the river and a small wood; ahead a handsome church tower dominates the view. This is All Saints', Aldwincle. A lake appears ahead, though it is not on the map. The path leads across a side weir and past Titchmarsh Lock; again, note the old mill beside it. Several boats are moored hereabouts. Follow around the northern end of the lake and head straight for the church tower; if you lose the footpath it's as easy to join the road for the few hundred yards into Aldwincle – spelt with a 'c' on the road signs and the map, but with a 'k' everywhere else.

All Saints' Church is disused, but addresses on the door indicate where the key can be obtained. It has a fine interior and is worth seeing if time permits.

Mill at Wadenhoe on the Nene (R. Russell)

The poet John Dryden was born in the old rectory opposite. Continue through the village (but be warned that the pub was converted into a dwelling house many years ago) to St Peter's Church, also worth a visit. Just past the church, a sign proclaims a footpath to Wadenhoe. Take it, but treat the next signpost with caution, being sure to keep to the top edge of the fields and head for the nearest corner of a wood. Keep to the upper edge of the wood; once past it, descend to the river. Soon the walk enters a beautiful wooded stretch of river bank with the occasional glimpse of another church ahead and above you. In a few minutes you find yourself immediately beneath this church and with the cottages of Wadenhoe just ahead.

This is another church worthy of a visit, much of it thirteenth century; but the keys may have to be fetched from the village. This is just over halfway and the King's Head, with its garden running down to the riverside, makes a welcome halt. It is a simple, unmodernised pub with good beer. Wadenhoe has several charming cottages, one with a dovecote, and Caroline Cottage has an extraordinary portico fit for a mansion. The village is small and takes only a few minutes to explore. Turn downhill before the polygonal cottage in the village centre, to a bridge across the millstream. Carry on to a cock-up bridge across the Nene and make for a stile in the corner of the field. You can divert across the next field to Achurch church (yes, this is a church-dominated walk) or continue alongside the hedge to a narrow nettle-filled path between two fields. Emerge by a farm; skirt the farmyard and join the road which has wide grass verges and takes you half a mile south to Thorpe Waterville. Again the view ahead is dominated by a tower – St Mary's, Titchmarsh.

At Thorpe Waterville turn right, cross the old bridge over the Nene and return alongside the river resuming your outward route. Alternatively, turn left onto the main road, head towards Thrapston and take a footpath across the fields for Titchmarsh. From St Mary's there is another path towards Thrapston that brings you out on the A605 just on the edge of the town.

For a shorter walk, leave your car at Thorpe Waterville and do the Aldwincle–Wadenhoe–Achurch section, about 3½ miles (6km).

11 RIVER·WYE

Time: 3¼ hours.

Start and finish: Goodrich Castle car park. In winter months start and finish can be by the single-track iron bridge on the lane from Goodrich to Symonds Yat East. Boots are recommended.

Approach: Goodrich lies ¾ mile (1km) east of the A40 about midway between Ross and Monmouth. The castle is clearly signposted.

Attractions: A circular walk along one of the finest stretches of the Wye. For nearly 8 miles (13km) it is within a few yards of the river through woodland and across meadows. A visit to Goodrich Castle is easily included.

OS sheet: 162

From the car park, which it is certainly advisable to use in summer months, walk back to the village, go straight over the crossroads, bear left along a lane, past the school and turn right to cross the playing field. Make for the left-hand corner of the next field, then cross another field to the churchyard. Go through the churchyard to a lane, turn right at a T- junction and left by a foot-path sign beside the Cross Keys. Keep right at a farmyard, cross a field and head for the left-hand end of a wood. Cross a fence and follow the line of a hedge, making for a stile in the corner of a field. Bear left and descend to the road; take the small road opposite for Symonds Yat East and turn down to the riverside between Ferry Cottage and the bridge. It is not as complicated as it sounds! Alternatively this point can be reached by walking along the B4228 from Goodrich village, but this is often very busy. In winter it may be possible to park by the bridge, but there is room for no more than three cars here.

Walk upstream. The first few yards may be rough and muddy, but you are soon on firm ground between the Wye and Coppet Hill. Now enjoy the unfolding scene as the densely wooded hills close in and the river winds between. Soon you are below the famous viewpoint of Symonds Yat Rock, one of the great limestone cliffs rearing above the river. Here the Wye Valley tourists – Wordsworth was one – would land and climb the hill for refreshments and the view, rejoining their boat on the far side of the peninsula, 4 miles (6km) by river but ½ mile (1km) overland. As you turn around the southernmost point of this loop of the Wye the Coldwell Rocks tower above on the opposite side. Beneath them is the course of the old Monmouth–Ross railway, opened in 1874 and closed in 1964, one of the finest of the many scenic railways which sadly and shortsightedly have been lost. The long-distance Wye Valley Walk uses parts of this line.

Styhead Tarn, Scafell Pike (Geoffrey N. Wright) (*see* page 49)
The northern crags of Cader Idris from Twr Du (Geoffrey N. Wright) (*see* page 55)

Now walk for about ½ mile (1km) through a wood, passing a monument to John Whitehead Warre, drowned in 1804 aged sixteen while swimming in the river nearby. The lengthy inscription is clearly legible and draws attention to John's piety and his parents' feeling of guilt at being unable to revive him. We are also told that apparatus and directions by the Humane Society for saving apparently drowned persons are available at Coldwell church. Unfortunately there has never been a church at Coldwell, so take extra care, please! Emerging from the wood, continue through meadows with the mellow stone buildings of Baynhams Farm above and a wooded hill euphoniously called Rosemary Topping on the further bank. Ahead a strange green tower can be glimpsed through the trees; this is part of the paper factory near Lower Lydbrook on the opposite bank. In the next stretch of woodland take the upper path if the river is running high.

Continue beneath the old railway bridge. The Lydbrook area was a busy industrial centre in early Victorian days, using the river for transport until the railway arrived. The Wye Valley Walk crosses the river here and you will soon pick up its waymarks as you approach the large youth hostel, once the vicarage of Welsh Bicknor. (To shorten the walk, take a path on the left here and follow it up the hill and along a lane back to Goodrich, completing a round walk of 6½ miles (10km).)

Carry on past the youth hostel and the pretty little mid-Victorian church of St Margaret, Welsh Bicknor; if open, go in to see the interesting thirteenth-century effigy. Beyond the far bank is Lower Lydbrook village and ahead on your side is Courtfield, home in the past of the old Catholic family of Vaughan, of which Cardinal Vaughan is probably the best known. Following the bend of the Wye enables the house with its chapel and inharmonious modern extension to be seen from three sides. It is now a seminary belonging to the Mill Hill Fathers.

You lose sight of Courtfield as you head north-west below a wood, with fine views across the Wye although some of the riverside development opposite is unfortunate. In about a mile (1.6km), enter Thomas Wood and soon pass the stone abutment of a bridge that once returned the railway to the far side. This wood ends by the next bend in the river: Goodrich Castle now appears on the near skyline with Kerne Bridge, built in 1828, in the foreground.

If you have left your car by the iron bridge, leave the riverside path at this point and ascend the steep hill following the power cables. At the top of the climb is a road. Cross to a lane opposite and follow this between attractive cottages. You will see a road below you; take one of the tracks leading down to this road and turn left along it to the lane to Symonds Yat East, the iron bridge and your car. Otherwise, carry on to Kerne Bridge and join the road. The farm across the road is on the site of Flanesford Priory. Take the lane on the right for Goodrich Castle, dating from 1160. Here Wordsworth is said to

The River Wye below Symonds Yat Pool (R. Russell)
River Swale at Gunnerside (R. Russell) (*see page 89*)

have met the literal-minded little heroine of *We are Seven*; and here he complained about the mock-Gothic rival to the castle, Goodrich Court, built in the early nineteenth century and now, apart from its gatehouse on the A40, demolished. There are splendid views over the Wye.

If more convenient, it is possible to begin and end this walk from Lydbrook Junction where the railway bridge is now a pedestrian crossing. For extensive exploration of this superb countryside there is the 52 mile (84km) Wye Valley walk from Chepstow to Hereford, and for the Chepstow to Monmouth part of the valley there is also Offa's Dyke Path.

12 UPPER·MEDWAY

Time: 2½ hours.

Start and finish: Layby at Ham Bridge on the B2110 Groombridge–Forest Row road in East Sussex. Boots are needed except in very dry spells.

Approach: Groombridge is 4 miles (6km) south-west of Tunbridge Wells, reached by taking the B2110 off the A264 East Grinstead road. From the south, use the A26 through Crowborough and take the minor road for Groombridge from Eridge station. Leaving Groombridge on B2110, cross the railway in ½ mile (.8km). A long S-bend follows, and a Medway tributary is crossed at Ham Bridge. The bridge has been widened and there is parking space for a few cars on the west side.

Attractions: This walk combines contrasting sections of two recognised routes: Forest Way, from Groombridge to East Grinstead, a 9½ mile (15km) linear country park created from an abandoned railway line; and the Weald-way, a 57 mile (92km) walk from Gravesend to Uckfield. There are two pubs in Hartfield on the route, and you are never more than ½ mile (.8km) from the infant Medway. The landscape – riverside meadows, gentle wooded hills, handsome farms with oasthouses – is superb.

From its source in the East Sussex Weald the Medway flows 69 miles (111km) to the Thames at Sheerness. It is navigable for 42 miles (68km) from Tonbridge. Here in its uppermost reaches it is normally a quiet little stream; it takes an effort to realise that Maidstone, Rochester and the great Chatham Dockyard stand on the same river.

OS sheet: 188

On the Groombridge side of Ham Bridge a path runs alongside the tributary stream to the firm and well-trodden track of Forest Way. In a few yards this crosses the stream and heads just south of west in nearly a straight line. Forest Way is constructed on the route of a single-track railway line, opened in 1866 and closed by Dr Beeching a hundred years later, that connected the London–Hastings line to the line from London to Seaford that now terminates at East Grinstead. The Way is maintained as a linear country park and there are benches and even tactfully constructed picnic tables here and there.

Pass under a bridge and continue on a series of embankments and cuttings with the river – this is now the Medway – always close by on the right. At Batts Green the old platform survives. Carry on, walking often through what seems a long green tunnel where the branches of the trackside trees meet overhead, crossing two streams by simple viaducts. Wooded hills rise on either side of the valley and to the south can be seen the churches of Withyham and Hartfield.

Forest Way on the line of the old railway above the river (R. Russell)

After 2½ miles (4km) the railway coal wharves, still in use, and Hartfield station now carefully converted into an attractive private house, are reached. Forest Way continues for a further 7 miles (11km) but leave it at the road and walk up the hill into Hartfield, a pleasant little village with a couple of rather upmarket pubs. Turn left to the lane to the church and look for an inscribed-stone 'public footpath' sign opposite the entrance to the churchyard. Follow the path across the field to a stile. On the far side of the stile the right of way runs through the middle of a field, sometimes sown, to another stile. Continue along the top of the next field beneath the large trees and break off for the far corner downhill, where there is a wartime concrete gun emplacement by a stream, with a stile to the road beside it. Cross the road, step a few yards toward the Withyham sign and climb a stile with a yellow 'WW' waymark – the Wealdway.

The path runs across the middle of the field – keep midway between a barn on the left and the stream on the right – to a waymarked gate. From here you can see a wooden gate and stile ahead, taking you across Forest Way. Continue forward, cross a footbridge over the Medway and make for the corner ahead where the river runs close to a bank. On this bank is a waymarked stile; cross it and take the track towards the farm buildings. Keep left of a barn and walk through the farmyard; this is Summerford Farm, of handsome red brick with three oasthouses.

Two gates face you over the road. Enter the right-hand one and keep to the left of the field as close to the wooded bank as possible. It may well be wet and muddy hereabouts. There is wire at the end of this stretch but if you turn towards the river there is a stile that takes you across a little stream, onto a narrow track and into a field. Head towards the farm – Hale Court Farm – and turn right at a three-way fingerpost.

Cross the river once, but immediately before a second crossing turn right alongside the tributary stream; the main river actually heads off northwards about 100yd (90m) from here. Cross the wire ahead (it should be protected). On an embankment in front is Forest Way, but the right of way over the field had been ploughed when I walked the route. If passage is impossible, it is no great problem to divert slightly to the stile and climb up to the track. Turn left and you are about 200yd (183m) from the car.

For a straightforward one-way walk with no need for map reading, simply continue along Forest Way from Hartfield for a further 6 miles (9.6km). In ½ mile (.8km) the line of a Roman road is crossed. Then on the north side across the Medway there is a deer farm and a new poplar plantation. Ashdown Forest lies to the south. Cross the Medway at Forest Row. The Way continues, passing woodlands and a lane marking the boundary between East and West Sussex, with Weir Wood Reservoir visible to the south-east. It ends close to the A22 on the eastern side of East Grinstead. You can return to the starting point by bus; service 291 connects East Grinstead and Groombridge at approximately 2 hour intervals, the journey taking ¾ hour. Sunday buses are less frequent and it is best to check beforehand.

13 RIVER·LARK

Time: The walk will take about 1¾ hours but can be extended through the forest for a further ½ hour or so.

Start and finish: The Forestry Commission car park near West Stow. Boots are not needed except after heavy rain.

Approach: West Stow is about 4 miles (6km) north-west of Bury St Edmunds. Take the A1101 Wisbech road from Bury and turn right at Flempton after 3½ miles (5.6km). At West Stow keep bearing left and follow a sign for West Stow Country Park. In about 600yd (550m) turn right at a Forestry Commission sign and leave the car in the car park some 500yd (460m) along.

Attractions: In an area not notable for good walking this route is full of interest. It includes part of the King's Forest, a few hundred yards of the Icknield Way, a stretch of the River Lark towing path, a reconstruction of an Anglo-Saxon village, and what must be the prettiest sewage works in the country. It is best avoided on summer weekends when parts of the route may be busy.

OS sheet: 155

Cherryground Lock with its unique crescent shape

There is a map of the King's Forest by the car park. It shows a forest trail and the walk begins by following the southern arm of this. The route is clearly indicated by yellow markers. The King's Forest was named in honour of George V's Silver Jubilee; it mostly consists of well-matured conifers, but it has also absorbed shelter belts of oak and beech planted well over a hundred years ago. Squirrels run across the path and watch from above. Follow the waymarked path across two bridleways. In a little under a mile (1.6km) the path begins to head northwards and crosses a straight east-west track. Take this track westwards; very soon you emerge from the forest and pass a ruined barn on the left in the corner of a large field.

Now follow a grass path along the southern edge of the forest, passing a group of impressive elderly beeches, to a stone-surfaced forest road. Turn left here; this is Icklingham Belt on the line of the Icknield Way, an ancient road from Norfolk to Dorset whose name was first recorded in AD903. This brings you in a few hundred yards to the minor road from West Stow; cross over and follow the path through trees to the second of two wooden farm gates on the left. Climb the stile and admire the lake ahead, created some years ago from a gravel pit and now stocked with coarse fish and populous with a variety of ducks. Make for the south side of the lake and soon the walk is on an embankment between the lake and the River Lark.

The Lark rises south of Bury St Edmunds and flows into the Great Ouse between Ely and Littleport. It was a transport route in the Middle Ages and was improved into a navigation in the early eighteenth century when locks and staunches were built, but most of the traffic came upriver and progress was often difficult and slow. It was further improved in the 1830s, but the opening of a railway to Bury took away most of its trade. A final effort to restore its fortunes was made in 1890, but this quickly failed. The upper river ceased to be used after 1894 and all trade had ended by 1930, although pleasure boats still use the lower river as far as Judes Ferry.

Although the lake on the left is enchanting to look at, keep a careful watch on the river. Very soon it begins to curve, and on the curve is the brick-built chamber of a lock. This is Cherryground Lock, built in 1842 by one of the Lark's improvers, Sir Thomas Geary Cullum, whose initials used to be visible on one of the coping stones. Now it is in poor repair – a great pity, for its crescent shape is unusual if not unique on English navigations.

You are now walking through West Stow Country Park with occasional discreetly placed notices giving information about the nearby flora and fauna. The riverside path goes past the site of a lock-keeper's cottage, demolished in 1979. A diversion can be made through the trees to view the reconstruction of an Anglo-Saxon village about ¼ mile (.4km) distant; this is no flight of fancy but a researched project by Cambridge University – the Lark Valley is known to have been a Saxon site.

Beside the river again you soon arrive at the remains of Lackford Staunch where a rising and falling gate, fitted into recesses in the brickwork, once controlled the water levels enabling boats to pass. At one time there were fourteen staunches on the Lark as well as eleven locks. The lakes to the south were created from gravel pits; one is a wildfowl reserve and another is used for sailing. The building a short distance away on your side of the river is the pump-house of a sewage works built in 1887 and supplied with coal brought up on the Lark. It is now preserved as a feature of the country park.

The path now leaves the riverside. Close to the pump-house there is a stile on the right; climb it and head diagonally through the trees away from the river, passing a large half-blasted oak, to arrive soon at the road. Cross and walk eastwards along the forest edge until a horse path heading north is reached. Take this, and look for a yellow marker on your outward track. Turn right and follow the track to the car park. If you have time to spare and would like to meet more squirrels, continue up the horse path until you meet the yellow markers of the northern arm of the forest walk and turn right there. This will add only fifteen or twenty minutes to the walk.

14 EAST·LYN·AND· HOAR·OAK·RIVERS

Time: 3½ hours (several variations possible).
Start and finish: Lynmouth. There are several car parks in the village, the nearest being at the end of Tors Road by the A39 bridge over the East Lyn. Boots or stout footwear are advisable.
Approach: Lynmouth is on the A39 North Devon coast road about 17 miles (27km) west of Minehead and within the Exmoor National Park.
Attractions: The spectacular, steeply wooded valleys of the East Lyn and Hoar Oak rivers in the National Trust's Watersmeet Estate. There are 30 miles (48km) of footpaths in all.
OS sheet: 180

Lynmouth was originally a fishing village which developed into a popular holiday resort in the Victorian era when its dramatic landscape drew many visitors. An early guide book describes the area as 'an immense gorge, into which the magnificent ravine of the East Lyn and the densely wooded but sequestered valley of the West Lyn abruptly descend; the twin streams, after heavy or long continued rains, assume formidable proportions and rush down to the sea with extraordinary speed and great uproar!' On the night of 15 August 1952, these twin streams created the Lynmouth flood disaster, when shops and houses were flooded to a depth of 10 feet (3m) and 34 people lost their lives. The flood changed the face of Lynmouth and evidence can be seen along this walk. Among the casualties of the flood was the hydro-electric power station, the largest in Britain when it was built in 1890.

From the car park in Tors Road follow the path on the north side of the East Lyn into the country. Cross to the south side at Black Pool Bridge in just under 1 mile (1.6km). Continue past the site of the Lynrock Mineral Water factory, destroyed in the flood, and look out for an earthenware ginger-beer bottle preserved as a relic. The next bridge, Chiselcombe, has been rebuilt, but traces of the earlier bridge can be seen. Soon Watersmeet, where the Hoar Oak Water meets the East Lyn, is reached. This is a Site of Special Scientific Interest frequented by herons, wagtails, dippers and kingfishers as well as by plenty of people in summer. Watersmeet House, built in 1830 as a fishing and shooting lodge, now incorporates a National Trust shop and a café, with beautifully sited tea gardens close by.

Now follow the south bank of the East Lyn on a path signposted Rockford, passing an old mine adit – a reminder of a vain nineteenth-century attempt to win ore – and some recently restored limekilns. Stone for Watersmeet

House was quarried nearby. Enjoy a splendid climb to a welcome seat and fine views across the valley. Keep forward for Rockford, crossing the river at Ash Bridge. The woodland consists mainly of sessile oak; look out for the rare Devon whitebeam and Irish spurge and various lichens, ferns and mosses. From time to time scree slopes interrupt the dense woodland. Tranquil pools, well known to local anglers, contrast with rapids and small waterfalls on the descending river.

The path climbs to a stretch of open hillside, a good place for a rest, then continues through woods to Rockford, a very small village with inn, craft shop and tea rooms. Cross by the bridge, not the ford, and turn right along the road through the village up the hill to the isolated St Brendan's Church. There are excellent views from the hilltop. Turn right at the T-junction and look out across the East Lyn valley to Butter Hill and Kipscombe Hill beyond. Now the lane descends to join the B3223 at Hillsford Bridge. Here the Farley Water meets the Hoar Oak Water and you are back in National Trust woodland. Take the path alongside the Hoar Oak signposted Watersmeet ¾/ Rockford 1¾. The river descends dramatically through a series of waterfalls

The East Lyn River (A. J. Russell)

to Watersmeet, forcing its way past huge boulders. Soon steps take you down to the meeting of the waters again.

From Watersmeet return can be by the outward path, but there are two alternatives if time permits. The shorter is to walk towards Black Pool Bridge along the north side of the East Lyn. This route incorporates a short stretch of Arnold's Linhay Path, a Victorian transport route on the line of a far older track from Lynmouth to Countisbury. The longer alternative is a hilly route across the Cleaves. For this, cross the A39 opposite Watersmeet House and follow a path across open country roughly parallel to the river to the north, zigzagging up and down hillsides and reaching the high point of Oxen Tor about ¾ mile (1.2km) before Lynmouth. The descent through woods brings you to the A39 a few hundred yards from the car park in Tors Road.

Information on the area is available from Watersmeet House and if you have a few days to spare there is much to see and do. Apart from the 30 miles (48km) of footpaths in the Watersmeet Estate, nearby is the cliff railway connecting Lynmouth to Lynton above, the wild Lorna Doone country and the Valley of Rocks. If possible, though, try to avoid the summer season; the area is at least as beautiful in spring or autumn and there are far fewer people around.

15 SEVERN·AT·IRONBRIDGE

Time: The riverside walk will take about 2½ hours, but with diversions and visits to museum sites a whole day is needed.

Start and finish: Car park at Dale End Riverside Park or at the Severn Warehouse nearby. Boots are not needed.

Approach: Ironbridge is fully signposted from Telford. If coming from the south, take either A442 or B4373 from Bridgnorth. Car parking is free. The car parks are ½ mile (.8km) west of Ironbridge.

Attractions: The Ironbridge Gorge is the birthplace of the Industrial Revolution. Here Abraham Darby was the first to smelt iron using coke as fuel, and several of the most important industrial sites are within 1½ miles (2km) of the riverside. The Ironbridge Gorge Museum is maintaining and restoring these sites and the walk is easily combined with visits to the museum's properties. One ticket admits to all of them. The walk itself is mainly along roads – and the road on the north side of the river is busy with traffic in the summer – but this is the only way to gain full enjoyment from this extraordinary area.

OS sheet: 127

Before beginning the walk – or before leaving the area – try to fit in a visit to Buildwas Abbey, about 1½ miles (2km) to the west of the car parks. Drive past the vast cooling towers of the power station, cross the bridge and the abbey is tucked away immediately on the right. There are good remains of the buildings, which date from about 1200. It is a peaceful and beautiful place and makes a moving contrast to the industrial sites in the Gorge below.

The Dale End Riverside Park has been created by the Telford Development Corporation from an area of rough ground; there is an attractive picnic area surrounded by splendid trees. On the opposite bank of the river can be seen the arches of the Severn Valley Railway viaduct tucked into the woods of Benthall Edge. Take the path alongside the antiques warehouse and emerge by a landing stage; there are occasional boat trips on the river from here. Cross the car park to the building that looks like a Gothic chapel but is in fact the Severn Warehouse, built by the Coalbrookdale Iron Company in 1842. It is now the interpretative centre of the museum and the best place to start from if you intend to visit the museum's sites. Beside the warehouse is what used to be Ludcroft Wharf; note the troughs which once held the iron rails of the horse-drawn railway from coal pits in Madeley. Most of the old wharves that lined the Severn have disappeared but one of the trows, the characteristic large sailing vessels of this river, has been salvaged and is now being restored by the museum.

The road along to the east used to be the wharfage, enormously busy in the eighteenth and early nineteenth centuries with riverside trade. There are converted warehouses and old pubs alongside, with limekilns behind the warehouse just past the Swan Inn. Across the river were boat-building yards, active until the 1860s. Soon you arrive at the Iron Bridge, of which you will already have had several glimpses. This, the most famous bridge in the country, was completed in 1779 and opened two years later. It was cast at the foundry in Coalbrookdale, but proved more costly than anticipated and it was some time before its example was followed. It attracted artists as well as sightseers and changed the whole pattern of road transport in the district. The tollhouse information centre is at the south end of the bridge. Opposite is the Tontine Hotel, built by the ironmasters who sponsored the bridge, and close by is the museum shop.

Continue along the lower road. In 1/3 mile (.5km) reach the Bedlam furnaces, built in 1757, originally powered by water pumped from the Severn and now gradually being excavated. Another mile of roadside walking (there is a footpath most of the way) brings you to a road junction. The left turn leads soon to the entrance to the Blists Hill Open Air Museum, covering 42 acres (17ha). Apart from what was there already, including a length of the Shropshire Canal and the Hay inclined plane, three blast furnaces, a mine and a brick and tile works, several buildings and items of machinery have been transferred here from nearby sites. Allow at least 1½ hours if you wish to explore.

At the road junction turn onto a path above the river. In about 400yd (.4km) you come to a short restored length of the old Coalport Canal. To the left is the steep slope of the Hay incline, rising 207ft (63m). At the top, tub-boats laden with coal or iron were drawn up onto wheeled cradles and lowered on rails laid on the incline while empty boats ascended. The machinery was controlled from an engine house at the top. This incline was one of three built on the Shropshire Canal and was last used in 1894.

By the basin at the foot of the incline is the entrance to the Coalport Tar Tunnel, another of the museum's sites. This was an enterprise of the ironmaster William Reynolds and was probably first intended as an underground canal. However, a spring of tar was struck about 300yd (274m) in, and tar was produced from 1787 until 1843. The total length of the tunnel is over 1,000 yards (914m), and for some years a horse-drawn railway was operated through it to the coal pits on Blists Hill.

Walk alongside the canal to the Coalport China works. Now restored as a museum, this was the home of the Coalport China Company founded by John Rose about 1795 and famous for fine quality decorative wares. If pressed for time, retrace to the basin below the incline and cross the river by the footbridge, noting the iron plaque telling in verse that it is a war memorial: Or continue along Coalport High Street for about 700yd (640m) to Coalport Bridge and cross there. This bridge replaced a rival to the Iron Bridge – the Preens Eddy Bridge, made of wood supported on cast-iron ribs and opened in

1780. It was largely rebuilt about 1818; its name is remembered in the picnic site on the south bank. Follow the riverside path, cross a field and make for the Boat Inn by the footbridge mentioned above. If you ascend the hill by the Boat and turn right along a track you come to a large house, The Tuckies, one of the oldest buildings in the Gorge and the home of William Reynolds, ironmaster, canal builder and founder of Coalport town. Below The Tuckies, but more easily reached from the riverside, is Maw's tileworks. This is now reduced to less than a quarter of its original size; in the 1880s it was the largest tile factory in the world. Now what's left houses a craft centre, which is well worth a visit.

You are now in Jackfield, once an important port and manufacturing centre and the home of hundreds of watermen who sailed or bow-hauled the Severn trows and barges. Little evidence of all this remains, apart from another tileworks, Craven Dunnills, which is soon reached. Restoration is taking place here, and the buildings now incorporate a Tile Museum. Close by, Jackfield Church contains examples of the local product. Half a mile (.8km) brings you to another important bridge. Built in 1908 this was the first

The Iron Bridge (Ironbridge Gorge Museum Trust)

large reinforced concrete bridge in England. Either cross here to rejoin the road a few yards east of the Bedlam furnaces and carry on back through Iron-bridge to the car park, or continue south of the river and cross by the Iron Bridge itself.

Several diversions can be taken including a walk up Coalbrookdale to see Abraham Darby's furnace and the Museum of Iron, an exploration of the narrow streets and alleys of Ironbridge town and of the Madeley Wood area behind the Bedlam furnaces or, south of the river, a tour of Benthall Woods with a visit to Benthall Hall, now owned by the National Trust. From all these walks there are glorious and often unexpected views of the Gorge below, and each provides a wealth of varied interest.

If you do plan to visit the Severn Gorge, and want to get the best out of the visit, it is advisable to read up about the area in advance. The Museum Trust publishes a range of guides: contact the Ironbridge Gorge Museum Trust, Ironbridge, Telford, Salop TF8 7AW. An excellent guide to walks in the Gorge by members of the Ironbridge and Coalbrookdale Society is obtainable locally. For the history of the area, Barrie Trinder's *The Industrial Revolution in Shropshire* and *The Darbys of Coalbrookdale* (both published by Phillimore, the latter in paperback) are recommended.

16 DERBYSHIRE· WYE

Time: 3 hours (several extensions are possible).
Start and finish: Ashford in the Water; layby in village centre or small car park behind church. Boots are needed.
Approach: Ashford in the Water is just off the A6, 2 miles (3km) west of Bakewell and 9 miles (14km) east of Buxton.
Attractions: Splendid open views across limestone country to begin with. Then the dramatic scene at Monsal Head and a riverside walk through Monsal Dale. Finally a woodland stroll above the Wye.
OS sheet: 119

The Peak District National Park is established walking country with clear waymarking on the many routes. It is rich in riverside walking – within a few miles of the chosen route are the River Lathkill, 3 miles (5km) south of Ashford; the River Bradford, 2 miles (3km) further south; and to the west there are several excellent walks alongside the Derwent. Near the southern edge of the Park the valleys of the Manifold and Hamps are full of interest, and Dovedale provides the best-known walk of all. However, most of the walks are well used; in holiday periods they may become quite crowded and the car parks, of which there are several, may be overflowing. Choose your time carefully, therefore; many walkers think the Peak District is at its best in the winter months.

Ashford in the Water is a pretty and well-kept village with plenty of places in which to eat and drink. From the centre, walk along Fennel Street and into Vicarage Lane. A signpost indicates a public footpath doubling back on the left; take this, along a track, across the middle of a field and over a stone stile to a walled track climbing steadily but gently upwards. As you ascend, look back from time to time to enjoy the view.

There are several stiles to climb; the track is clearly waymarked and in just under 2 miles (3km) arrives, with little warning, at a point close to Monsal Head at the very edge of Monsal Dale. You seem to be standing on the rim of a huge deep bowl. Below you catch glimpses of the Wye, spanned by the five-arched viaduct of the old Midland Railway branch line to Buxton. The valley sides are steep and thickly wooded. It is a wonderful place.

Continue along the narrow path on the edge of the slope. This brings you to an opening onto a minor road near the village of Little Longstone, where refreshments can be obtained at the Monsal Head Hotel. Below this opening, steps have been cut, descending to the bottom of the valley. Cross the river by the viaduct. This is now part of the Monsal Trail created on the line of the old railway which closed in 1968. The trail runs from Bakewell to the

Derelict bonemill beside the Wye (R. Russell)

Wyedale car park about 2 miles (3km) from Buxton. The many tunnels – you will see one of them behind you as you walk onto the viaduct – have been closed, but alternative routes have been signposted. The trail keeps close to the river through Miller's Dale and Chee Dale and makes a splendid extension to your walk; or leave it for another day and take in Tideswell Dale as well.

On the right, at the far side of the viaduct, walk down to a footbridge by a weir and admire the ducks. The path through the Dale takes the opposite direction; so with the Wye on your left walk away from the viaduct, now 80ft (24m) above, into the wooded valley, passing weirs and shallow rapids. Fin Cop rises steeply above the opposite bank to a height of 1,072ft (327m); there is an Iron Age settlement on top. All too soon you emerge close to a stone wall bordering the A6. Cross the road and go through the small car park opposite, to a stile on the far side. From here the path is waymarked by the familiar yellow arrow with '3' on it. Head across limestone, up an incline, then into Great Shacklow Wood, catching glimpses of the river below close to the A6. In about a mile (1.6km) the track descends to the riverside and crosses an onrush of water emerging from a tunnel; this comes from the abandoned Magpie lead mine a mile (1.6km) away in the hills above. Next a derelict watermill is reached with two iron wheels still in place. This was a bonemill, crushing bones for manure. At the riverside are the remains of a pumping station also with an iron waterwheel, and by the bridge a gauging point for the river.

Continue parallel to the river, passing the site of a mine where the stone called 'black marble' was once quarried. The path emerges onto a minor road to Sheldon; follow a footpath beside the A6 and cross Sheepwash Bridge into the centre of Ashford. Note the stone enclosure at the bridge side where sheep were once penned during the washing process. The bridge dates from the mid-seventeenth century. Ashford church is worth a visit, though much of it was rebuilt in the 1870s. It contains a table made from the local black marble.

By following other waymarked paths the walk can be extended through Deepdale – a dry limestone dale – to the little village of Sheldon. From Sheldon it is about 1½ miles (2km) to Ashford by footpath or minor road.

17 River · Tees

Time: The walk should take no more than 3 hours, but you may wish to spend some time at High Force. Boots are recommended.

Start and finish: The west end of the hamlet of Holwick, 3½ miles (5.6km) from Middleton-in-Teesdale, on the south side of the Tees.

Approach: Holwick is at the end of a 3 mile (5km) No Through Road that leaves B6277 ½ mile (.8km) south of Middleton-in-Teesdale. Leave the car at the beginning of a track leading to the fell, just where the road makes a right-angle turn.

Attractions: An energetic walk along the northern slopes of Holwick Fell with fine views of Teesdale. Then you join the Pennine Way along the river-side in the opposite direction, passing a vast and active quarry, High Force, England's mightiest waterfall, and Low Force; a most fascinating stretch of Teesdale.

OS sheet: 92

Go forward along the track, through a gate, and onto the fellside with Holwick Scars above on the left. There are wide views ahead and to the north; this is a sparsely populated area and the white-painted farms and cottages stand out brilliantly in the sunshine. In about a mile (1.6km) the Upper Teesdale Nature Reserve is reached with a convenient notice board outlining the local geography. Continue through the Reserve until a notice directs you off the hard track along a green path to the right. You are now at over 1,300ft (400m contour) and it is probably squelchy underfoot. For some time you will have been aware of a large quarry ahead; this is on the far side of the Tees and you will pass close by it on the return.

Soon the Blea Beck is crossed; it may be necessary to search for stepping stones after rain. Reach drier ground – a good place to pause and enjoy the ever-changing views – then begin to descend to cross two smaller becks. To the right can be seen two footbridges across these becks close to the Tees. Cronkley Scar now rises ahead. Closer and forward right can be made out the line of the Pennine Way on a small, steep incline near the river.

On the level ground at the foot of your descent look out for a path crossing at right angles and follow this to the right, through a wall and until it merges with the Pennine Way at the top of the rise. Turn right onto the Way and descend, soon coming to a line of duckboards across the mud. Cross the two footbridges seen earlier and continue along the riverside. Over the river the quarry has taken a huge bite out of the hillside, disfiguring the landscape but making its own aggressive and formidable statement to the eye. You can find relief by looking south where Bleabeck Force tumbles down to the Tees.

East of the quarry, woodland takes over the far bank and the noise of vehicles and machinery blends with the roar of water ahead. In a few minutes you are by the upper reach of High Force where the Tees falls 70ft (21m) over an outcrop of the Great Whin Sill, that great sheet of dolerite traversing some 80 miles (129km) from Burton Fell in the Pennines to the Northumbrian coast. This is not the highest, but for volume and pace is the most impressive, of England's waterfalls – at least of those with uninterrupted fall. There are several good viewpoints, all of them easy to reach. Moreover you are on the free side; folk across the river have had to pay an entrance fee to reach the falls from the B6277 road.

The path continues on duckboards through juniper bushes, now above the river hurrying through its gorge. Soon you will see a bridge across the Tees. Either descend to it and follow the riverside path for almost a mile (1.6km), past the lesser falls of Low Force then turning right by Winch Bridge across fields to the end of the road at Holwick, from where it is a few hundred yards to the car, or stay on the upper level if time is pressing, walking past a farm, through fields and past the grounds of Holwick Lodge, part of the Earl of Strathmore's estate, to the end of the Holwick road.

It would be a pity to visit this area without seeing the other massive waterfall on the Tees – Cauldron Snout. This is only about 6 miles (9.6km) upstream from High Force and it can be reached on foot by following the Pennine Way westerly from the point you first joined it on the walk. If you have no time or energy for this – it is not all the easiest of walking – return from Holwick to Middleton-in-Teesdale, take the B6277 Alston road and after 7 miles (11km) turn left at Langdon Beck. This road takes you across a cattle grid to a car park near Cow Green Reservoir. From here follow a nature trail alongside the reservoir, past the dam, to the surging cascades of Cauldron Snout. They are still impressive, although the building of the reservoir has diminished the flow – as indeed it has at High Force.

Winch Bridge over the Tees below High Force (R. Russell)

18 River·Swale

Time: The shorter walk should take 2½–3 hours; with the extension to Keld, visiting the waterfalls, allow at least 6½ hours.

Start and finish: Centre of the village of Gunnerside on B6270 Reeth to Kirkby Stephen road. Boots are recommended.

Approach: Gunnerside is 6 miles (9.6km) west of Reeth on B6270. From the south, approach by taking the narrow and hilly minor road from Askrigg in Wensleydale, signposted Muker, and turning right on reaching B6270. Space for parking is available in Gunnerside alongside the gill.

Attractions: A lovely stretch of Swaledale in the Yorkshire Dales National Park with superb views. Two (or three) of the best of the Dales villages are included. You tread part of the old Corpse Way to Grinton and can incorporate a length of the Pennine Way if you wish.

OS sheet: 98. For the longer walk, 92 is also necessary.

Leave the village on B6270 heading for Muker. In about 300yd (274m) the bridge over the Swale is reached. Don't cross it, but take the opening on your right and descend to the path by the river. Follow this through a small meadow ablaze in summer with wild flowers, across a stile and until it leaves the immediate riverside making a Z-bend with a short steep ascent, resuming its original direction in a field above the Swale. Continue westward through fields and stiles in the drystone walls until a small cluster of buildings is reached. This is Ivelet. It is well worth descending the hill, about 500yd (457m), to see Ivelet Bridge, a graceful narrow stone single span reputedly haunted by a headless dog. Close by is a large stone on which coffins used to be rested on the long trek from Upper Swaledale to Grinton church, for many centuries the only church in the Dale. This is the old packhorse route known as the Corpse Way.

Back in Ivelet resume the path through fields heading west; there is a signpost for Muker. Soon the village comes in sight through the trees. The path begins to swing northwards, keeping parallel to the Swale and above it, with Muker on the left. You may notice another track coming in from above to join yours. On the right the hills rise steeply and the valley is beginning to narrow. Look out for a footbridge across the river below. To visit Muker, cross here and follow a path across five small fields. There are a couple of good tea rooms and a pub in the village, as well as the Swaledale woollen shop.

Return across the footbridge and, for the shorter walk, retrace your steps as far as a sign 'Gunnerside by road'. Head uphill to where a narrow metalled road begins and follow that along the hillside back to Gunnerside. There will be very little traffic – perhaps none at all – as this road serves only a handful of cottages and a couple of farms. This route is about 150ft (46m) higher than the outward path and the views along the Dale are correspondingly wider, with the river glinting through the trees below. The road brings you into the village a few yards from your car. To avoid any road walking, take an alternative path back, fingerposted Ivelet Bridge. This takes you as far as the bridge, keeping close to the river, but you lose the open views. At the bridge, walk uphill to rejoin the outward path.

Footbridge over Swinnergill

For the extended walk, continue from the footbridge along the east bank of the Swale. Ivelet Wood comes down almost to the waterside. After a mile (1.6km) of easy walking along the valley floor, a footbridge is reached over Swinnergill, bubbling down from the moors. Across the bridge are old lead workings. Where the track forks, follow the higher path which takes you below ruined Crackpot Hall – the name having no reference to its owner, but derived from Old Norse meaning 'hole of the crows'. The steep hill opposite is Kisdon and deep in the gorge below you as walk onward through a gate is the waterfall, Kisdon Force, which you will soon be visiting.

The path now descends to cross East Gill by a footbridge just below the three levels of East Gill Force. Then cross the Swale and head uphill in the upstream direction along a narrow path leading to the tiny village of Keld. This is little more than a square of cottages with a farm at the end. A path through the farmyard leads to steps descending to Catrake Force, worth seeing especially after rain.

To return, retrace from Keld towards the bridge over the Swale. You will previously have noticed a double Pennine Way signpost and one of the options for the return to Muker is to take the Pennine Way, ascending the slope of Kisdon Hill and walking at 1,180ft (360m contour) for nearly 2 miles (3km) until a track descending south-eastwards towards Muker is reached. Alternatively, keep to the track closer to the river alongside a stone wall. As this track descends, an obvious break in the wall is seen with a clear path heading down at an obtuse angle on the far side. Follow this down to Kisdon Force, the grandest of the falls on the Upper Swale, dramatically set beneath steep cliffs in a thickly wooded gorge.

Return to the wall and the track downstream towards Muker. The setting and scenery, as elsewhere along this walk, are beautiful beyond words. In a little under 2 miles (3km) the footbridge is reached and, perhaps after calling at the village for refreshment, cross to take either of the return paths to Gunnerside as described above.

On this walk, please remember to keep in single file through fields and to use either stiles or gates. Never climb a drystone wall.

COASTS

Walking along the coast has always had wide appeal. Not only is a coast route usually easier to follow than a winding lane, but there is often an irresistible desire to see what is behind the next headland and find an unspoilt bay or hidden cove. It is surprising how many such places do exist and how empty the coast can be once a concrete promenade gives way to natural features. In East Anglia, Hunstanton and Walton-on-the-Naze have packed summer beaches only a short walk from the undisturbed landfalls of migratory birds. In Cumbria one of Britain's main seabird colonies is only a few miles' walk from Whitehaven harbour once well known for coal mines and industry.

Crops are grown and cattle reared within yards of the sea. A coastline, like all countryside, is constantly changing. Even areas unsuitable for farming, such as the dunes on the North Norfolk Coast Path, respond to the seasons with a purple carpet of lavender in summer and golden reeds in winter. And not only are coasts subject to more dramatic temperature changes than many other parts of the country, but the cliffs are under relentless attack from wind and sea. Sandbars can disappear overnight after being a feature for half a century. Alternatively, the sturdy cliffs on the Kent and Sussex border were deserted by the sea several hundred years ago as successive storms helped silt up old estuaries.

The National Trust's Operation Neptune has done much to protect the coast from new development. It is only since the early 1970s that a number of official long-distance paths, promoted both by the Countryside Commission and local councils on their own initiative, have helped to open up significant stretches of coast which were hitherto either so inaccessible or badly signposted that the inexperienced felt uncertain about the status, safety or even exact line of old coast paths once used by fishermen and smugglers. There are now well over 1,000 miles of waymarked coast path in the British Isles.

The best coasts are said to be in Ireland, even if the waymarking there is more patchy. The finest of all Ireland's sweeping beaches is probably Magilligan Strand in County Londonderry, but across the Irish Sea similar wide beaches can be found in Lancashire where the sand is hard enough for serious hockey matches to be played on the beach rather than on the readily available grass. Hockey is also played on North Yorkshire's Scarborough beach, where low tide reveals not just sand but a contrast of rocks in the same bay and a steeply rising cliff. Both these beaches feature in this chapter along with other high cliffs, sand dunes, flat

Pembrokeshire Coast near St David's (Geoffrey N. Wright)

OXNEY FERRY

LIST OF TOLLS

	s	d
EVERY CARRIAGE, WAGGON or MACHINE WITH 4 WHEELS	1	0
" " " WITH 2 WHEELS		6
EVERY HORSE, MULE or ASS		1
CATTLE Each		1
SHEEP or LAMBS Per Score		3
PIGS Each		1
FOOT PASSENGER		½
ENGINE	1	6
TRUCK, WAGGON, MACHINE or PLOUGH Drawn by same	1	0
LORRY- STEAM or MOTOR	1	6
TRACTOR	1	0
MOTOR COACH or CHAR-A-BANC	1	6
MOTOR CAR	1	0
MOTOR CYCLE		2
TRAILER or SIDECAR		1
HAND TRUCK		1
BATH CHAIR		1
TRICYCLE or BICYCLE. Each Way		1

salterns, nature reserves and abandoned Kent cliffs.

Samples of the main waymarked paths are included in this section of walks where an attempt has been made to combine two essential ingredients – the best stretches and, where not on a peninsula, the likelihood of reasonable public transport at opposite end to the car. Sometimes, as in the case of the Old Kent coast walk, the trip back can be enjoyable for its speed as well as the panoramic view of the recently walked path.

The seaside is often associated with children and whilst the shorter circular walks could serve as an introduction to walking, both children and adults should always remember that a coast walk is enjoyable only so long as cliffs, tides and winds are respected. Wandering from the path can be very dangerous.

19	North Norfolk Coast Path	6 miles (10km)
20	The Naze, Essex	5¾ miles (9km)
21	Old Kent Coast, Kent and East Sussex	8 miles (13km)
22	Pennington, Hampshire	7 miles (11km)
23	Rame Peninsula, Cornwall	9 miles (14km)
24	Oxwich, West Glamorgan	3½ miles (5.6km)
25	Cumbria Coastal Way	7 miles (11km)
26	Scottish East Coast, Grampian	3 miles (5km)

19 North·Norfolk· Coast·Path

Time: 3 hours.
Start and finish: The starting point is the church at Thornham, the finish is the car park next to Hunstanton bus station.
Approach: Hunstanton and Thornham are north of King's Lynn on the A149. Walkers are advised to leave the car in the car park next to Hunstanton bus station (or the promenade car park on Wednesdays) and travel to Thornham on the Coastline bus (July and August) or Birds bus (daily except Sundays).
Attractions: This is a section of one of the more recent long-distance paths and features both the North Sea and The Wash. The loss of the railway and declining public transport in Norfolk has helped to preserve the area. There is now a coastal nature reserve at the north end of the Roman Peddars Way, and this is still a gateway to East Anglia for migrating birds. In August the dunes are a mass of purple sea lavender and, although Hunstanton beach can be crowded in the summer, the less accessible beaches to the east have plenty of empty space.
OS sheet: 132

At Thornham turn north between the King's Head and the mostly fifteenth-century church which has a beautiful traceried door and an unusual Hanoverian coat of arms. Beyond the bakery turn right where the lane divides. At a sharp bend, leave the road by going left onto a curving path. Cross the footbridge and follow a raised path westwards. To the north are reed-covered marshes. On reaching another lane, turn right for the harbour where the only building is a coal store. Coal was once landed here and villagers came down to buy whenever they needed more fuel.

At the end of the harbour road turn left onto a path which crosses a sluice gate, then turn right to pass iron barriers. Follow the top of the high embankment, built in 1860 to assist in drainage, which soon bears westwards. At the far end, where another path comes up from the south, continue north with the bank. On approaching the sea and the Holme Dunes, the path rises on a wooden boarded surface to enter the confines of the nature reserve; it then turns west to run along the back of a wood. Soon it drops down the bank to join another path in a dip on the seaward side. The area is planted with young pine trees. After passing a collecting box beside a sandy cross-path, the way is over open ground. Bear half-right towards an old bomb shelter, and ascend onto another bank where the way is again boarded. This useful wooden surface continues for the next mile (1.6km) as the path rises and falls on top of the sandy bank. There is an occasional optional diversion to prevent pressure on this next sandy stretch of the coastal path. To the left, and getting nearer, is the church tower at Holme next the Sea. The windmill on the hill behind is on the Peddars Way which runs down into Holme. Ahead is the lighthouse on the high cliff at Hunstanton.

The path runs nearer to the beach at Gore Point – site of a now disappeared shingle bank. Still keep forward when the wooden surface ends and after ¼ mile (.4km), when level with a brick tower, take the right-hand path where the way divides and join the wider track below the bank. On reaching a wide cross-track leading to the beach, turn left to walk inland through a golf course. Beyond a gate the way becomes metalled.

Just before a bridge turn right to follow a stream. The waterside path runs along the side of a caravan park before crossing a footbridge to the golf course. Keep by the water as much as possible and, at the far end, join a road which passes the golf clubhouse. The path becomes uneven before entering Old Hunstanton and passing the Le Strange Arms and the next-door Ancient Mariner Inn.

After a few yards, turn right off the road to follow a wide path down the side of a wood on the right. The path becomes rough as it bears left onto the rising cliff; but the way is soon over grass, passing the lighthouse and ruined St Edmund's Chapel built by the saint to mark his landfall here from Germany in 850. Continue along the cliff top and, when the grass ends, take the foot-path on the seaward side of the café. The path curves round to the road at the town centre.

Further reading:

Robinson, Bruce. *The Peddars Way and North Norfolk Coast Path* (HMSO 1986)

20 THE·NAZE

Time: 3 hours.

Start and finish: Station Yard car park (operated by Tendring Council) next to Walton-on-the-Naze station.

Approach: Walton-on-the-Naze is at the end of the B1034 which leaves the A604 between Colchester and Harwich. On entering Walton-on-the-Naze turn right up Church Road next to the church to find Station Yard car park.

Attractions: The word 'Naze' comes from an old English word for 'nose' and it is thanks to recent efforts by the Essex Naturalists' Trust and others that this nose-shaped walk has been saved, not only for walkers, but as a landfall for migrating birds and a home for the Essex skipper butterfly and the emperor moth. The route involves a small unspoilt town, a hill and an expansive marsh. The 70ft (21m) East Cliffs, rich in fossils and being eaten away by the sea, are unique on the Essex coastline. From the tip of the 'nose' there are views towards Harwich and Felixstowe. There is little shelter from the sun, but the easterly winds off the North Sea are usually less fierce on the return path behind the hill.

OS sheet: 169

The station is on a high cliff. Walk north along The Parade which runs downhill giving a view over the pier. At the bottom of the hill, the shops are huddled together behind the seafront houses. The Information Bureau and the end of High Street mark the beginning of Princes Esplanade. After ¾ mile (1.2km) the traffic turns inland, whilst the walk continues along East Terrace at the side of the Naze Mariner.

Beyond the coastguard station, the way is along the back of the beach huts and up onto the rising cliff. At the top, behind the shelter, is the start of a footpath passing along the back of new houses to Sunny Point, once famous for its convalescent home. Ahead is the walk's orientation point, the Naze Tower, built in 1720 by Trinity House as a landmark for navigators.

Keep forward over the grass along East Cliffs and observe any warning notices about keeping away from the crumbling edge – the wartime blockhouses on the beach were originally standing on the cliff top. Ahead is the first glimpse of the Haven ports 5 miles (8km) across the water. After ½ mile (.8km) the cliff loses height. At the end turn north-west onto a fine grass-covered sea wall. Just inside is one of the Essex Naturalists' Trust nature reserves, whilst on the seaward side is a series of lagoons formed when the present wall was built inland from the old one. At the end of the new wall it is still possible to turn right onto the Naze's most northerly point. This is a superb spot for observing both birds and the large ships from the continent.

The Wharf behind Walton-on-the-Naze (Leigh Hatts)

The walk continues eastwards along the older but still pleasant sea defences – a grass path behind a low wall. To the south there are views across farmland whilst Cormorant Creek, below the wall, is drained of water at low tide. After ¾ mile (1.2km) the path turns sharply south. Across Walton Channel is Horsey Island which can be reached by road at low tide. The Naze Tower is now over to the left and Walton is ahead with the church tower, only a century old, silhouetted against the sky.

At the wharf, keep forward to find a stile leading to the continuation of the coastal footpath. Here the shock of finding a hidden caravan park is usually relieved by the sight of sheep keeping the grass down. The path curves east and south round the inner backwater, known as the Old Mill Pond. Looking east here one is aware of how narrowly the Naze is joined to the mainland. After passing a line of waterside backgardens, turn up North Street to reach High Street. Go right as far as the church, then climb up Church Road to the Station Yard car park.

21 OLD·KENT·COAST

Time: 4 hours.

Start and finish: Appledore church or station is the start of this walk; it finishes in Rye, at the car park in Cinque Ports Street.

Approach: There is a car park in Rye's Cinque Ports Street near the rail and bus station where Hastings & District buses run to Appledore church. Trains to Appledore run hourly. Those wishing to park at Appledore and catch the train at the end of the walk, can park at Appledore station. It should be noted that the station at Appledore is 1½ miles (2km) outside the village.

Attractions: This walk, part of the Gravesend–Rye Saxon Shore Way, follows the old coastline and crosses the former sea bed to visit the Isle of Oxney which was surrounded by significantly navigable waters as late as Tudor times. The landlocked town of Tenterden, still further north, is a Cinque Port on the grounds that Henry VIII's ships were built at Small Hythe where, in spite of the silting up, barges operated until early this century. But flooding does occur in winter when nature reasserts itself, as readers of E. F. Benson's Mapp and Lucia books will recall.

OS sheet: 189

Leave Appledore station on the 'London' side to pass the pub and follow the road westwards. To the left, just beyond Blackmore Farm, is the start of a parallel footpath which offers a handy alternative to the road walk into the village. When the road passes alongside the Royal Military Canal, the foot-path joins to run close on the left side. Cross the bridge over the canal to enter Appledore which was once a port. The church is mainly fourteenth century, having been rebuilt after a French attack from the sea in 1380 which has left the interior with a sense of space if not balance behind the early sixteenth-century door.

Walk up the road opposite Appledore church. (Do not be tempted up the brick path beyond the iron kissing-gate near the beginning.) Just before the road drops down, go left through double gates at Court Lodge farm and at once turn right through another gate. Head for the right-hand side of the mound ahead.

Drop down off the old coastline to cross a wooden stile and a footbridge below. Keep by the ditch (right) to follow a path to the far left-hand corner near the lonely telegraph pole in front of the buildings. On reaching the Reading Sewer cross the bridge into the next field to follow the sewer (left) towards the Ferry Inn ½ mile (.8km) away. At a road, turn across the bridge to the eighteenth-century Ferry Inn; there was once a ferry from the Isle of Oxney and Appledore, and when the water receded barges were operated along the Reading Sewer to the village.

Opposite the pub, take the track which leads back to the water and on to a pumping station. Keep to the right of this building but leave the wide Reading Sewer and follow the smaller dyke (left). After a short distance, cross this dyke by a bridge and follow the concrete path. On approaching farm gates, near a pylon, leave the concrete and continue ahead just inside the field by the wire fence (left). At the field corner go over a stile and cross open ground to a second stile by a road.

Walk up the drive of Luckhurst opposite, and when the drive swings to the left keep ahead through a small wooden gate. Keep forward under the trees and where the buildings (left) end, turn left over a stream into a field. Bear half-right across the field in the direction of Stone church. On the far side do not enter another field but follow the ditch (right) to the end of the existing field. Cross another ditch and bear half-right across a new field towards the white weatherboarded house in the line of houses. Beyond iron gates is the Crown at Stone-in-Oxney.

Walk up the road opposite between the Old Post House and the Crown, and when the lane bends sharply right take the raised pavement which leads to the viewpoint at Stone church. Continue up the lane and at a T-junction go over the wooden stile ahead.

Keep to the side of the field and cross another stile at the far end where there are magnificent views from this south side of the 'island' across to the 'mainland'. Bear half-left down a sloping field to a further stile over the brow of the hill. Still continue half-left, and beyond a wooden gate follow a curving cliff path down to another wooden gate. Keep to the right of the mound ahead and walk in the direction of the farm buildings down a sloping field to a wooden stile in the fence below, at the end of a ditch. Cross this stile and a footbridge, and follow the ditch (left). Cross another ditch into a second field and at the far end go left onto a track. At an isolated brick building turn right off the track to follow a ditch down the side of an open field. At the far end bear left to follow another drainage ditch, the Kent Ditch, which marks the county boundary. At the next field corner bear right from Kent into Sussex, to follow the parallel ditch and road. Beyond an iron gate and a stile, turn left over a bridge to reach the road.

Go right along the road to reach Iden Lock ½ mile (.8km) away. Turn left before the River Rother bridge to cross the lock and bear right. Now follow the Rother for 3 miles (5km) into Rye. To the right are rising cliffs and, after a mile (1.6km), a first view of the hill town crowned by its partly Norman church.

On reaching a road bridge, cross over the water and bear left into Fish-market Road where a path climbs up into the old town of Rye. Beyond the Landgate go left to reach the car park and bus and BR station in Cinque Ports Street.

Jonathan Swift's house and Candlestick Chimney, Whitehaven, seen from the path (Leigh Hatts) (*see* page 110)

22 PENNINGTON

Time: 3 hours. The twisting path is best taken slowly, allowing time to enjoy the surprise views and the wildlife.

Start and finish: The walk starts at Milford-on-Sea beach car park; it finishes at Lymington where buses run back to Milford-on-Sea.

Approach: Milford-on-Sea lies on the B3058 and is well signposted from the A337. The beach car park is easily reached from the centre of the village by driving south along Sea Road.

Attractions: This route, which is part of the Solent Way, begins in Christchurch Bay before following the salt marshes, where salt was produced for over eight centuries to the 1860s, to Lymington's famous yacht marina. The path, which is a bird-watcher's paradise, has views of both Hurst Castle, which can only be reached along the shingle Hurst Beach, and the Isle of Wight. Only occasionally during very high tides should the walker find any difficulty.

OS sheet: 196

From the car park which is on the seafront promenade, turn eastwards to walk onto a shingle spit – now greatly strengthened with rocks and concrete blocks – which divides the sea from Sturt Pond. On reaching the second footbridge on the left, leave the high path to cross the bridge over the Sturt Pond channel.

Follow the waterside road ahead and keep forward onto a track when the road turns inland. Just before the end of the sea wall, turn left to reach Keyhaven – a yachting hamlet with just The Gun inn for refreshment. Take the easterly road, opposite the inn, to cross a bridge. After a short distance, turn right off the road and follow a footpath along the edge of the water. Here, by Keyhaven Marshes, the path is mainly at beach level and at its nearest to Hurst Castle where Charles I was held prisoner in 1648.

Soon the way is on top of a sea wall giving a better view inland over the flat countryside, whilst the shelter of the Isle of Wight across The Solent becomes more apparent. The scene ahead changes as the path turns south-east. Later, running in a north-easterly direction, the path affords a sight of the Esso Oil Refinery flame 11 miles (17.5km) away at Fawley on Southampton Water. Eighteenth-century Pennington House can be seen nestling in trees on the far side of Pennington Marshes to the left. Meanwhile The Solent, sometimes a crowded water, always has its permanent feature – the regular Lymington–Yarmouth ferry.

Boat at Thornham Harbour (Leigh Hatts) (*see* page 95)
Raised path by River Rother near Rye (Leigh Hatts) (*see* page 99)

After a mile (1.6km) the path begins an uncertain 180 degree turn to follow the side of a narrow creek, giving a view of Lymington's church tower away on high ground. Turn sharply right over a stile to stay with the creek which, unless the new floodgate is closed, is tidal up to picturesque Creek Cottage and its Tudor barn, once used for salt storage. Turn left before the next stile only if intending to visit The Chequers public house beside the road. Otherwise, climb over the stile ahead and walk across the front of Creek Cottage to follow a path through a tunnel of trees. Beyond a row of former saltern cottages, the way becomes surfaced and passes Eight Acre Pond (known as Eight Pans Pond in salt-manufacturing days). Beyond Maiden Cottage do not follow the road left, but go right to reach the water again.

Keep to the left side of the inlet and follow the sea defences round more marshland. After five turns there are good views across reeds to the main Lymington river channel. Where the path meets Lymington marina, go right along the signposted permitted path along one side of the harbour. At the far end turn right behind the building to walk along the second side of the marina and reach the river at the end of the saltwater swimming pool.

Beyond the slipway, by the Royal Lymington Yacht Club, bear half-left to follow Bath Road into the town. Near the Ship Inn the road narrows to become Quay Street and pass a tea shop. Turn right up a cobbled hill to High Street where the bus station is on the left.

Further reading:
Hatts, Leigh. *The Bournemouth Coast Path* (Countryside Books, 1985)
Shurlock, Barry. *The Solent Way* (Hampshire County Council, 1984)

23 RAME·PENINSULA

Time: Allow 5 hours to include a lunch stop and looking at the views.

Start and finish: Mount Edgcumbe car park is the starting place; the walk finishes at Millbrook where a regular bus service runs along the edge of Millbrook Lake to Mount Edgcumbe.

Approach: Mount Edgcumbe car park is at the end of a headland and is reached by turning south off the A374 at Antony and following the B3247 to its eastern end. But those approaching from the east and wishing to avoid a long drive across the Tamar Bridge and through Saltash, can leave the car in Plymouth and cross to Mount Edgcumbe on the Cremyll passenger ferry which sails at least hourly from Admiral's Hard, Stonehouse.

Attractions: The Cornwall Coast Path starts at Mount Edgcumbe, a park which Samuel Johnson described as one of the finest situations in Great Britain, and passes through the unspoilt fishing villages of Kingsand and Cawsand which face each other across the old Devon–Cornwall boundary. The walk leads on to a lonely chapel on Rame Head before reaching the undeveloped beach of Whitsand Bay.

OS sheet: 201

Leave the car park (or ferry) and walk to the gates of Mount Edgcumbe. Beyond the gates at once turn left to pass under an archway and along a short hedged path to reach the Orangery built in the 1780s. Mount Edgcumbe House, dating from 1549, continues to be the home of the Earls of Mount Edgcumbe. Continue on, to follow the sea wall. After passing between the Battery and Block House, the path is alongside a hedge.

Beyond the gate follow the concrete road up onto the wooded cliff and, when the road swings inland, keep ahead past the pond to take the rough cliff path which starts by Milton's Temple. The path emerges at a wooden gate. Keep forward, with a folly to the right, and soon there is a view ahead of another headland. The path runs downhill to bear right with the cliff, and the way is briefly at beach level before climbing again and passing near Lady Emma's Cottage – to the right in the trees. The path is a little inland from the cliff before log steps take the coast route up through the trees to join a higher path. Turn left to follow a woodland zigzag up to Earl's Drive. Go left again and keep on this wide way which passes under an arch and affords occasional views down through the trees to the sea. On passing a Gothic summerhouse – known as Picklecombe Seat – at the head of the valley, look down to catch sight of nineteenth-century Fort Picklecombe which was part of the Devonport Dockyard defence.

Where the way divides, go left, but keep ahead at the second junction.

Kingsand seen from Cawsand across the old Cornwall–Devon border (Leigh Hatts)

Here the path emerges into the open and onto grass with a sudden view of Kingsand and Cawsand nestling in the corner of a bay like an Italian village. The path runs down to a stile where walkers must join a lane for a few yards before turning right to another stile on the far side. A gently rising path enters a wood where the way then descends into the open, giving another view of the villages ahead. The main path runs over Minadew Brakes below another fort.

On reaching Kingsand turn left and follow any of the narrow charming lanes to cross the invisible old county boundary into Cawsand, which has a model square and a store selling ice cream made with clotted cream. Turn left by reaching the church, up a lane which soon loses its metalled surface and runs through a tunnel of trees. On approaching Bayfield Cottage the way is briefly metalled. Where it divides, bear right onto a rough track which climbs through cliffside woods to reach a metalled road. Go left and follow the road to a sharp bend above the roof of Adelaide Chapel at Penlee Point. The 'chapel' was probably built in the early 1800s as a picnic house for the future Queen Adelaide.

When the road next turns right, at a hairpin, keep ahead over a stile. The path, on the side of the cliff, is mostly between gorse, and halfway along this most southerly cliff of the area there is a signposted path leading to the medieval church at Rame. But the coast path is still ahead, passing a stone wall near a coastguard station. The coast path turns at the base of Rame Head but keep ahead up the steps to visit the little fourteenth-century chapel – often lost in mist – dedicated to St Michael, Cornwall's patron saint. This is the nearest mainland point to the Eddystone Lighthouse, and Rame Head once maintained a flaming beacon.

Having turned away from the headland walk south for a few yards, then bear left to a wooden stile beyond a hump. After stepping stones the way narrows and leads to nearby Queener Point where the path turns a corner and the walker is confronted with a sweeping view of Whitsand Bay. Further round the corner there is a handy seat. The ledge path affords a view down onto the few buildings in Polhawn Cove including a long greenhouse above a small fort. When the way divides beyond a stile, turn left down a narrow path which leads to steps and at the bottom cross a drive and go down a few more steps. Beyond a gate turn right to pass along the back of a white cottage. At a junction of paths bear right for a few yards before crossing a stile on the left. The grass way runs ahead for ½ mile (.8km) before becoming rougher and climbing the cliffside. On reaching the road – a military road built to link all the forts – turn left, and after 100yd (90m) the left-hand verge affords views down onto the chalet homes dotted on the cliff.

Some 200yd (180m) before reaching Rame View Café (which serves clotted cream teas), turn right up a concrete path. The way appears unexciting until there is a surprise view down onto Millbrook and St John's Lake. The path becomes rough at a gate and later passes through a farmyard at Treninnow. At a metalled crossroads go left down a lane into Millbrook. Turn right at the bottom and follow the main street to the bakery and café opposite the Devon and Cornwall inn. Keep forward, with the café to the left, to the bus shelter by a garage.

Further reading:

Harris, W. Best. *From Cremyll to Crafthole* (Plymouth: The Author, 1981, obtainable from local shops)
Pyatt, Edward C. *The Cornwall Coast Path* (HMSO, 1976)

24 OXWICH

Time: 2½ hours.
Start and finish: Sea front car park at entrance to Oxwich village.
Approach: Take the A4118 out of Swansea and beyond Penmaen turn south at The Towers, a partly ruined castle lodge. On approaching Oxwich turn left into the car park.
Attractions: On the map the route looks deceptively short and easy, but there is much rising and falling on the cliffside and wonderful views to be contemplated. The church and castle at Oxwich and Oxwich Point can all be visited without touching a road. Oxwich has a tiny population of less than 200, its life revolving around the Post Office where the many services offered include flask filling. Oxwich Wood appears loveliest in autumn just as the holiday crowds are thinning.
OS sheet: 159

Walk past the Post Office and ahead at the crossroads. After a short distance turn left through a gate to enter Oxwich Wood. A path runs quickly up into the trees giving occasional views of the sandy bay below. Try to keep to the recommended paths both for the sake of the flora and to avoid the hidden quarries created during nineteenth-century limestone working.

The path divides by a stone ruin. Descend the left fork until the top of a long flight of steps leading down to St Illtyd's Church is reached. The chancel is believed to be a sixth-century Celtic cell, and the font to have been brought here by St Illtyd himself. The ceiling is decorated with a rainbow added by a theatrical scene painter for Lilian Baylis who had noted the almost daily rainbows on The Gower. At low tide it can be seen that the building, in good Biblical tradition, is built on rock.

The walk continues beyond the top of the steps on a path that weaves through the trees, giving more glimpses of the bay, before descending steeply by steps to a lower path which leads to Oxwich Point. On the way one can see the site of a massive rockfall caused by the quarrying. At the Point there is a small shelf of grass on which to pause and identify the coves and headlands on a map.

Beyond here the path, passing through growth affected by strong winds, has views down onto rocks at low tide, and this cliff is said to be the best on The Gower for flowering plants in spring. A stile marks the end of an area cared for by the Nature Conservancy Council; take the higher of the two paths. The low buildings seen briefly on the cliff top are the remains of a wartime radar station. At another divide, again keep to the higher path which broadens out as it rises in a curve. There is a first view of Port-Eynon Point to the west.

Take a last look back before finally turning the corner below a rock. A barely visible path runs due north over the grass – generally kept short by sheep. Here is the best view of Port-Eynon Point, and on climbing over a stile one sees headlands on both sides. Beyond gateways, go over a firm farm track by a pond to find an OS triangulation station – a concrete post. This point is 260ft (79m) above sea level and on a clear day Lundy Island, 35 miles (56km) away off the Devon coast, can be seen to the south-west.

Now join the parallel farm track on the left. Beyond a gateway there are more views at field entrances and suddenly, after ½ mile (.8km), Oxwich Castle rises up over a farmyard. The castle, now partly ruined, was rebuilt in the early Tudor period when Penrice Castle was abandoned.

Although a public footpath runs through the farmyard and then left through a gate to the road, this is little used and always excites the dog! It is easier to go ahead down to the road. (But those wanting to stand back from the castle walls and obtain a good long view could turn left before reaching the road onto a path leading to Oxwich Green.) Turn right at the road, which offers a good view over the reeds on the freshwater marsh before entering Oxwich village.

25 CUMBRIA·COASTAL·WAY

Time: 3½ hours.

Start and finish: The start is St Bees car park next to the station at the bottom of Main Street. The finish is Whitehaven, where there are buses and trains back to St Bees. Boots should be worn.

Approach: St Bees car park is on the south side of the level crossing, next to the station, on the B5345 south of Whitehaven.

Attractions: St Bees, an unspoilt village on a rising cliff above a Benedictine priory, may owe its existence to the arrival of the refugee Irish princess Bega in about 900. The high cliff walk is one of great contrasts, passing through one of the country's largest seabird colonies before encountering a quarry and even a disused coalfield which runs under the sea, on the cliff above White-haven. Much of this route is expected to become part of the Cumbria Coastal Way.

OS sheet: 89

Cross the railway line and head towards St Bees Priory which has a magnificent Norman west door. Just before the church, turn left onto a footpath which passes through two kissing-gates to another road. Go left for the sea front, and turn north along the promenade to Gutter Foot where a bridge crosses the Rottington Beck. Go over the stile, and then a second (ladder) stile on the left, to make the steep climb up the edge of the cliff. Behind are increasingly extensive views of St Bees – the priory partly sheltered by a hill whilst the village is more exposed on the far side of the valley. This is the nearest point to the Isle of Man, which can sometimes be seen to the south-west.

At first the path is outside the cliff fence but later, across one of the many stiles, it runs just inside and there is a view across land to the lighthouse at North Head. The path bends inland down the side of the Fleshwick Bay inlet below St Bees Head, where a stream runs down into the sea which at high tide rushes up between the cliffs. It is clear where many walkers scramble down and up at low tide, and where others go to the top of the valley. The official crossing is somewhere between the two, with the public footpath running along the top of the north side. From St Bees Head there is a view down onto unusual red sandstone and a beach said to contain semi-precious stones.

The 300ft (91m) cliff between the Head and the lighthouse houses an exceptionally large seabird colony and is therefore normally alive with bird sound. This reserve, the only place in England where the black guillemot can be found, is in the care of the Royal Society for the Protection of Birds (RSPB), who provide observation areas from where birds can usually be seen massed below the sandstone ledges. Pass between the fog warning station and the lighthouse, built in 1822 and giving out a light seen on the Isle of Man.

At North Head, a stile takes the path outside the fence. The way is narrow but with a ledge below; this is where sheep have fallen and become birds' food. Ahead is the first sight of Saltom Bay cliffs and Whitehaven's stone pier. Do not go all the way to the headland, but cross a stile on the right. Walk on, with the promontory to the left, and on the far side still keep away from the edge by bearing slightly right up to a stile. Here the path continues outside a fence. Ahead on the skyline is the Marchon chemical works which provides local employment in place of brickmaking, fishing and mining. The way is occasionally narrow, but at one point completely sheltered from the sea. A series of stiles takes the path in and out of fields and, after a mile (1.6km), the path is suddenly above a quarry. Follow the path round to the quarry cottages – usually surrounded by hens.

The way is now down the good path below the cliff. But before reaching the bottom, go left down hidden steps indicated by a large plaque unveiled in 1985 when a very short section of the Cumbria Coastal Way was inaugurated. A path skirts a mound to run across the bottom of a surprise coal tip and then over a disused conveyer. There was mining in this area from the seventeenth century until 1984.

Strike ahead to find a path running along the cliff top. There are good views down onto the beach. Between the old Kells and Ravenhill pits the path runs onto a concrete road. The best route to the town centre is half-right up a narrow enclosed footpath which turns inland. Cross two road junctions and keep ahead up a short residential road. Bear right and left round the building ahead and continue east to the Brewers Arms perched high on the edge of a hill. Go half-left down a footpath to join a metalled way running down into Whitehaven; part of the path is paved with Whitehaven bricks. At the bottom go right to the Dusty Miller in the town centre.

Bear left along the main road – Strand and Tangier Streets – to reach the bus and BR stations.

26 Scottish·East·Coast

Dunnottar Castle

Time: 2 hours.
Start and finish: Stonehaven (but buses run from near Dunnottar Castle back to Stonehaven).
Approach: The A92 from Aberdeen passes through the market square.
Attractions: Stonehaven is a typical Scottish town unharmed by too many modern shop fronts and to its south, but unseen from the harbour, is Dunnottar Castle resting on a 160ft (49m) rock almost surrounded by the North Sea. Once, a walk south to Crawton would have been recommended, but cliff falls have made the way beyond the castle a little less certain. However, the walk to Dunnottar remains clear and provides the best views of the unusual castle. This, together with the bird's-eye view of Stonehaven, makes this 3 mile (4.8km) return walk one of the most rewarding on the east coast.
OS sheet: 45

From the market square turn south down Alladice Street which crosses Carron Water and leads directly to the Sheriff Court House. Turn left, right by a school, and beyond New Street take the curving footpath up the hill to join the coastal road and look down on Stonehaven. There are seats for those who want to linger. Follow the pavement up the hill to obtain a better view of the harbour and Garron and Downie Points embracing Stonehaven Bay.

Where the road turns sharply, keep forward up an enclosed path. On Black Hill, where Cromwell's army once camped, is a pillared war memorial to the dead of both world wars. The path rounds the hill to reveal Dunnottar Castle across the headlands. To the east is the top of Downie Point. From a kissing-gate a path leads up to the war memorial viewpoint, whilst the walk continues down to a stile. From here the way is unenclosed and is on the side of the cliff round Strathlethan Bay. The footpath does not continue to rocky Bowdun Head, but crosses a stile and field to a wooden footbridge spanning one of the many streams which pour off the top of this high coast. Keep by the fence, and from the stile at the far end of the next field there is the best view yet of the once impregnable Dunnottar Castle jutting out at the end of Castle Haven.

The path (subject to change only near a spring used by the castle) follows the outside of a fence round this last bay before the high ground opposite the castle itself. Entry – which is normally possible daily throughout the year except on Saturdays – is either by the steep path or by the more recent steps which descend to almost sea level. The rock's church, visited by St Ninian, probably preceded the castle which dates from the fourteenth century when it was the seat of the Keiths, the Earls Marischal of Scotland. Mary Queen of Scots and James VI (I of England) both visited here, and the Scottish crown and regalia were hidden in the castle during the Cromwellian period until smuggled out during the 1651 siege which ended in partial damage of the fortress.

Whilst most walkers will not be continuing on the more difficult coast path beyond the castle, many will wish to cross the bridge over a dramatic canyon to the south where two streams fall down the rocky sides. Old Hall Bay, at the end of a faint path beyond the bridge, affords a sight of the southern aspect of the castle.

There is a bus stop 400yd (366m) inland by a lodge at the end of a path from the castle. The return to Stonehaven, by way of the outward route, is downhill with panoramic views beyond Black Hill.

Stonehaven from the path (Leigh Hatts)

Moorlands·and·Hills

Don't think of moorlands and hills, in the context of this book, as merely supporting cast to the big mountains, to be tossed aside when weather or other circumstances indicate that a real challenge is possible. Whilst they are often accessible on an off-day or when mist clings to the higher tops, they have a character all their own and many of them demand the respect, and soon gain the affection, sometimes reserved for the real mountains.

Selection of a mere nine examples was appallingly difficult. Despite the fact that the downlands of southern and south-eastern England are covered elsewhere, and other moorland walks appear under various disguises, many fine walks have had to be omitted. Lack of space rules out the Malvern Hills and the Howgill Fells, for example. The nine walks included do, however, include a wide enough range of hill and moorland environments to satisfy most tastes, from bleak upland plateaux and rolling heather moorland to the more intimate, smaller scale landscape of, for example, the northern Cotswolds.

It is as well to emphasise this range of environments because some of the walks described, even though they do not traverse great mountains, are quite serious expeditions which require some experience and route-finding ability. The Cheviot ridge, the mid-Pennines around Tan Hill, and the wilds of southern Dartmoor all fall into this category. On the other hand, the North York Moors walk, along the Hambleton Hills, is rarely far from habitation, and the Cotswold walk actively seeks out a succession of superb villages.

Having emphasised the need to be prepared for a challenge, and to recognise the unique merits of these moorland walks, it should also be made clear that these are essentially walks to be enjoyed rather than endured. None of them is excessively long and one or two, such as that on the delightful Quantock Hills, are not only comparatively short but also capable of further truncation if a very brief walk suitable for even the youngest walkers in the family is required.

Many of them are, indeed, ideal family walks – neither too elevated nor containing too steep ascents for the youngest, eldest or least agile. Although the Cheviot route, seventeen miles (27km) of hard walking from Alwinton, is clearly too long for such occasions, there are many opportunities within

The path from Snowshill to Great Brockhampton looking west to the main Cotswold ridge (M. Dunn) (*see* page 134)

these walks. Try, for example, the Quantock Hills route: not too long, not too trying a climb, and with a magnificent panorama from Wills Neck, or the walk from Peebles to Kailzie Hill, quickly freeing itself of the town and bearing the reward of marvellous views back over the almost encircling Tweed valley.

The lower altitude of these moorlands and hills means, too, that they have been more hospitable to man through the ages, so that the marks of ancient cultivation and settlement are thickly scattered on the slopes. There are prehistoric hillforts: Clennell Street, the road to the Cheviots from Alwinton, is guarded by two. Burial mounds abound, and there are more curious survivals too – the stone row at the head of the Erme valley in Dartmoor, for example, or the strange dykes on the Hambleton Hills.

The shape of hills tended to confine through ways to certain specific routes, which quickly became definitive and in several cases saw continuous use for many centuries. The Hambleton drove road in the North Yorkshire moors, though it derives its name from the Scottish droves of the eighteenth century, was a prehistoric ridgeway, as was the Portway over the Long Mynd in Salop. Medieval packhorse trains first beat out some of the tracks around Tan Hill in the mid-Pennines, and they reused ridgeways and through routes in the Peak District. The monks of Buckfast Abbey are credited with the creation of Dartmoor's Abbot's Way as a through route. And drovers, as we have seen, were again responsible for the wide, high track leading south from Peebles through Dryhope to the English border.

The ruins of Edale House and the Noe Valley (see page 129)

The hand of contemporary man is also near at hand in many of these routes, nowhere more so than in the Cotswolds where classic stone-built villages such as Snowshill and Stanton add much to the pleasure to be derived from the walk. But this is also true of the Peak District in historic (though now very popular) Edale and Castleton, and of the Cheviots where Alwinton is a quite magnificent unspoilt hamlet to be savoured at leisure. Often – and this is nowhere better illustrated than at Alwinton, whose Rose and Thistle is a gem of a pub – the village inn is the focus of this contemporary social dimension to moorland walking. The Tan Hill Inn, isolated in the mid-Pennines and the highest inn in England, is a classic focal point for a series of excellent walks.

These nine are, without exception, stimulating and satisfying walks, but inevitably there are highlights which are etched particularly vividly in the memory. One such is the feeling of pure joy on reaching Wills Neck, highest point of the Quantocks, and savouring the extraordinarily varied panorama of fertile valleys and rolling moorland, with the backdrop of Exmoor hills and sea. Others concern more intimate facets of the landscape – the discovery of the marvellous packhorse bridge at Ravensett in the mid-Pennines, for instance, or the gaunt Blackhouse Tower in its remote setting in the Southern Uplands. Every walk has its share of these distinctive treasures and traverses the superb landscape of British hill country.

27	Southern Uplands, Borders	14 miles (22km)
28	Cheviot Hills, Northumberland	17 miles (27km)
29	Mid-Pennines; Cumbria, North Yorkshire, County Durham	8 miles (13km)
30	North York Moors	8 or 16 miles (13 or 26km)
31	Peak District, Derbyshire	15 miles (24km)
32	The Long Mynd, Shropshire	8 miles (13km)
33	Cotswold Hills, Gloucestershire	6 miles (9.6km)
34	Quantock Hills, Somerset	6 or 9 miles (9.6 or 14km)
35	Dartmoor, Devon	12 miles (19km)

27 SOUTHERN·UPLANDS

Time: 6 hours should be sufficient for the main walk, via Kailzie Hill and Black-house (add a further hour or so for the 3 mile (5km) diversion to Dryhope).
Start and finish: Start in the High Street at Peebles (253404); finish at Innerleithen (330366). Frequent buses link the two towns.
Approach: Peebles lies at the junction of the A703, running south from Edinburgh, and the A72 from Biggar to Galashiels.
Attractions: Glorious open walking with exceptional views above the Tweed valley, and with a wealth of historical interest in Peebles itself, at the ruined border towers of Blackhouse and Dryhope, and at Traquair House, the oldest inhabited house in Scotland.
OS sheet: 73

The long, bare and gently graded ridges of the Southern Uplands are today deserted, but were once followed by ancient tracks of some importance. Over Kailzie Hill passed the busiest of the Scottish drove roads on its way from Falkirk Tryst to the English markets; whilst the track leading north-east from Blackhouse to Traquair and Innerleithen formed part of the only road south from the Tweed to Ettrick and the Borders in the early eighteenth century.

The drovers had many ways of reaching the Borders from Falkirk, but the most important made for the Pentland Hills, which were crossed at the pass known as Cauldstane Slap, then Peebles, Kailzie Hill and Dryhope, then via St Mary's Loch to Teviothead and the Cheviot Hills. We join the route at the Royal Burgh of Peebles, where the town kirk is built on the site of David I's twelfth-century castle, and where an emergency session of the Scots parliament was held in 1346.

Start at the kirk and cross the impressive Tweed Bridge, turning right into Springhill Road. On the left is Victoria Park, part of the King's Muir, where the rights of common grazing, so important to the drovers, were confirmed in a charter signed by James IV in 1506. Springhill Road becomes Glen Road as it skirts suburban housing, but where the Glensax road leaves to the right it becomes an enclosed stony track, level at first but then losing height quickly down a muddy slope into Gypsy Glen, where the Haystoun Burn is crossed on a modern footbridge.

The track gains height steadily, passing through a little wood and then two gates, from the second of which there is a superb view back to the north, over Peebles and the Tweed valley. Down to the east, again close to the Tweed, is the old ruined tower at Glentress. The track continues to the south, at first as a classic wide drove road between low drystone walls, but later as a narrow path through heather. Just to the right of the path is the cairn on the top of

Kailzie Hill, a fine viewpoint for the Glensax valley and the bare ridges and rounded hills of the Southern Uplands.

To the left Cardrona Forest and its Sitka spruce becomes a prominent feature of the landscape, but the drove route along the top of the ridge is treeless as it makes for Kirkhope Law, Birkscairn Hill and – leaving the ridge but keeping well above the Quair Water – Whiteknowe Head and ruined Blackhouse Tower in the valley of the Douglas Burn. Blackhouse, the seat of the Douglas barony by the eleventh century, was once the most heavily settled part of Ettrick Forest; here, too, the 'Douglas tragedy' occurred, when the elder daughter of the house eloped and her father and seven brothers were all killed by her lover.

The track following the drove road leads south-west across South Hawkshaw Rig to Dryhope Tower, where the substantial remains of a fortified house typical of the Borders can be seen. Mary Scott, an ancestor of Sir Walter Scott and known as the 'flower of Yarrow', was born here. On the way down to Dryhope there is an excellent view of St Mary's Loch in its shallow trough amongst the green hills of Ettrick Forest.

Returning to Blackhouse, take the path leading between the farm and a small wood and climbing gently above the Craighope Burn onto the long, flat south-easterly ridge of Deuchar Law. This is the 'Muir Road', the direct route from Ettrick and the south to Dalhousie and Edinburgh in the eighteenth century. The track – now part of the Southern Upland Way long-distance footpath – contours above Glenlude, climbs gently to the flat summit of Blake Muir above the valley of the Quair Water, and slowly descends to Kirkhouse and, in another mile (1.6km), the hamlet of Traquair and fascinating Traquair House.

Inhabited since at least 1209, when William the Lion held court there, Traquair House is well worth a visit, not least for the strong ale produced in 200-year-old oak fermenting vessels which were rediscovered by the laird in 1965. The final stage of the walk bears north from Traquair, then crosses the River Tweed to arrive in the centre of Innerleithen, some 6 miles (9.6km) from Peebles.

28 CHEVIOT·HILLS

Time: 8 hours.
Start and finish: Alwinton village green (921063).
Approach: From the B6341 between Elsdon and Rothbury take the Coquet valley road to Harbottle and Alwinton.
Attractions: Magnificent open walking on ancient border tracks used in the past by raiding parties, drovers and others, climbing to the main Cheviot ridge at Windy Gyle.
OS sheet: 80

Take the road leading west into upper Coquetdale for ½ mile (.8km), then the bridleway cutting across the shoulder of Middle Moor (the site of the former hamlet of Aldenscheles, now taken over by the military, is down on the left at Quickening Cote) to the solid Georgian farmhouse at Shillmoor. From here there is little alternative to the valley road, following the River Coquet in its rocky trench, past Barrowburn – where the monks of New-minster, who held the grazing rights here in the thirteenth century, had a fulling mill – to Slyme Foot, south of Rowhope.

Slyme Foot is nowadays deserted, merely a quiet junction of old ways, but in the eighteenth century there was an inn here, where the local farmers are reported to have spent their time drinking and gambling. The left-hand track is The Street, later called Clattering Path, one of the ancient tracks running from Coquetdale across the border into Scotland. It is more convenient, however, to bear right, past the remarkably isolated farmsteads of Rowhope and Trows, and then left up a well-defined path which climbs to meet the Pennine Way at the border fence close to Windy Gyle.

The summit of Windy Gyle (2,032ft, 619m) with its huge cairn is unmistakable, and it forms an excellent vantage point for views north into Scotland, north-east to the massive bulk of the Cheviot itself, and south into the dissected hill slopes running down to the Coquet valley. This exposed spot was a meeting place for the Wardens of the Marches on days of truce, and Russell's Cairn commemorates Lord Francis Russell, killed here in 1585 by John Forster at one of the more unruly Border trysts. The way then lies across the damp peat moorland to the north-east, following the Pennine Way (described on the map as 'undefined' but actually beaten out by the passage of long-distance walkers into a wide, black and at times boggy path close to the border fence) for a mile (1.6km) until, at a cairn, Clennell Street approaches from Outer Cock Law, crosses the fence and begins its descent southwards to Alwinton.

The Usway Burn and Hazely Law (M. Dunn)

Clennell Street is one of the most impressive of all the border tracks, and boasts an impressive pedigree to match. Undoubtedly of prehistoric origins, it was never Romanised, but returned to favour in.Saxon and early medieval times – in a charter of 1181 it is described as 'the great road of Yarnspath' – and was used by the monks of Newminster on their way to the sheep pastures in Kidland and by cattle rustlers and border raiders during the Border wars. Later, drovers travelling south from Falkirk tryst shared the route with whisky smugglers distributing the illicit produce of clandestine stills hidden in the side valleys of upper Coquetdale.

Clennell Street descends the slopes of Hazeley Law in company with the Salter's Road (known in the thirteenth century as the Thieves Road) until the latter veers left towards Alnham; down in the forest to the right are the waterfalls of Davidson's Linn, near Rory's Still on the Usway Burn, one of the best known sources of illegal whisky. The track is threatened by encroaching plantations on its way down to the Barrow Burn valley and the area known as 'The Middle'. This junction of important medieval tracks was once bustling with activity, with a drovers' inn and a cockpit amongst its attractions. Now there is only a sense of isolation amidst magnificent scenery, particularly where Clennell Street crosses the Usway Burn, which is much bigger than expected, with deep pools and miniature waterfalls.

The route climbs gradually away from the Usway Burn on a fine green rake, making for the coniferous plantation ahead and entering it by means of a dilapidated stile. Once in the forest the path improves and then joins a pleasant track which swings round the head of a small valley and, back on the open moorland for a while, becomes more stony as it contours round a minor hill. A second section through the Forestry Commission's Kidland Forest follows, with no views but with the compensation of fast level walking as far as Wholehope.

Wholehope is now a desolate sight indeed, a collection of roofless buildings and haphazard cattle enclosures; yet it was once a shepherd's cottage and overnight cattle stance for the drovers, and more recently functioned as a youth hostel. It commands wide views south, with the broad track of Clennell Street plainly in view across green sheep pasture, descending to a gate in a rather damp hollow, and with a typical Cheviot stell, or circular cattle enclosure, in the valley of the Alwinton Burn to the right.

The track rises after the gate and crosses a none too obvious cross dyke, probably constructed in the sixteenth century to block the return of Scots cattle raiders. To the left Clennell Hall, much altered but still incorporating a fourteenth-century peel tower, can be seen amongst the trees in the Alwin valley; across the valley is one of the hillforts which protected the route in prehistoric times. The ditches of the other are in sight ahead, crowning a small hill which forms the foreground to a fine view southwards to the Simonside Hills. Clennell Street now descends to pass between two farms, cross the Hosedon Burn and enter Alwinton across the village green, conveniently close to the excellent, unchanged Rose and Thistle Inn.

29 MID-PENNINES

Time: Allow 3½ hours for this Tan Hill circuit, which includes a couple of quite steep sections.

Start and finish: The Tan Hill Inn (897067), on the minor road between Reeth and Brough.

Approach: From Appleby and Brough by the minor road heading south-east, signposted Tan Hill; from Richmond via Reeth and Arkengarthdale; from Kirkby Stephen and Keld via West Stonesdale.

Attractions: Varied walking on old packhorse routes and coal roads in the remote mid-Pennines, centred on the highest inn in England.

OS sheet: 91

The Tan Hill Inn, in its remote situation on the borders of North Yorkshire and County Durham, with Cumbria less than ½ mile (.8km) away, has long been a magnet for thirsty travellers. Historically it has catered for packmen and colliers; nowadays this highest inn in England has attractions for Pennine Way walkers, real-ale drinkers and even double-glazing salesmen. But it is also notable for its position at a focal point in an intricate network of pack-horse routes and coal roads, many of them, these days, no more than green lanes or narrow tracks and the preserve of walkers.

Had it not been for an accident of geology, the inn might (like a number on the Hambleton drove road in the North York Moors, described on page 127) have catered for the drovers until the coming of the railways and then slowly declined and faded out of existence. But thin seams of coal in the millstone grit break through the universal blanket of glacial drift at Tan Hill, and the colliers – active in the area from the thirteenth century – created the network of rough roads to Brough, Kirkby Stephen, Bowes and Barnard Castle.

Leave Tan Hill by the road to Keld, but quickly fork right onto a path traversing open and often soggy moorland on its way to meet, accompany and finally cross the Stonesdale Beck. This path is the remnant of busy Jaggers Road, a packhorse route from Barnard Castle and Bowes to Kirkby Stephen. The green track crosses the southern summit of Roberts Seat at 1,759ft (536m), close to the scanty remains of the long-abandoned gamekeeper's cottage known as Roberts Seat House, and then (paved in the most difficult sections) descends steeply to the superbly unspoilt hamlet of Ravenseat.

The pack trains went west from here, crossing the beck on a fine packhorse bridge, but the Tan Hill walk keeps to the eastern side of the beck and follows

(overleaf) *The packhorse bridge at Ravenseat* (M. Dunn); (inset) *Wain Wath Force on the River Swale* (M. Dunn)

its sometimes rocky course down almost to its confluence with the Swale, just below the rugged stone hamlet of Hoggarths. The path contours above the well-wooded slopes above the river and its impressive cliffs here, though there are fine views of the stepped waterfall and rapids of Wain Wath Force.

Go straight across the twisting Tan Hill road at one of its hairpin bends, then turn left to follow a field path into West Stonesdale, another glorious, solidly built Yorkshire stone hamlet. A few yards north along the road another path leads down to and crosses the Stonesdale Beck, then rises obliquely to join the track carrying the Pennine Way near Low Frith.

The track – quite deeply eroded in places now that it has to contend with the Pennine Way traffic – keeps to its bench above the deeply incised beck, with magnificent views across the open rough grazing of Stonesdale Moor. This is classic mid-Pennine country – uninhabited moorland with, on the lower slopes, a network of stone-walled fields and occasional solitary trees.

Above High Frith the track dips down towards the beck, then climbs again onto the plateau and heads towards Tan Hill, which is now only a mile (1.6km) or so away. On the right are disused mineworkings – the remnants of a coal industry which can be dated back to the thirteenth century and which at that time supplied Richmond Castle. Four hundred years later the collieries around Tan Hill were in the ownership of Lady Anne Clifford, and the coal was then carted to Appleby Castle. The last pits closed during the 1930s.

One of the larger coal workings was Kings Pit Colliery, just to the east of the Tan Hill Inn, and indeed the inn was once known as Kings Pit House. The present building, whose outbuildings once housed two more inns, dates from the eighteenth century; but this junction of important trade routes has probably been the site of an inn since at least the thirteenth century.

Walkers not satisfied with the 8 mile (13km) circuit described, can stand on the rock outcrops to the north of the inn overlooking the barren swampy moors of Stainmore Forest and plan further outings: along the path to Sleightholme, once part of a busy way from Barnard Castle to Kirkby Stephen; past the coal workings to Great Punchard Head and Eskeleth, following the ancient route between Richmond and Appleby; or from Sleightholme to Eskeleth in the footsteps of the Scottish drovers. Together these three walks make up a second and more challenging 12 mile (19km) circuit, just as typical of the bleak and solitary mid-Pennine hills.

30 NORTH· YORK· MOORS

Time: 3 hours for the main walk, with up to an extra 4 hours for the extension to Black Hambleton.

Start and finish: The large car park at the top of Sutton Bank (515830). There is a National Park information centre here.

Approach: The car park lies immediately north of the A170 Thirsk to Scarborough road.

Attractions: Easy walking on well-marked paths and a wide green drove road on the western scarp of the North York Moors, with very wide views across the Vale of Mowbray to the Pennines.

OS sheet: 100 (or Outdoor Leisure Series sheet 26).

The western scarp face of the North York Moors, from Black Hambleton south to Sutton Bank and Roulston Scar, is a welcome and familiar sight to travellers in the Vale of York. But it is even better underfoot, with a combination of easy walking on clearly defined paths and magnificent views west across the Vale to the Pennines, and east into the heart of the moors.

Sutton Bank, marvellously situated at the edge of the scarp but now largely occupied by its massive car park with an extensive National Park information centre, is soon out of sight on the way to Hambleton Hotel, ½ mile (.8km) along the A170. Turn left here, along a bridleway leading past Hambleton House, still used as a racing stables but now the only reminder of the days when Hambleton Down racecourse was referred to as the 'Newmarket of the North'. The most valuable race, the Queen Anne Plate, was transferred to York as early as 1755, and the last meeting took place in 1811.

Northwards from the stables a fine green lane points to Dialstone Farm, previously a drovers' inn and meeting place for the racing fraternity; the dial stone, a primitive weighing machine for jockeys, can still be seen in a wall opposite the farm. There is then a stretch of road walking, albeit along a single-track lane which is relatively free from traffic, and which has assumed the name of Cleveland Road. From near the top of Sneck Yate there are panoramic views across the Vale, and the route passes Hesketh Dike, a mysterious low earthwork.

Now the road peters out into a wide grassy drift between white limestone walls, leading in ½ mile (.8km) to the High Paradise turning. For the extension of the walk to Black Hambleton keep straight on along the drove road here, past the quarries on Dale Town Common and the stump of Steeple Cross, situated at the junction of the drovers' route (this section of which was once known as the Lord's Tongue) with the green lane connecting Kepwick and Helmsley. Monastic connections are commonplace here for Friar's Cross, for which there is now little or no evidence on the ground, stood only a few hundred yards to the west.

About a mile (1.6km) to the north stood Limekiln House, another of the inns catering for the drovers; now, with its adjacent cattle stance, merely a few heaps of rubble. Northwards from here the track, enclosed between limestone walls, runs along the edge of the escarpment above Whitestone Scar before climbing through heather to the right of the drove road to the summit of Black Hambleton. There are fine views, particularly to the north-east and east, where there is a fine panorama of the North York Moors, and to the north, where the drove road can be seen for miles on its way to Scarth Nick and the Cleveland plain.

Return from Black Hambleton via the drove road, the spring-line villages in the Vale of Mowbray catching the eye, to the High Paradise Farm access road. Turn right here, passing the farm and then, in company with the Cleveland Way, contouring through forestry below the top of the scarp slope and above Low Paradise Farm, to cross the road at Sneck Yate Bank. A good path now follows the edge of the moor, with a steep drop on the right towards Boltby, past Cleave Dike and an Iron Age hillfort near Little Moor, to the top of Whitestone Cliff. The cliff, with a face of about 120ft (36m), is well known amongst the climbing fraternity.

Nestling at the foot of Whitestone Cliff is the attractive, tree-fringed Gormire Lake which, like many others, is reputed to be bottomless. To the south is the stark, almost vertical cliff of Roulston Scar (bearing on its far side the nineteenth-century Kilburn White Horse, a conspicuous local landmark) and, detached from the escarpment, the pyramid peak of Hood Hill with its thickly wooded summit. To the west, in the far distance beyond Gormire Lake and the Vale of Mowbray, the blue outlines of the Pennine hills can be discerned on a clear day, with Great Whernside prominent despite being 32 miles (51km) away.

The path bearing the Cleveland Way, very well marked at this point as it meanders gently between hawthorn trees at the top of the steep scarp slope, nears the top of Sutton Bank and, across a strip of woodland and the Dialstone road, reaches the end of the walk at the massive tourist car park on the busy road to Scarborough.

31 PEAK·DISTRICT

Time: 6 to 7 hours.
Start and finish: Castleton (151829).
Approach: Castleton lies on the A625 Sheffield to Chapel-en-le-Frith road. There is ample car parking in the village.
Attractions: The walk utilises a superb cross-section of paths and tracks in the Dark Peak and includes Peveril Castle, limestone caverns, medieval Edale Cross on the flanks of the Kinder Scout massif, and the start of the Pennine Way.
OS sheet: 110 (or Outdoor Leisure Series sheet 1, 'The Dark Peak').

Fascinating though it is, Castleton is rather overrun by tourists in summer and is perhaps only worth exploring on a winter's day, when the magnificent situation of its Norman castle can be seen in the context of the town it protected. Castleton was, in fact, a Norman new town, though not a particularly successful one since it never expanded to fill the space inside the town ditch, the remains of which can still be discerned in places. But Peveril Castle, on the limestone cliff overlooking the town, successfully fulfilled roles varying from defensive fortress to royal hunting lodge and mansion before it suffered later neglect.

Castleton's fortunes have revived with the onset of tourism, much of it directed at the limestone caverns which pepper the surrounding area – Blue John, Speedwell, Peak (already described as 'a marvel of England' in the twelfth century), and Treak Cliff. The entrance to Speedwell Cavern lies on our route, ½ mile (.8km) west of the village, on the former saltway and later turnpike road piercing the Winnats Pass. This narrow road has had to accept massively increased traffic since the collapse of the main A625 on the slopes of Mam Tor, accurately described as the 'shivering mountain'.

A footpath keeps fairly close to the road through the dramatic limestone scenery of the Winnats, then runs roughly north-west to the col between Mam Tor and Rushup Edge. A fine ridge walk along Rushup Edge now ensues, following the line of a prehistoric trackway past a burial mound on Lord's Seat to the A625 and, 100yd (90m) further west, the fine packhorse route connecting Tideswell and Hayfield. This excellent track, walled in places and eroded away into a sunken hollow-way in others, crosses Roych Clough and skirts the Kinder moorland on its way to Mount Famine.

Just before Mount Famine, turn off to the right where a path leaves the northern slopes of South Head, then descend to and cross the River Sett immediately above South Head Farm. At the top of the opposite slope this path meets the packhorse track from Hayfield to Edale; turn right here, climbing slowly to cross the Oaken Clough Brook at Stony Ford and reach Edale Cross at about 1,750ft (533m) on the southern flanks of Kinder Low.

Edale Cross, almost certainly early medieval, is virtually intact, having lost only part of one arm. It appears to have originated as an internal boundary marker of the royal forest of High Peak, indicating the spot at which the forest's three wards (Longendale, Hopedale and Campana or Champion) met. But it also served to delineate the eastern limit of the lands held by Basingwerk Abbey in Flintshire and, more recently, it has helped to guide packmen, traders and now ramblers across the exposed and largely featureless slopes of the Kinder Scout massif.

The alternative route of the Pennine Way, especially useful in mist and rain, comes in from the north at Edale Cross and then coincides with the packhorse track, parts of which are roughly paved, as far as the top of Jacob's Ladder, a steep eighteenth-century descent into the Noe valley. The pack trains veered right here, zigzagging down a marvellous stony track to Edale Head House (now in ruins) and, lower still, the packhorse bridge over the River Noe.

The route is now obvious as an elongated light-coloured scar past Lee House to Upper Booth and then across fields below Broadlee Bank to Grindsbrook Booth and the scattered village of Edale. Isolated until the coming of the Manchester to Sheffield railway in 1894, Edale is now very conscious of its position at the start of the Pennine Way long-distance foot-path, which was officially established in 1951.

Edale church, south of Grindsbrook Booth, was not consecrated until 1633; until then the packhorse route to Hollins Cross and Castleton also served as a corpse road. Now it is a fine, short but quite steep path, reaching the ridge between Mam Tor and Lose Hill at about 1,250ft (380m), a climb of some 500ft (150m) from the Vale of Edale. Across the valley there is an excellent view of the Kinder plateau, while to the west the position of the low ramparts of the Iron Age hillfort enclosing much of the summit of Mam Tor can be picked out.

The path descends equally steeply from Hollins Cross into Hope Vale, again paved in places with rough slabs. Gradually it becomes enclosed and at times is confined as a deep sunken way, now known as Hollowford Road. As the outskirts of Castleton are approached, the lane from Losehill Hall joins from the left and Hollowford Road, now surfaced, crosses the stream – presumably this was the ford in a hollow which gave the road its name – and enters the village to the east of the market square, at the end of quite a challenging walk in the Dark Peak.

32 THE·LONG·MYND

Time: 3 to 4 hours.
Start and finish: The main car park in Church Stretton, just west of the railway station (545936).
Approach: Church Stretton lies immediately west of the A49 Shrewsbury to Hereford road, some 12 miles (19km) from Shrewsbury.
Attractions: Deep green valleys and an empty moorland plateau, with a combination of ancient trackways and popular tourist paths.
OS sheet: 137

The hills of south Shropshire all have their own special attractions; Wenlock Edge, for example, has its long wooded scarp, Caer Caradoc has its hillfort and historical associations. But the Long Mynd is in a class of its own – a level plateau of tussocky grass, bilberry, bracken and heather, deeply dissected by a series of extraordinary, isolated valleys. It has the feel of a mountain, and indeed the girth of one, since it is some 9 miles (14km) long and 4 or 5 miles (6 or 8km) wide. It comes as a disappointment to learn that the highest point is a mere 1,695ft (517m) above sea level.

At the crossroads in Church Stretton turn right, then left after ¼ mile (.4km) onto a minor road heading up the Cardingmill valley. After a while, the way along the valley floor opens out and it is possible to walk on grass parallel to the road, which can be very busy in the summer and at weekends. Pass the last buildings, ford the stream and climb to the left of the car park, quickly gaining the rocky ramparts at the end of the ridge and gaining also a fine view into the side valley below the Devil's Mouth, with its sparkling reservoir.

A marvellous green path runs along the side of the ridge, keeping a constant height and gradually converging with the Cardingmill stream and the main tourist track into the hills. Across the valley the Iron Age hillfort of Bodbury Ring can clearly be seen. At a confluence keep to the right, on the ancient Mott Road from Church Stretton, and climb steadily up the quieter upper section of the Cardingmill valley onto the Long Mynd plateau. Soon a complex junction is reached: not only do the Mott Road and the Portway meet here, but also an old drove road which ran north-east down to All Stretton.

The Portway, a Bronze Age trackway which seems to have provided a link between the Kerry Hill ridgeway and the north, was reused in medieval times as a drove road carrying four-footed traffic from the collecting centres of Montgomery and Plowden to market in Shrewsbury. The droves climbed up Black Knoll from Plowden, traversed the inhospitable top of the Long Mynd at Pole Bank, and finally dropped down off the plateau to reach the main valley road at Leebotwood, where the name of the Pound Inn is a reminder of former times. The Portway can still be followed along the crest of the Long Mynd, but is now partly metalled and therefore forms only a small part of this walk.

Before following the Portway south, however, it is worth tramping north for about ⅓ mile (.5km) over the heather moor to Robin Hood's Butts – tumuli of no great physical distinction, but with fine views over the plateau to the Caer Caradoc earthworks, the Lawley and the serrated Stiperstones ridge. Turn south past the Mott Road junction to further tumuli, a junction with the metalled road from Ratlinghope to Church Stretton and the OS triangulation station on the summit of the Long Mynd at Pole Bank (1,695ft, 517m), in the middle of a large and generally featureless plateau. On the left is Boiling Well, where a small spring signals the start of the picturesque Ashes Hollow, one of the finest Long Mynd valleys.

Despite the unremarkable nature of the immediate vicinity, with its gentle heather- and bilberry-covered slopes, Pole Bank has the considerable virtue reserved for summits, namely a magnificent all-round panorama. On a clear day the distant hills glimpsed from here include the summits of Snowdonia, Cader Idris, the Brecon Beacons, the Malverns and the unmistakable pyramid of the Wrekin. Nearer to hand are Caer Caradoc, Wenlock Edge, Clun Forest and the Stiperstones.

The view east from above the Mott Road (M. Dunn)

The way continues south, past the trees at Pole Cottage and alongside the Plowden road (still the Portway) for about a mile (1.6km) to a signpost where the track down Yapsel Bank to Minton branches off on the left. Take this excellent track, passing a well and then yet another burial mound as the ridge narrows, with Callow Hollow to the left and Minton Batch to the right, and descending Packetstone Hill. Finally the track descends quite sharply to the Saxon hamlet of Minton, with its manor house, castle mound and open green.

From Minton take the country lane, narrow but rarely used, to Little Stretton, where there is a remarkable thatched black and white church. Then follow the B4370, rather busier but with the compensation of fine views of the surrounding hills, back to Church Stretton, a rather prim and proper tourist resort of the Victorian era, at which time it was briefly popular as a spa. Even the half-timbered houses date largely from this period, although the church has a Norman north doorway known as the 'corpse door'. The town is, however, an unrivalled and marvellously accessible centre for walking in the hill country of southern Shropshire, and especially the Long Mynd.

33 Cotswold·Hills

Time: 3 hours.
Start and finish: The village of Stanton (067342), which has a car park on
the road to Broadway.
Approach: Stanton lies ½ mile (.8km) east of the A46 Cheltenham to Strat-
ford road, some 2 miles (3km) south-west of Broadway.
Attractions: Although this is an easy and quite short walk it includes sections
under and along the prominent Cotswold scarp south of Broadway, passes an
Iron Age hillfort and visits a number of delightful stone-built villages.
OS sheet: 150

Begin the walk at the cross in Stanton, one of the most appealing of Cotswold
villages (partly because its attractions have not been destroyed by commer-
cialisation). The village has a number of late medieval Cotswold stone
houses, some of them converted from barns, and a much altered church. The
latter appears to have been founded in Saxon times, but the earliest remaining features are Norman, and most are fifteenth century. Inside there are two
pulpits, from one of which John Wesley is said to have preached. The cross
itself has a medieval base, perhaps dating back to the fifteenth century, but
the shaft is an eighteenth-century replacement.

Take the alley leading from Stanton cross to the church, and at the north-
east corner of the churchyard take a walled path, quickly turning left over a
footbridge and following a field path northwards to the village of Laverton.
Turn right and follow the road through the village, and at a minor crossroads
carry straight on along a track which becomes an excellent path with a hedge
on both sides. Where this reaches a country lane, turn right to enter the
village of Buckland with its pleasant stone cottages and fine church, noted
for its seventeenth-century canopied pews and ornate fifteenth-century font.
The rectory is a claimant for the title of oldest parsonage in England.

Follow the road up through Buckland, curve uphill around a wood and
then, having reached the plateau close to some prominent barns, walk south
on a well-defined and very straight bridleway which forms part of the
Cotswold Way long-distance footpath. Where the Cotswold Way leaves to
the right, keep straight on, skirting Buckland Wood (look back from here
over Buckland to the rounded outline of Bredon Hill) and then keeping to a
farm track bounded by woodland to the right. At the hamlet of Great Brockhampton keep to the right of the houses, then swing sharply left, away from
the track, to find a footpath which leads above a small pond and in ½ mile
(.8km) reaches the outskirts of Snowshill.

Tan Hill Inn, the highest inn in England (M. Dunn) (see page 123)

Unlike some of the villages at the foot of the scarp, Snowshill is regarded as part of the Broadway tourists' itinerary, largely because of Snowshill Manor, owned by the National Trust and open to the public on certain days. A mainly Tudor house with a William and Mary façade, it has attractive terraced gardens and an extraordinary series of collections, from toys and musical instruments to clocks and bicycles. The village itself, arranged around a triangular churchyard and green, is typically Cotswold, with stone cottages and colourful gardens.

Retrace your steps to the edge of Snowshill, but instead of taking the track to Brockhampton keep on the road under Oat Hill until, at a sharp bend, a bridleway leads straight across the plateau. After ½ mile (.8km) turn left, then immediately right, on a substantial track which makes for Shenberrow hillfort. One of seventeen Iron Age hillforts along the Cotswold scarp, Shenberrow is neither the largest nor the most impressive, covering only 3 acres (1.2ha) or so and defended by ramparts which have been considerably damaged in succeeding centuries. It comes as a surprise to find a substantial farm against the southern edge of the fort; as a result it is necessary to go around the fort to the right, with glimpses of the low and rather unimpressive bank and ditch, the former now surrounded by a field wall.

Go through a gate and turn left on the Cotswold Way, into the fort through a gap in its northern defences and then, beyond the southern tip of the fort, down a steep wooded slope on a waymarked eroded path into a quite deep valley. The path is easy to follow, and indeed is well waymarked, as it descends through the wood. After rain it can be muddy in places. Keep right at a junction of paths after emerging from the wood, and cross a large field, heading for some old gateposts and a wooded dell. There are excellent views from above the gateposts across buttercup fields to Stanton and the Vale of Evesham.

The way lies over a stile, then cuts through the wood – Stanton Reservoir is just to the left – to emerge on a track which can be followed past marvellous mellow stone cottages into the village of Stanton. The cross and car park lie to the left; uphill to the right is the Mount Inn, well known for its locally brewed real ale and for the views from its gardens.

The remote hamlet of Ravenseat in the Mid-Pennines (M. Dunn) (see page 123)
Looking north along the ridge of Black Hill in the Quantocks to the Bristol Channel (M. Dunn) (see page 140)

The Cotswold Way above Stanton (M. Dunn)

34 QUANTOCK·HILLS

Time: Allow up to 3 hours for the basic walk, and a further 1½ hours for the extension to Wills Neck.

Start and finish: The car park at Holford village green (154410).

Approach: From Bridgwater take the A39 to Holford village, turn left at the Plough Inn and follow the road signposted Hodder's Combe to Holford village green.

Attractions: Easy walking with astonishingly wide views along the crest of this compact range of hills, coupled with visits to two of the most attractive of the Quantock combes.

OS sheet: 181

Retrace your steps from the village green for 100yd (90m), then turn sharply right and follow the road into the delightfully sylvan Holford Combe. On the right a former tannery has been cleverly converted into an hotel, with the waterwheel still visible. Where the tarmac ends at the last houses, continue ahead on the stony track between thick hedgerows. At a clearing turn right, fording the stream, and climb through woodland and then bracken, with increasingly fine views, to the Black Hill ridge.

To the east lies the well-wooded head of Holford Combe, and beyond it Woodlands Hill; north is the end of the Black Hill ridge and the deep bowl of Hodder's Combe, backed by the Bristol Channel and the hills of south Wales; westwards is the broad track leading quickly to the backbone of the Quantocks, the ridge leading south-east from West Quantoxhead towards Lydeard Hill. Beyond the top of Black Hill the way reaches the ridge route at Crowcombe Park Gate, where the main walk turns right and the longer walk taking in Wills Neck turns left to follow the ridgeway south.

Wills Neck is about 1½ miles (2km) away, and the ridgeway – first tramped by prehistoric travellers, referred to in Saxon charters, but later used as a drove road too – heads directly towards it, skirting the top of Great Hill and then running between ancient beech trees to Triscombe Stone. On the way there are fine views over the Brendon Hills, and later the massive quarry which has eaten into the northern slopes of Wills Neck. Beyond the car park at Triscombe Stone keep to the drove road, now a sunken track hemmed in by a drystone wall in places, as it skirts the head of Cockercombe, part of the Forestry Commission's much-criticised Quantock Forest.

At a junction of three tracks veer right, climbing gradually through heather to reach the summit of Wills Neck (the Weala's ridge, named after the local Britons driven back to this ridge by the Saxons in the seventh century). At 1,261ft (384m) this is the highest point in the Quantocks, and

The Quantock drove road near the Triscombe Stone (M. Dunn)

it has magnificent all-round views as a result. Dartmoor lies to the south-west, Dunkery Beacon and Exmoor above the Brendon Hills to the west, the sea to the north, and the Mendips to the east. Closer at hand there is the heather moor of the main ridge, subsiding gently into the softer, more intimate landscape of the southern Quantocks around Broomfield.

The southern Quantocks lie on Morte Slates, Wills Neck and the main ridge on more durable Hangman Grits, and it is the gritstone ridge which is now followed towards the sea, past Triscombe Stone back to Crowcombe Park Gate and then rejoining the main walk, north-west to Thorncombe Hill. Some of the many Bronze Age round barrows on the Quantocks are scattered along the ridge here. This is wild, open country above the steep western escarpment, with the superb villages of Crowcombe and Bicknoller hidden in the lower slopes.

The classic ridge-walk continues around the forked head of Hodder's Combe, losing height and then climbing quite sharply to the wooden stake of Bicknoller Post, one of the traditional meeting places for the Quantock staghounds. Beacon Hill, the last summit seawards, is an easy ⅓ mile (.5km) north from here; it boasts the widest view over the Bristol Channel, with the islands of Flat Holm and Steep Holm prominent. Then, after returning to Bicknoller Post, there is time for a last glance at the view, from the Brendon Hills round to the unmistakable skyline tumulus on the ridge of Longstone Hill, before plunging down a well-marked track into the upper reaches of Hodder's Combe.

The gentle descent along Hodder's Combe forms a fine climax to the walk, though it can be marshy at times and the stream has to be crossed on occasion. It is a gentle, well-wooded landscape, in stark contrast to the bare heights above: the path, later developing into quite a sizeable track, traverses oak woodland with an undergrowth of bilberries before meeting the straggling outliers of the village of Holford, and finally the village green.

To the left here, for those needing another diversion, is Holford's dog pound and, on a rather larger scale, Alfoxton – home of William and Dorothy Wordsworth for a year, and now an hotel. The Wordsworths traversed the hills around here repeatedly, taking walks which Dorothy reported as extending 'for miles over the hill-tops, the great beauty of which is their wild simplicity'. Few who wander the open heights of the Quantocks nowadays would disagree with that.

35 DARTMOOR

Time: 5 hours.
Start and finish: Start at Buckfast Abbey (741674); finish at Princetown (591735).
Approach: From the A38 Buckfastleigh junction (2 miles (3km) south-west of Ashburton) follow signs for ½ mile (.8km) to Buckfast Abbey.
Attractions: The Abbot's Way is a classic walk of southern Dartmoor, over clapper bridges and tors, and past medieval crosses and abandoned farms to the grim setting of Princetown.
OS sheets: 191 and 202 (or Outdoor Leisure Series sheet 28, 'Dartmoor')

Although the monks of Buckfast Abbey undoubtedly used this path across the moor on their way to Tavistock and Buckland Abbeys, they were by no means the first to travel along it, and in this respect its name is misleading. Parts, at least, were in use in prehistoric times when southern Dartmoor was quite thickly populated, and even the crosses marking its course may predate its monastic uses. But the monks certainly did use the Abbot's Way, along with packhorse trains in the later medieval period, and even now it remains comparatively little changed – testing in places, marshy near the headwaters of the Plym, but otherwise a magnificent walk over open moorland.

Buckfast Abbey, however, combines medieval ruins with a modern church (its history is complicated, culminating in a late nineteenth-century revival inspired by the French Benedictines). The Abbot's Way is represented at first by the road past Hockmoor to Cross Furzes, where a rough track dips quite sharply into a wooded valley. Here the Dean Burn is crossed on a simple but strikingly picturesque clapper bridge constructed of massive slate slabs.

The route of the Abbot's Way is now waymarked very clearly across fields and rough pasture to a gate at Water Oak corner, at the edge of the moor. Slant up to the right here, on a path which improves gradually to reach a tall guide-post overlooking the Avon reservoir. The path skirts the northern edge of the reservoir, with the low mounds of a Bronze Age settlement in the bracken to the right. Another ancient settlement can be picked out more clearly as the path, now stony in places, descends into the Avon valley at Bishop's Meads, fords the Western Walla Brook, and approaches Huntingdon Cross.

The cross, presumably monastic in origin, is disappointingly squat and now apparently functions mainly as a meeting place for the black cattle of the area. To the west the Abbot's Way crosses the Avon, by ford or clapper bridge according to choice, and makes its way across the barren, featureless and sometimes boggy moor, passing the remains of the tramway which used to serve the china-clay works at Red Lake, and the stone row at the head of the Erme valley.

Further marshy areas now have to be negotiated, at Blacklane Brook and Erme Pits, before the Abbot's Way climbs beyond Erme Head to skirt around the southern shoulder of Great Gnat's Head and then cross the Plym valley, fording the river close to the derelict remains of tin workings only ½ mile (.8km) from its source on Crane Hill. The way then slowly climbs again, heading north-east for ¼ mile (.4km) before turning quite sharply to the north-west and dropping down to Nun's Cross Farm.

The small, low farmhouse at Nun's Cross was built by Richard Hooper in the 1870s, when he enclosed the surrounding land and began the long and ultimately unsuccessful struggle to improve its productivity. The remains of the field walls, constructed of granite blocks with a turf capping, which surround the farmhouse can still be traced. Within a few decades Nun's Cross Farm was in ruins, and although some repairs have been carried out to the building it no longer functions as a farmhouse.

The Abbot's Way continues to the north-west of the farm and in 200yd (180m) or so, at an important junction of tracks across the moor, reaches Nun's Cross. Originally this was known as Siward's Cross, and as early as 1280 was referred to in documents granting Buckland Abbey rights over adjacent land at Walkhampton. The tall granite cross, reinforced by iron struts as a result of nineteenth-century vandalism but nonetheless an impressive survival, probably originated as a forest boundary marker and was later claimed by the monks as a useful guide-post when they linked existing paths to form the Abbot's Way.

A notably straight path now takes the Abbot's Way through a rock-strewn landscape of close-cropped grass and purple heather, and past a number of boundary markers, to the delightful outcrop of South Hessary Tor. Straight in front is the grim sight of Princetown and, beyond the town, Dartmoor Prison. The town, surrounded by bleak moorland, lies at 1,400ft (427m) and owes its origins to Sir Thomas Tyrwhitt, whose granite quarries and estate at Tor Royal were adjacent. Tyrwhitt also built the prison, opened in 1806 to house prisoners of the Napoleonic wars; it was closed in 1816, but was reopened for long-term prisoners and has since been considerably enlarged, even becoming a tourist attraction in its own right.

Black cattle at Huntingdon Cross, Dartmoor (M. Dunn)

CITY·HERITAGE

This is the 'odd man out' among the chapters of this book, forsaking the rural or wild for an urban environment. Note well the word 'heritage' in the title, for no British town would be more worth visiting than another were it not for what Sir John Summerson describes as 'the enormous, obstinate and overwhelming legacy of the past'. Incredibly insensitive redevelopment during the 1950s and 1960s has ruined many urban treasures, but although for many places conservation has come rather late in the day, it is possible to find and enjoy what has survived in some cities. More and more areas, often whole streets, have been returned to pedestrian use only; and sensible towns, through the creation of ring-roads, are keeping heavy traffic away from sensitive places. Many civic authorities actively promote the enjoyment of their streets and buildings by the publication of useful walk guides, and there is little doubt that increasing numbers of people are discovering the pleasures of exploring towns and cities on foot – the only sensible way of seeing and appreciating their legacy from the past.

My choice of cities has been dictated partly by the need to have a fair geographical spread, partly by the need for variety in terms of townscape qualities, but predominantly by 'heritage' character, easier to feel than to define in words. One of the old university cities had to be included, and Cambridge is less industrially afflicted than Oxford. As the supreme Georgian city Bath had to be in, as had Newcastle for its unique Victorian city-centre content. Edinburgh is by far the most romantically situated city in the list while Durham, the smallest, has no British equivalent. But I am biased, having spent memorable years at university there, absorbing – among other things – the reassuring influence of cathedral and castle on the rock above the river.

Because of limitations imposed by length, it is impossible to give precise and detailed instructions for the entire routes of these walks. I have often restricted myself merely to trying to point out the general way. As you walk the streets of these places you will be aware of city character – an amalgam of geography, history, buildings, spaces and people. Visually, these create townscape, taken in the broad canvas or in the intimate view. Shapes, colours, textures, lines, elevations, scale; all these enter the reckoning. Often it is details that delight: Georgian fanlights, window shapes, doorknockers, cobbles and stone flags, inn names and signs, the unexpected sight

Northumberland Place, Bath (Geoffrey N. Wright) (*see page 153*)

of cathedral or church framed between buildings, date-panels and inscriptions, leafy gardens or courtyards, water or skylines. Often, a certain part of a walk is best done at a particular time of day – the best section of York's walls, north and east of the minster, in the morning; the Cambridge 'Backs' in late afternoon or early evening. Bath stone seems most luminous on a June afternoon, Newcastle's riverside at dusk in autumn.

City walking is very tiring. Measure it in hours not miles for, being rarely straightforward, it is slower than country walking. Boots are very comfortable, though they may look out of place and shoes may seem more appropriate. One piece of advice: avoid all temptations to mix exploring a city heritage with shopping, otherwise you will find yourself lumbered with irritating packages. Restrict yourself to window shopping! A pub lunch, bar snack, or a meal at a small restaurant gives a welcome break, and reminds that cities are for people, not merely assemblages of buildings serving an idea, although they are that, too. Without the people, a city street becomes mummified.

I am tempted to list towns by personal preference, but will restrict myself to particular streets or views presented in no particular order of merit:

The Cambridge skyline from the Backs.
Canterbury Cathedral framed through Mercery Lane.
York Minster from the north-east corner of the city walls, and York's 'snickelways'.
Edinburgh from Calton Hill.
Bath's Lansdown Crescent.
Durham, either from the Observatory or the railway station.

And for friendly vitality, sense of purpose, and the music of local dialect – Newcastle. Good walking, and remember, streets are to be enjoyed!

36	York, North Yorkshire	3 miles plus 1½ miles (5 plus 2km)
37	Bath, Avon	4 miles (6km)
38	Cambridge, Cambridgeshire	2½ miles (4km)
39	Canterbury, Kent	3 miles (5km)
40	Durham, County Durham	2½ to 3 miles (4 to 5km)
41	Chester, Cheshire	2½ miles (4km)
42	Norwich, Norfolk	2 to 3 miles (3 to 5km)
43	Newcastle upon Tyne, Tyne and Wear	3 miles (5km)
44	Edinburgh (Lothian)	4 miles (6km)

36 YORK

Time: Allow 2 hours for each of the two parts of this walk.
Start and finish: Bootham Bar for each part of the walk.
Approach: Bootham is the north-west entrance to the city, reached from the A19. Car parking is available at various places outside the city walls.
Attractions: The walls and streets of one of Europe's finest cities.
OS sheet: 105

York's city walls are more extensive and higher than those of Chester, more aloof from the everyday life of the city, more demanding and rewarding to walk. Old fortified gateways through them, called 'bars', provide stepped pedestrian access; this access closes at dusk each day. Bootham Bar is the oldest entrance into York, being on the site of the Roman north gate. The other three bars are medieval; all have been restored.

Climb onto the wall, prepared for a 3 mile (5km) walk, most of it sufficiently above street level to reduce the noises of a busy city to an acceptable amount. Walk clockwise, first north-east, then south-east, to Monk Bar. This is the best part of the whole wall, Roman based, and most striking in the first part of the day when morning sunlight illuminates the eastern elevations of the nearby minster. In mid-autumn the foliage of the tree-fringed gardens within the walls glows golden against silvery-grey stone.

At Monk Bar, descend to street level and up the opposite side. Almost immediately, just outside the wall, is an early nineteenth-century ice-house. Past the remains of a Roman corner-tower, the medieval wall vanishes for between Layerthorpe Bridge and the Red Tower, former marshland by the River Foss made a wall unnecessary. Walk along Foss Islands Road to pick up the wall again at Red Tower, the only substantial brick-built section, and continue to Walmgate Bar with its unique surviving barbican, or outward extensions. Go past the Elizabethan house above, and walk westwards along the wall to the minor entrance of Fishergate Bar and the Fishergate postern tower with splendid, distant views of the minster. Beyond there, between the River Foss and the Ouse, the castle protected the city. Cross Skeldergate Bridge (road) to the artificial mound of Baile Hill, originally topped by the Conqueror's timber castle, and rejoin the medieval wall there.

Bitchdaughter Tower and Victoria Bar (nineteenth century) soon follow as the walk continues north-westwards to Micklegate Bar, its Norman arch above the road by which kings entered York from the south. At Toft Tower the wall swings north-eastwards, past the station on the left, to North Street postern tower above the river. This section, above grassy ramparts daffodil-gay in spring, colourful with flower-beds in summer, offers wonderful views

St William's College (Geoffrey N. Wright)

ahead of the minster. Cross the river by Lendalgate Bridge, turn into Museum Gardens diverting north for the beautiful ruins of St Mary's Abbey, and pick up the wall again by the Roman multangular tower beyond which the medieval wall is outside the Roman one and there is an impressive cross-section of all the walls, excavated and identified. At normal ground-level, follow the outside of the wall past Tudor King's Manor, official residence of Henry VIII's Council of the North, whose restored courtyards should be explored before moving into Exhibition Square and Bootham Bar.

After this elevated view of York, take your ease, and food – there's no shortage of good eating places nearby – and prepare for a street-level foray full of medieval flavour, exploring some of what Mark Jones recently described as 'snickelways' ie narrow alleys which evolved to allow York's townsfolk to move around their city. Between Bootham Bar and Clifford's Tower, ½ mile (.8km) to the south-east, over fifty such snickelways reveal the secret York. This walk uses only a few.

Go through Bootham Bar into High Petergate, and turn through the covered passage by the Hole-in-the-Wall pub into the quiet charm of Precentor's Court, framing a delightful view of the minster's west front with early afternoon sunlight glancing across its Gothic west towers. At the end, turn left into Dean's Park, north of the minster, past the Minster Library into Minster Yard, passing the Treasurer's House (National Trust) on the left, with

York Minster and City Walls from above Station Road (Geoffrey N. Wright)

a quick glance down cobbled Chapter House Yard before reaching College Street and its gloriously half-timbered fifteenth-century St William's College.

Turn right into Goodramgate and soon, on the right overhanging the pavement, is Our Lady's Row of 1316, the oldest surviving houses in York. Beyond them a wrought-iron gateway dating from 1815, in an older brick arch, leads to Tonge's Court and lovely Holy Trinity Church. Continue down Goodramgate to King's Square with trees, street musicians and fish-and-chips; and at its farther corner be prepared to be funnelled into The Shambles where, even in 1830, there were twenty-five butcher's shops! While you can pursue an in-and-out policy between shops on the right, it is simplest to go directly to the end, into Pavement, across Piccadilly (divert to Merchant Adventurers' Hall), Coppergate and down Castlegate to Clifford's Tower and the elegant Georgian buildings round the 'Eye of York', (two of which house the remarkable Castle Museum).

Go down to the river and walk northwards along South Esplanade and King's Staith into Low Ousegate, left along Spurriergate and Coney Street to the Mansion House by St Helen's Square. Turn right along the square and ahead into Stonegate. Past the entrance to Little Stonegate turn, near the overhead sign of the Starre, into Coffee Yard, a splendid snickelway, long, narrow and with tunnels. At the end, go left into Grape Lane which leads to Low Petergate, left again to the Stonegate crossing at the junction of the two principal Roman streets – a marvellous place, a peopled place, cheerful, colourful, lively. The minster beckons along Minster Gates, formerly Book-binders' Alley. Cross Minster Yard and enter the cathedral by the south door. Amongst all its great glories, do not miss the crypt. When you emerge, a few yards' walk along High Petergate will return you to Bootham Bar.

37 Bath

Time: At least 2 hours, but 3 or 4 would be much better.
Start and finish: Bath Abbey in the centre of the city.
Attractions: The walk passes through elegant eighteenth-century town-scapes, and includes a short section along the towpath of the Kennet & Avon Canal. Choose an afternoon in late May or early June.
OS sheet: 172

Bath was the queen of English cities, and is probably unrivalled in Europe as the survivor of an elegant age. Bombs damaged much; postwar development – another name for legalised rape – piled on more indignities, but, not quite too late, common-sense conservation has exerted sufficient influence to save the gracious showpieces – the billowing curves of crescents, terraces, tall houses, textured honeyed stones of walls and pavements, all greened with lawns and trees and in the grandly theatrical setting of the Avon valley. By heading generally north-westwards and working in a wide clockwise loop, this walk misses the worst of the urban destruction and the graceless modern buildings of the southern part of the city.

The abbey, an early sixteenth-century replacement of a monastic church, co-cathedral since the thirteenth century with Wells, bestows a Tudor benediction at the beginning of the walk whose route moves northwards into High Street and, opposite the Guildhall of 1775, turns left into Northumberland Place, ablaze with flowers in summer and full of continental flavour. Turn right at the end into Union Street, with a glimpse northwards up Milsom Street with its shade of Jane Austen visiting the library, and shortly left along Upper Borough Walls, past a fragment of medieval walling.

Almost immediately turn into Trim Street, past Wolfe's House, under St John's Bridge into cobbled intimate Queen Street, left into Wood Street, soon entering Queen Square and, walking up its eastern side, appreciate this first of many climaxes on the walk. John Wood the elder's first great Bath venture, 1729–36, used the whole of each side of the square and treated it as though it were a single monumental palace, the northern one the most impressive, looking across greenery in the middle where trees were added later.

Northwards, now, past Wood's own bow-windowed house of 1740 into Gay Street, climbing steadily to the Circus, the second climax, started by the elder Wood in 1754, the year he died. This English version of the Roman Colosseum turned inside-out is the first circular space in British town planning. Walk round it completely before leaving by its western exit, Brock Street, with characteristic town houses, which suddenly and magnificently opens onto the younger Wood's Royal Crescent (1767–74), a semi-ellipse of terraced houses on a hillside site, south-facing over a spacious lawn to what would have been a green idyllic landscape, now the tree-clad Victoria Park. Black-painted iron railings, lamp-holders, boot-scrapers; sandstone flags on wide pavements and setts in the sweeping road; white paint on window frames, glazing bars, Adam fanlights – it is a symphony of texture all the way round the crescent, right at the end up Marlborough Buildings to Cavendish Place and Cavendish Road with, near the top, a glance along Cavendish Crescent.

Above this, across Summerhill Road, take the steps to Somerset Place, highest point of the walk, leading eastwards to Lansdown Place West, Lansdown Crescent and Lansdown Place East (1789–92). This bravura townscape triad of wriggling terraces – convex, concave, convex – has urn-capped railings above steps descending to basements, and across the wide pavement and road a steep drop to trees and shrubs. Join Lansdown Road, go past the Lansdown Grove Hotel and left to Camden Crescent, with views over the chimney-pots of Belvedere to the wooded hills of Bath's distant southern skyline. Look for a path across Hedgemead Park below, dropping into the traffic noises of London Street; go left along Walcot Parade, elevated and urbane. At its eastern end cross the road by the traffic lights into Cleveland Place, and across the River Avon by the 1827 Cleveland Bridge with its two pairs of toll-collectors' lodges.

This part of Bath east of the river, known as Bathwick, dates largely from 1788 to 1820 and shows terraces rather than crescents. Continue along Bathwick Street, left at the end into Beckford Road, and where this climbs to cross the Kennet & Avon Canal, gain access to the canal towpath up left, turning right onto it beside Sydney Gardens. The canal, completed in 1810, passes through short tunnels beneath Beckford Road and Sydney Road, rings and grooves on the walls marking where chains were suspended on Sundays to stop barge traffic. Observe, too, the masons' marks, the rusticated stonework of the arches, the trim iron bridges of 1810, the keeper's cottage by the top lock as you walk southwards, crossing to the opposite side of the canal and eventually reaching Sydney Wharf.

Climb the steps to George Street, turning towards the city by Vane Street and Edward Street into Great Pulteney Street, 1788–94. Wide and handsome, this is another noble climax, with two tiny red accents of rare, hexagonal Victorian pillar boxes. Walk south-westwards to Laura Place and its fountain, into narrower Argyle Street and down steps to the riverside below Pulteney Bridge, 1769–74, Adam's unique contribution to Bath's architecture, carrying roadway and shops. Follow the Avon southwards to North Parade Bridge, climb to road level again into North Parade, turn immediately left by Duke Street into South Parade, cross Pierrepont Street into Lilliput Alley, then the quiet oasis of Abbey Green, and northwards past the statuary of the Roman Baths to Abbey Churchyard – backwards in time from the Georgian to the Tudor mode. A dozen feet below lie the pavements, streets and baths of Roman Bath, Aquae Sulis, where it all began.

38 CAMBRIDGE

Time: Allow at least 3 hours.
Start and finish: Market Hill by St Mary the Great Church.
Attractions: Although Cambridge was a regional centre for 1,000 years before the university was established, today Cambridge and its university are inseparable. This walk concentrates on the medieval colleges, unique in the way they relate to their setting, separating the busy country town from the River Cam and the grassy, tree-graced Backs.
OS sheet: 154

Note: The colleges are the homes and places of study of undergraduates and senior members of the university carrying out research, who ask that their need for privacy and quiet is respected. College courts only are open to visitors during daytime, and normally close at 5pm. Most college courts are closed during university examinations, mid-May to mid-June.
Warning: Bicycles ridden apparently by madmen are the greatest hazard of this walk!

Every weekday seems to be market day when brightly awninged stalls display an astounding range of goods and products to entice the eye beneath the tall tower of St Mary the Great, the University Church. Turn your back on it all, walk down Peas Hill to Benet Street, and right to St Benet's Church whose Anglo-Saxon tower is the city's oldest building. Turn along Trumpington Street by the long frontage of Corpus Christi College, detouring through its beautiful archway into the New Court of 1825, and down a few steps into the irregular quadrangle of Old Court, Cambridge's best evocation of what a four-teenth-century college was like.

Continuing southwards along Trumpington Street, notice beyond St Botolph's Church the water-filled gutters, part of a seventeenth-century scheme for supplying water and for cleaning the city ditch which was then part of the town's boundary. Trumpington Street winds its southwards course – a spine road descended from meandering town paths – past Pembroke College on the left whose chapel of 1663 was Wren's first architectural design and therefore the first Classical building in Cambridge. One of the delights of the town is the repeated discovery of colleges, and particularly their gardens, tucked away in unexpected places yet always invitingly approach-able. Every court and fellows' garden vies for the brightest display of roses, geraniums, phloxes and pinks, Michaelmas daisies, waving grasses, shrubs and the shade of tall trees. Colour and greenery complement weathered stone and brick, and this is seen to perfection at Pembroke.

Peterhouse, almost opposite, is Cambridge's oldest college, founded in 1284. Walk beyond it to see the magnificent frontage of the Fitzwilliam Museum, 1840, and make a mental note to see its treasures on another occasion. Opposite, Fitzwilliam Street with its modest, white-brick terraces is an early nineteenth-century gem. Continue southwards as far as Lensfield Road for the fun of seeing Hobson's Conduit, an ornate fountain-head associated with seventeenth-century water supplies to the town.

Retrace steps as far as Silver Street on the left, then enter Queens' Lane for Queens' College, founded by two queens in the mid-fifteenth century. Beyond its impressive gatehouse is the Main Court, then the charming Cloister Court, the earliest cloistered walk in Cambridge. Leading from Queens' across the river is the unique Mathematical Bridge of 1749, built of wood but without nails. When dismantled in 1867 to see its structure, inquisitive Victorians had to use bolts for its reassembly.

Work westwards beyond the river to Queens Road, beside the Backs – once common pasture for Cambridge townsfolk, but from the sixteenth century gradually acquired by the colleges for gardens, lawns and walks. Their greenery is the perfect foil for college buildings; the whole scene is beautiful in any season, unequalled anywhere for the impression of space, the trees, the water and the cool, learned formality of gracious architecture. It is the city's unforgettable town-mark.

From Queens Road turn right through King's back gate, cross the river or, yielding to temptation, sit upon the bank and watch the punts glide by the

Wren's Library, Trinity College (Geoffrey N. Wright)

King's College Chapel

willows, the occupants curtseying beneath King's and Clare bridges and ducklings taking early learnt evasive action. Walk the yellow-pebbled path to King's College Chapel and, entering, sit quietly at the back and marvel at the glory of the vaulting, spraying into fans of stone, as sunlight floods through southern windows to stain the still air and soaring arcades.

Detailed directions are now out of place; let instinct guide, taking you in a northwards course from the west end of the chapel, past Clare College and Old Schools, with a diversion townwards to James Gibbs' Senate House, 1722, designed for university meetings and degree ceremonies. Here, in June, undergraduates crowd anxiously to see posted their examination results. Return to Trinity Lane and so to Trinity, largest of all Cambridge colleges. Apart from its huge, majestic Great Court with fountain, its chapel with so many memorials to the famous – Newton, Bacon, Tennyson, Macaulay – make time for Wren's Library, 1676–90, and gravely walk the length of its paved arcade.

Emerging from the Great Court, through the Great Gate into St John's Street where gown meets town again, turn left into St John's College through its gatehouse ornamented with carvings of heraldic beasts. Go through its three successive courts to Kitchen Bridge, 1710, with its view of the graceful Bridge of Sighs, built in 1831 to give access to New Court across the river. Return through the courts to St John's Street, turning left to Bridge Street corner for the rare round church of the Holy Sepulchre; turn right into Sidney Street, until Market Street is reached, for a return to St Mary the Great and a final blessing on the walk. Sit quietly and reflect on the loveliness of this city of stone and brick and stained glass – its water, bridges, green lawns, gardens and trees representing seven centuries of ordered beauty designed by man and dedicated to the service of learning.

39 Canterbury

Time: Allow 2 to 3 hours.
Start and finish: West Gate.
Approach: Travel via the A2 (London road) or A290 (Whitstable road).
There is a convenient car park in St Radigund's Street.
Attractions: The procession of archbishops and pilgrims spans eight centuries.
As the centre of English Christendom, Canterbury's roots go back another
five centuries, yet all the while it has been a working, often prosperous, town.
This short walk tries to embrace these parallel threads.
OS sheet: 179

Wise walkers should look upon their visit to Canterbury as a pilgrimage.
Though the cathedral is rarely out of sight during this walk it is probably best
to leave it towards the end, a natural climax, so that you enjoy the many
sudden little surprises with which Canterbury rewards you: glimpses of the
River Stour, medieval stonework, later half-timbering, colourful gardens and
lawns and – inevitably but usefully – neat plaques on walls or stones set in
pavements, as pointers to a persistent past.

Almost everything of interest lies within the medieval walls, which themselves are superimposed upon, and therefore hide, the Roman ones. Nothing
remains of the gridiron pattern of Roman streets, yet the present alignment
is relatively simple to understand, with the main axis only ½ mile (.8km)
long orientated north-west to south-east, a straight road now largely pedestrianised called consecutively St Peter's Street, High Street and St George's
Street. Crossing this at right angles, with the two arms slightly offset, are
Castle Street and St Margaret's Street to the south-west, with Palace Street
and Northgate opposite, running parallel to the River Stour. The walk
explores the two western quadrants first, then follows the town walls from the
Norman castle at the southern end of Castle Street anticlockwise to the
north-east quadrant, dominated by the cathedral precinct.

Directions of the 'turn left, turn right' type are tedious to read. Trying to
follow them detracts attention from the interest of the surroundings, and the
many surprises already hinted at are diminished by being anticipated. Within
the suggested guidelines all you have to do is follow your instincts, use your
eyes to look around at shapes, textures, materials, colours, street names, inn
signs and the plaques on the walls.

Beyond West Gate, St Dunstan's Street is, for a short distance, as pretty as
anything in Canterbury, the historic approach by penitents as well as pilgrims.
Through the gate and into St Peter's Street with its brick half-timbering –
nothing spectacular; then left along St Peter's Lane into the north-west quad-

rant for Blackfriars, some small public gardens by the Stour, a footbridge, a lock gate, the Miller's Arms, and back towards St Peter's Street by way of Mill Lane and Blackfriars Street, with its neat brick terraces and delicate fan-lights. Cross the river by The Friars, and in St Peter's Street again you'll be unlikely to miss The Weavers – half-timbered, gabled, sixteenth century – by the river and, opposite, Eastbridge Hospital, open, splendidly late twelfth century in its hall and undercroft, where poor pilgrims paid fourpence a night for a probably uncomfortable lodging.

High Street, the secular heart of the old town, is fronted by tall gabled buildings, mainly Victorian except for the noble Queen Elizabeth's Guest Chamber dated 1573 with its cheerful and artistic frieze at second-floor level. Turn your back on delightful, ancient Mercery Lane, and potter away down St Margaret's Street into Hawks Lane for Stour Street to see the Poor Priests' Hospital, a thirteenth-century almshouse for celibate clergy (weren't they all, then?), opposite Beer Cart Lane. Good modern houses follow at Temple Mews, then Maynard and Cotton's Almshouse (1700), as you work towards the flinty castle keep overlooking the busy roundabout on Rheims Way.

Stately lime trees grace Dane John Gardens, the best open space within the walls, bordered on one side by charming Castle Row on the other by the wall, reached by an easy slope to the enigmatic Dane John Mound. Walk north-wards, past bastions, with the ring-road outside the walls and modern development forming an unfortunate foreground to the cathedral beyond Burgate.

Before entering the precinct, walk beyond the wall, across Broad Street to Longport and St Augustine's Abbey ruins. Excavated, their outlines bared and identified, these footings and walls of ancient brick and stone spanning almost a thousand years up to the Dissolution are in their way as moving as the great cathedral itself. Return to Burgate, enter the modern precinct of Long Market, St George's Street, briefly touch High Street, then Mercery Lane. Although restored and modernised, its flavour is medieval, and all nine buildings on the west side were originally the Chequers' Inn, a thirteenth-century hostelry for pilgrims. Pause for the view up Mercery Lane to Christ Church Gate, before walking there, past the cobbled, colourful Butter-market, and through the emblazoned arch into the precinct. The transition from the secular world of medieval and modern Canterbury to that of pre-cinct, cathedral, holiness and martyrdom, requires time to adjust. Use it quietly, thankfully. Your own thoughts will accompany you through the solemnity of English Christendom's main church. The outside is beautiful; inside it is breathtakingly glorious. Words cannot match the eloquence of its stones, its glass, its memories, its mysteries.

Anything which follows is anti-climax, but a walk north-westwards by Sun Street, Palace Street and King Street will reward with more unexpected delights, and good navigation should return you to the familiar sights of Blackfriars by the River Stour. St Radigund's Street, and your vehicle, are here closer than West Gate, for which you may be quite relieved!

40 DURHAM

Time: Allow 2 to 3 hours.
Start and finish: Framwellgate Bridge. There is car parking within 250yd (230m) in Milburngate or Framwellgate.
Approach: Every view focuses on the cathedral. Because this can be seen from all directions, arrange the walk so that you see it from the east and south in the late morning, and from south-west or north-west in the afternoon.
Attractions: This is not only a walk but an experience. Britain has no medieval group to compare with that of the cathedral, castle and monastery rock-perched high above the wooded River Wear; thus this easy walk savours a thousand years of history and great natural and man-made beauty. The fortress on the rock, physically and spiritually, is the heart of Durham. Girdled by a horseshoe loop of the river, the ½ mile (.8km) long peninsular plateau is only 300yd (275m) across its northern neck, between the two medieval bridges of Framwellgate and Elvet, both now for pedestrians only.
OS sheet: 88

Cross Framwellgate Bridge and wander with the crowds up Silver Street into Market Place, the civic centre of the town, cobbled, pedestrianised and modestly dignified mid-Victorian. Turn right into Fleshergate, soon becoming Saddler Street, and wander up Saddler Street for 200yd (180m) as far as Owengate, to enjoy some rather nice Georgian and Victorian shop fronts. You will glimpse the cathedral up Owengate, but resist the temptation to go closer. Instead, return down Saddler Street, descending right to Elvet Bridge which, until the Reformation, had two chantry chapels, and a fortified tower at the city end. Dating from c1190, the bridge is probably the oldest in the country and linked Durham with the then new borough of Elvet.

Continue ahead into Old Elvet, now a pleasant street of Georgian houses and hotels, and the focus for the famous Miners' Gala held each July. Turn right into Court Lane and New Elvet, along Church Street to St Oswald's Church, for a fine eastern prospect of the cathedral. South-westwards from the church, follow a riverside path round the 'outside' of the river's loop until you reach Prebends' Bridge – three-arched, graceful, 1778, and now for pedestrians only. From it is obtained one of the classic views, down-river, of the cathedral above its wooded banks – a sylvan scene attributable to the dean and chapter who have cherished and landscaped the river banks for two centuries. Pause by the plaque on the north parapet, which records Sir Walter Scott's oft-quoted praise of Durham.

Across the bridge, on the right, felled trees provide unusual seats in a lawned setting by the river, ideal for picnics and summer-used for students'

Shakespeare productions. Walk up the cobbled road from Prebends' Bridge, beneath the 1778 Watergate Arch which replaced the Bailey Gate in the medieval wall, and into South Bailey, most of whose eighteenth-century buildings house various colleges and societies of the university, but which were formerly town houses of Durham gentry. Particularly noteworthy are numbers 14, 18, 19, 20 and 22. St Mary-the-Less, opposite, is a charming little twelfth-century church.

College Gateway on the left, a monastic gatehouse rebuilt in the early sixteenth century, leads to College Green to be visited later. South Bailey here becomes North Bailey, and at St Mary-le-Bow, mainly a late seventeenth-century rebuilding and now the Durham Heritage Centre, Bow Lane descends daintily to Kingsgate Bridge while Duncow Lane, which we now follow, takes us to Palace Green and the cathedral. Walk anticlockwise round the spacious green, grateful to the great Bishop Flambard who cleared it of domestic property soon after 1100. The palace was the castle, home of the Prince Bishops of the Palatinate from Norman times until 1836, when Bishop van Mildert founded the university and gave the castle and its precincts for university use. All buildings round Palace Green are now university property and include, on the east side, eighteenth-century Abbey House and seventeenth-century Bishop Cosin's Hospital and Hall. On the opposite side are the former Exchequer and Chancery, Bishop Cosin's Library, the Diocesan Registry and the seventeenth-century Grammar School, now the Music School. The castle fills the northern side.

So, to the Norman cathedral, with awe and wonder. Even its majestic, dourly northern exterior cannot prepare you for that first breath-stopping gasp when you enter. Nothing in Europe can compare with its vastness, its monumental grandeur allied to a confident, direct simplicity. Walk its hallowed stones with reverence, pondering the logistics of its construction (largely finished in forty years), and its nine centuries of proud history. Do not miss the simple memorial to St Cuthbert behind the High Altar, and that to the Venerable Bede in the exquisite Galilee Chapel. Find time, too, for the Cathedral Museum in the Dormitory to see, among other treasures, Cuthbert's seventh-century exquisite pectoral cross and the coffin in which he was buried.

Emerge, eventually, through the cloisters on the south side, to College Green, mainly of Georgian and early Victorian properties housing cathedral clergy round a lawn, trees and a pump. From the south-west corner, take the 'Dark Entry', a tunnel leading from the former monastic complex to the river bank near Prebends' Bridge. Cross the river and walk along its west bank to the weir which connects the corn mill with the fulling mill opposite, both eighteenth-century rebuildings of former priors' mills, and another classic western viewpoint for the cathedral. Retrace steps to the bridge and climb the ramp to Quarry Heads Lane. For a gloriously rural view of Durham, walk southwards a short way, go through a gate on the right, and climb the field path to the Observatory, a really rewarding detour for a little-known view of

the cathedral from an elevated position. If time presses, and energy flags, walk north-wards from Quarry Heads Lane along South Street, whose eighteenth- and nineteenth-century houses enjoy a supreme view of Durham's soaring towers above the fore-ground trees. Continue along South Street and down to Framwellgate Bridge. To put the icing on the cake, climb to the railway station above Milburngate for the greatest rail-traveller's view in Britain – across the Victorian town to the medieval fortress on the rock, glowing in mellow afternoon or evening sunlight.

Durham Cathedral from the banks of the River Wear (Geoffrey N. Wright)

41 CHESTER

Time: Allow at least 2 hours.
Start and finish: Watergate on the western edge of the city. Car parking is available outside the walls near the Roodee.
Approach: By the A548 via Sealand Road and New Crane Street.
Attractions: One of the best two walled cities in England, Chester's street pattern is Roman, its appearance apparently medieval, its Rows unique, its reality largely Victorian. Chester developed on the site of a Roman fort at the head of the Dee estuary where the Roman harbour, now the famous Roodee racecourse, was still important in medieval times. The Roman walls formed the basis of the thirteenth-century city walls, whose 2 mile (3km) circuit marks the first part of this walk, followed by a closer look at the main streets. Chester is thus explored at two levels.
OS sheet: 117

Watergate dates from 1788, and near it were the riverside quays. Go through it and turn north into City Walls Road, which soon rises to wall height, passing Sedan House with its sedan-chair porch, the elegant Georgian brick terrace of Stanley Place and, beyond the Royal Infirmary, gain access to the city wall. Continue northwards, over the railway line to Bonewaldesthorne's Tower, the Spur Wall and the Water Tower, all early fourteenth-century work. After turning eastwards, descend from the wall for a brief diversion across Tower Road to Canal Basin, where the Shropshire Union Canal joins the River Dee. Canal boats, a boat-repair yard, wharves, an elegant iron roving bridge and the constant appeal of waterside activity make this corner a place to linger by and explore leisurely before returning to the wall-walk.

This continues eastwards, past Goblin Tower, over the inner ring-road by St Martin's Gate, past Morgan's Mount, over Northgate Street with a good view of Bluecoat School nearby, to King Charles' Tower in the north-east corner; so-called because Charles I saw from here the defeat of his army at the battle of Rowton Moor in 1645. Below, the canal and its towpath turn the corner of the wall soon to leave it, however.

The walk continues southwards along the wall, whose parapet here has many inscribed stones. Cross Kaleyard Gate above the cathedral precinct, and by now you will realise how vital a part the wall plays in Chester's everyday life. Local folk use it; like visitors, they appreciate its peaceful and convenient elevation above the busy streets. On it one enjoys a sense of detachment, almost of contemplation, only interrupted by the need to descend steps and ramps to the street-level world. Its height allows one to see 'behind the scenes', making more public the backs of offices, workshops and shops –

Roving Bridge canal basin (Geoffrey N. Wright)

rather better, incidentally, than looking down on car parks and vacant lots.

At wall height but outside it, Mercia Square is a pleasant, umbrella-gay piazza with shops at two levels. Opposite, by the cathedral gardens, is the 1975 bell-tower, the first free-standing English bell-tower since the fifteenth century and a rare contribution to the city's heritage. The wall's crossing of Eastgate has a splendidly ornate, brightly painted clock commemorating Queen Victoria's Diamond Jubilee supported on playful ironwork, with a marvellous view along Eastgate. Nearby, Newgate Steps lead down to relics of the Roman town, the amphitheatre and Roman Garden, a green oasis of quiet.

Farther south, the inwards view from the wall gives a glimpse of seventeenth-century Chester in the gabled houses in Park Street. Reaching the river, swing south-westwards, past Bridge Street, descending to Castle Drive. Follow the road round the edge of the castle grounds, past Harrison's model of his Grosvenor Bridge, to observe the same architect's monumental, Greek Revival rebuilding, 1788–1822, of the Norman castle – a complex of buildings housing offices, courts and barracks.

Detour down Grosvenor Road to see the fine Grosvenor Bridge, at its time, 1827, the largest single-span arch in Britain (200ft, 61m). Return to Nun's Road, northwards to Watergate, and head for the town centre along Watergate Street, least commercialised of the four main streets. Contrasting with its Georgian houses is Stanley Palace, 1591, with finely carved woodwork on its east front. Across Nicholas Street (ring-road) turn right along Weaver Street, and second left into Whitefriars, full of modest Georgian charm, parish-boundary marks, fire plaques and some half-timbering.

This leads to Bridge Street. Digress down Lower Bridge Street to appreciate more seventeenth-century half-timbering before retracing steps northwards to The Cross, meeting point of the sensibly identified *via decumana* (Northgate) and *via principalis* (Eastgate). The High Cross, re-erected in 1975, occupied this site from 1407 until the Civil War. Here, city, history and people meet, as they have done for centuries. Here, too, is the meeting of the Rows, raised and galleried walkways with shops at first-floor level, medieval in origin, so civilised in concept. Their unique dignity not only gives additional grandeur to buildings, but doubles the shopping density, so packing a small area with a lot of people. In their own way, they extend the height and advantages of the city walls into the town centre itself. Take your fill of them in all directions from The Cross; see if you can find a tunnel from Watergate Row leading to quiet, sequestered St Peter's churchyard, emerging by the City Club. As you explore Northgate be sure to visit the cathedral and the dignified calm of Abbey Square to its north. I suspect, however, that your abiding impression of Chester will be secular rather than ecclesiastical. Many cities have cathedrals; none other has the Rows and the prodigies of mid- to late-Victorian half-timbering which, superficial though this later magpie work may be, adds a memorable exuberance to Chester's unrivalled townscape.

The Cross and the Rows (Geoffrey N. Wright)

42 NORWICH

Time: Allow 3 hours.
Start and finish: Norwich Castle.
Approach: Easiest from the Inner Ring Road from the south, opposite the A11 roundabout, St Stephen Street and Red Lion Street.
Attractions: This is a walk through the second most essentially medieval British city (York claims first place), where restoration, repair and restrained modern development has rehabilitated and revitalised an historic inner city area of great character. Unlike Durham, however, it has not solved its traffic problems.
OS sheet: 134

Make no mistake: within the old walled city, Norwich is a jumble of medieval streets, with no coherent pattern; it is, therefore, pointless to give detailed instructions. I shall merely guide you in certain directions and suggest you then follow your own inclinations. But first, a strong recommendation: go round the Inner Ring Road to the north-east, and seek the magnificent viewpoint – appreciated last century by George Borrow – from the open elevation of Mousehold Heath, preferably in the morning. This reveals the spire and towers of Norwich in the context of their East Anglian setting – 'a fine old city' indeed.

The best close viewpoint is the highest point within the walls, the artificial mound crowned by the castle keep, Norman in origin, refaced 1837–9 in Bath stone. Mightily impressive it houses a superb museum, while the mound allows you to check your bearings. Westwards across Castle Meadow and hidden Castle Street is the Market Place, dominated on its southern side by St Peter Mancroft, on its west by the City Hall (1938), arguably as Sir Nikolaus Pevsner wrote, the 'foremost English public building of between the wars'. But even its tall campanile cannot compete with the soaring grace of the cathedral spire, ½ mile (.8km) to the north-east. As the eye roves round the arc, so at street-level will the walk wind through the medieval maze, its progress measured by the towers of ancient churches and the splendid signs of scores of friendly pubs. It used to be said of Norwich that you could do a different church every Sunday of the year, and a different pub every night. If the numbers are now less, the ratio seems the same!

Thread your way to the Market Place, large and busy and full of coloured awnings above serried rows of stalls. On higher level, noble stately St Peter Mancroft dominates, as it has done for five centuries. Go inside and reflect on its glories. Out again, walk right round Market Place, past City Hall and down to the Guildhall, flinty and fifteenth century, with the best at its eastern end. St Giles' Street running westwards starts as half-timbered, becomes Georgian. Go down Willow Lane to Cow Hill and return east along Pottergate where, set back, is the famous Maddermarket Theatre with its Elizabethan-style apron stage and one of the finest amateur theatre companies in existence. Continue along into Bedford Street, looking for Bridewell Alley on the left (north), where some modern shop fronts betray, through their deeply recessed doorways, timber-framed houses above and behind. The Mustard Shop is a re-creation of an early Victorian interior, and the Bridewell Museum, formerly a fourteenth-century merchant's house, later a Bridewell or prison, then a factory, now houses an excellent folk and industrial collection.

Medieval churches abound, and former friary buildings now enjoy, literally, secular use. Head north now, along George Street, over the river, turning right into Colegate, once the home of prosperous wool merchants. The fine Georgian houses now have other uses, which is far better than suffering decay; and on the north side there are reminders that Norwich was, and is, a stronghold of nonconformity. The Octagon Chapel, designed by local architect Thomas Ivory, dates from 1756, and nearby is the Old Meeting House, built by early Congregationalists in 1693.

Pull's Ferry

At the eastern end of Colegate turn right into Wensum Street, recross the river, and look for Elm Hill on your right. This is the best-preserved medieval street in Norwich, cobbled and lined with colour-washed, often half-timbered Tudor buildings, with some Georgian refronting. Most shops, inevitably, sell antiques. At the top, having appraised it from the higher end, turn left into Princes Street, also timber-framed with Georgian features, its curving north side showing a delightful sequence, leading the eye to the cathedral. Where the eye leads, let the legs follow, into Tombland – no sinister connotation, merely a former open space – with a slight backtrack beneath Augustine Steward's house of 1530 into Tombland Alley.

Cross the main road, go through the fifteenth-century Erpingham Gate into the sylvan Upper Close and the glorious cathedral. Ponder, within its dignified beauty, the sheer logistics of shipping from Caen in Normandy the lovely white limestone of its exterior. As a whimsical afterthought, consider that the top of the spire, 315ft (96m) above the ground, is only 14ft (4.2m) lower than the highest land in Norfolk. By the south door, on the outside, Nurse Edith Cavell's simple grave commands more poignant respect.

Walk southwards into Lower Close, where some former priory buildings survive – all flint, brick and pink tiles, glowing in sunlight. Turn north past, but well beyond, the eastern end of the cathedral, to Bishopsgate and the Great Hospital, still keeping north to Riverside Walk. Turn east, and follow the edge of the park along Riverside Walk past medieval Cow Tower to Bishops' Bridge, oldest of Norwich's bridges. At picturesque Pull's Ferry, site of the watergate, turn right to the two cathedral closes again, and through St Ethelbert Gate across Tombland into Queen Street, exchanging a cloistered calm for throbbing city commercialism. Above Bank Plain you will, relieved, recognise the castle, four-square and eight centuries proud on its guardian site.

43 Newcastle·upon·Tyne

Time: Allow 2 to 3 hours.
Start and finish: Beneath the High Level Bridge.
Approach: Ideally from the south, via the A1(M). Branch off on the A1(M) near Birtley along the A69 signposted 'Gateshead/Newcastle', then A6127.
Attractions: Modern developments have not completely obliterated what is arguably the most attractive industrial provincial city in England. Its planned centre, 1825–40, is outstanding, yet there is still a complex of medieval streets.
OS sheet: 88

If you have not been able to appraise Newcastle on your approach, do so now. From Quayside take the Tyne Bridge lift to road level, and walk southwards above the river. Turn round and be rewarded with the most exciting visual experience of any English industrial city: the great river, spanned by six bridges in less than a mile (1.6km), steep northern banks with their layers of buildings at different levels summarising eight centuries of history, from the late Norman keep of the castle to the concrete-and-glass office blocks nearby. Older still was the Roman crossing of the river on the site of the 1876 Swing Bridge, which these days so rarely needs to swing. From medieval times Newcastle grew northwards and upwards from the river in a series of phases, each transport-based.

First phase was the river, for Newcastle originated with boats. Then, from the 1840s, the railway, after Robert Stephenson challenged the Tyne in the grand manner, his High Level Bridge bringing both rail and road from the south to the city's new heart farther up the hill, around which Victorian Newcastle developed and prospered for a century. Finally came the motor car, with more brutal townscape changes of the 1960s and 1970s, taking commerce and commuters even farther from the Tyne.

Exploring the riverside first, there is unexpected half-timbering at first in The Close, then a remarkable range of mainly early seventeenth-century, four- or five-storeyed, timber-fronted houses with continuous window ranges, unique in Britain. Around and especially above are extraordinary, neck-aching scenes – bridges, towering office blocks and warehouses. Quayside, east of Tyne Bridge, has more of these, many empty. Continue eastwards, where on Sundays a bustling market enlivens the area, and turn up Broad Chare, widest of the river-leaving streets. Explore its alleys and steps, and peep into the little courtyards and buildings of trim Trinity House.

Steepled, graceful, elliptical, but deserted All Saints' Church commands another wondrous view. Walk westwards, guided by the lantern-tower of St

Nicholas' Cathedral, to The Side and Dean Street, northwards into Grey Street, gradually gaining height towards the hub of Newcastle's early Victorian growth. (In this walk, avoid straying too far east; that way are the new roads and aggressive underpasses.) Grey Street, 1835–9, is full of Corinthian and Ionic splendour, Richard Grainger's best creation in the city – a graceful, majestic curve reaching to the focus of the Grey Monument, with the handsome Theatre Royal portico just below. Grainger, a developer and builder, with John Dobson as architect, and with the backing of John Clayton, the Town Clerk, gave Newcastle its orderly, elegant Victorian centre, making it the only major English provincial city to enjoy such a planned layout with majestic buildings all faced with splendid sandstone masonry. Although too much has gone, particularly at Eldon Square, sufficient survives, maintaining dignity and detail. The area is not over-trafficked, so walking these city streets – lively, peopled, friendly and musical with Geordie accents – is pleasantly satisfying.

Go through Central Arcade, an Edwardian gem, into Grainger Street, westwards by Nelson Street and the double bow-windowed pub, the Collingwood, to Grainger Market. This hive of covered alleys between permanent stalls is friendly, intimate, human scaled – an early Victorian supermarket. Emerge into Clayton Street, turn right into Newgate Street, left at St Andrew's Church in its plane-tree'd churchyard. Seek Stowell Street, which looks thoroughly unprepossessing until, walking along it, you realise it follows a considerable length of medieval wall, built during the Scottish wars

Blackfriars

of the fourteenth century. Heber Tower, Durham Tower and Morden Tower survive, and in Bath Lane a foreground of lawns and flowers adds a colourful foil.

Nearby is Blackfriars – a restored, revivified courtyard complex incorporating many conventual buildings of a medieval Dominican friary and now housing craft workshops, a restaurant and an Information Centre. A large Chinese supermarket is next door. Return along Stowell Street into Gallowgate, where the huge stands of Newcastle United's famous football ground are a beacon leading you to Leazes Terraces. This fashionable development of 1829 by Grainger, is in the form of a long rectangle of outward-facing, impressive, three-storey houses, inspired by Regent's Park in London. Like all their contemporaries in the city they are sturdily faced with Northumberland sandstone, honey-gold after cleaning yet still dwarfed by the towering concrete stands of St James's Park.

Walk eastwards, along Leazes Crescent towards Leazes Park, King's Road and the university, which is an attractive complex of buildings spanning almost a century from 1888, on a campus agreeably close to the life of the town and thus sharing a sense of community. The Haymarket, immediately south, has a metro station offering a quick return to Central Station; better by far to walk down Northumberland Street and Pilgrim Street, with a chance to enjoy Grey Street again, to Mosley Street and St Nicholas' Street, dropping down by the Black Gate to the castle keep, with a sight nearby of the superbly Greek Revival Moot Hall, built a generation before Grainger's work. A paved and stepped path, offering more fine riverscapes, descends steeply between cliffs of tall brick buildings to The Close and the start of the walk by the river, beneath those massive bridges that are Newcastle's townmark.

44 EDINBURGH

Time: Allow 5 to 6 hours.
Start and finish: The Castle (east entrance).
Approach: It seems presumptuous to tell anyone how to get to Edinburgh, one of the world's greatest capitals and the most romantically situated city in Britain. Car parking is available off Lothian Road at the west end of Princes Street.
Attractions: Princes Street Gardens separates the two halves of this walk with Calton Hill, the hinge that links them, dominating the eastern end. Nature, in the form of volcanic hills, has given Edinburgh an almost theatrical setting, exploited with exceptional brilliance. The castle, crowning volcanic crags, has been a defensive site for 2,000 years. To its east and south is Old Town, and the first part of this walk concentrates on the famous 'Royal Mile', the central spine linking the castle to the Palace of Holyroodhouse. Although much of Old Town has gone in the name of road improvements, university expansion, and modern development, sufficient remains to give a startlingly medieval flavour to the townscape.
OS sheet: 66

From west to east, Royal Mile descends gently, first as Castle Hill then through Lawnmarket, High Street, Canongate, and finally as Abbey Strand. Four centuries of street scenery, albeit with a few gaps, conversions, restorations and dismal reminders of what has gone, frown down on wide pavements and granite setts – except in the lower parts where tarmac has regrettably been allowed to intrude. In distance, this royal and ancient highway may be but a mile (1.6km), but on no account must it be rushed. Savour it slowly, lingeringly, lovingly, for there is nothing else in Britain to match it. Pause often, to look upwards at the towering tenements, downwards at the setts; notice the texture of rubble sandstone, the dignity of Georgian masonry, the turrets and steeples, gables, windows, inscriptions above doorways. Explore the tunnelled yards and courts burrowing behind street frontages; appreciate the townscape value of open spaces and small squares, and perhaps bemoan the apparently unpeopled nature of the Royal Mile. Shops there are – many with attractive fronts – but the vibrant liveliness with which Old Town once teemed has vanished; so, left with the buildings, make the most of them. To name but a few, from west to east: Tolbooth Church, Outlook Tower (and don't miss Ramsay Gardens behind), Gladstone's Land, Lady Stair's House, Sheriff Court, City Chambers, St Giles, the Mercat Cross nearby, Tron Kirk, John Knox's House where High Street narrows ino Canongate and sixteenth- and seventeenth-century buildings crowd in – Moray House, Huntly House and Acheson House on the south side, Canongate Tolbooth, Canongate Church and White Horse Close on the north. Here, Abbey Strand goes ahead to Holyroodhouse beneath the crags of Arthur's Seat, while our walk branches off, down Horse Wynd, left in Calton Road and over the hidden railway, to Regent Road.

Almost opposite the Burns Memorial, the Grecian façade of the Royal High School is a classical curtain raiser for what follows. Backtrack up Regent Terrace, curl round Calton Terrace and emerge, triumphant but tired, on Calton Hill, where a partial Parthenon commemorates the fallen in the Napoleonic wars and the tall, round monument remembers Nelson and gives a superb, aerial view of the city. Calton Hill is the ideal place for a midday break, but if you haven't brought your own lunch, you will have to descend to street-level for it.

Westwards, beyond the foliage of the nearby slopes, stretches the planned geometry, formal squares, terraces and crescents of New Town, Scotland's equivalent to Bath, but rather less ravaged. After the Nor' Loch was drained about the middle of the eighteenth century – its former site now occupied by Princes Street Gardens and the railway – New Town was designed to house Edinburgh's wealthier citizens and their servants who were anxious to leave their medieval homes in Old Town. The young James Craig's plan of 1767 was based on three broad thoroughfares, Queen Street, George Street and Princes Street, aligned east-west and parallel to each other, with intersecting streets forming a gridiron pattern between St Andrew's Square at the east and Charlotte Square at the west. The plan was outward-looking – northwards towards the Forth, southwards to Old Town. This southerly view from Princes Street across the gardens is spectacularly theatrical, presenting a skyline of towers, spires and gables rising from east to west to their thrilling climax of the castle, irradiated in late summer evenings by a golden glow.

But leave Princes Street to the last. Descend Calton Hill south-westwards to Waterloo Place, walk westwards and soon turn north into St Andrew Street. From there you can indulge yourself, perhaps experimenting with the 'zigzag' walk initiated many years ago by the master-tramp, Stephen Graham, in which you take first left, first right, first left and so on. Work your way west-wards and slightly northwards through the living city of Georgian Edinburgh, recognising it as an ideogram of the United Kingdom, specifically illustrated in its street names.

Many architects, mainly Scottish ones, contributed to its cool formality and splendid spaciousness. The first New Town was complete by the end of the eighteenth century, the second New Town developed north-westwards over the next forty years. Work your way in that direction, to Heriot Row, Royal Circus, the masterly Moray Place, the flowing curves of Ainslie Place and Randolph Crescent, returning southwards by Charlotte Square – whose north side, by Adam, 1791, is one of the greatest of his architectural creations – to the west end of Princes Street. Now relax in the sheer self-indulgence of an eastwards stroll along one of the most famous shopping streets in the

world, architecturally rather a mishmash
and really quite ordinary, but scenically
superb.

At its east end, when you reach the
North British Hotel, cross over and be
tempted by the modern, exciting colourful
Waverley Market, spikily spectacular and
great fun, followed by the appropriately
Victorian splendour of the Scott Monument.
Amble through Princes Street Gardens,
constantly making little southwards forays,
and at the west end, turn into Lothian Road
which will lead you by Castle Terrace and
Johnston Terrace to your starting point,
where a final glimpse down Lawnmarket
confirms how Old and New Town are such
perfect foils for each other.

Ramsay Garden (Geoffrey N. Wright)

CANAL·WALKS

Walking canal towing paths is walking through industrial history. From 1760 to 1840 canals were the main arteries of trade and industry in Britain. By 1845, however, railways were rapidly extending, forcing the canals into unprofitable rate-cutting and eventually out of business. A few traded on into the twentieth century but the development of road transport affected them severely and by the late 1960s, apart from a little short-haul carrying, commercial boating was finished.

The canals themselves, however, were by no means dead. Although hundreds of miles had been abandoned, many of which had been filled in, there was still plenty of water for the pleasure traffic which increased spectacularly in the sixties and seventies. Moves soon came to restore and reopen waterways hitherto regarded as lost. The British Waterways Board, the national controlling authority, supported by strong voluntary movements, is intent on retaining and improving our canals and adding to their mileage, and the future of the system now seems secure.

All canals were constructed with towing paths, for horse-towing and the use of maintenance staff. With a few exceptions these paths are not rights of way, but the Waterways Board is happy for people to use them provided they take them as they find them – which, owing to shortage of funds, is not always in the best condition.

Towing-path walking is generally easy. Surfaces vary and the going in places may be rough or muddy even in dry weather so boots or stout shoes are generally needed. Hills are gentle, occurring only at flights of locks; access is simple and you should never get lost. Sometimes you can plan a circular route but mostly you return the way you came. This is not a disadvantage; things often look different from another angle and there is the opportunity to examine items at greater length. There is much to see: locks, with a variety of paddle gear, bridges of different designs and materials, aqueducts, weirs, canal cottages, tunnel portals, the sites of wharves and docks. On most stretches there are pubs every few miles. And there are boats, especially traditionally decorated narrow boats, 70ft (21m) long but only 7ft (2m) in beam, many converted from old working boats, moored or on the move, bringing extra life and colour to the canal scene.

Horse-drawn narrow boat on the Caldon Canal (British Waterways Board) (*see* page 191)

It adds greatly to the interest if you brief yourself beforehand. The Nicholson/ Ordnance Survey guides cover the navigable system in three volumes and there are guides to all the major canals and many of the lesser and non-navigable ones. The best sources of information are British Waterways Board and the Inland Waterways Association (addresses below). There is an excellent Waterways Museum at Stoke Bruerne in Northamptonshire and the Boat Museum at Ellesmere Port, Cheshire, has a fine collection of old working craft.

For fascinating city walking there are over 30 miles (48km) of the Regent's and Grand Union canals in London; Birmingham has a large network of canals, and Manchester, Stoke-on-Trent, Liverpool, Leeds, Bath, Leicester and Nottingham can all be explored from towing paths. The Leeds & Liverpool Canal takes a lonely route across the Pennines as well as intersecting Burnley, Blackburn and Wigan. The Rochdale and Huddersfield canals, both being gradually restored, also cross the Pennines by spectacular routes. The Midlands have retained most of their narrow canals and their junctions – Fradley, south-west of Burton, Fazeley near Tamworth, Hawkesbury near Coventry and Braunston and Napton between Daventry and Warwick – make good starting points for exploration. The Grantham Canal provides a gentle ramble between Grantham and Nottingham and the Louth Canal penetrates remote Lincolnshire. In Surrey and Sussex a long-distance footpath, the Wey-South Path, uses much of the towing path of the Wey & Arun Canal, while in Kent you can inspect the old defence line of the Royal Military Canal from Winchelsea to Hythe. Most south-western canals have long been abandoned but you can trace over 30 miles (48km) from Bude towards Launceston or follow the recently reopened 11 miles (17.5km) of the Grand Western Canal at Tiverton.

Wales has three canals of outstanding scenic beauty: the Brecon & Abergavenny in the Brecon Beacons National Park, the Montgomeryshire and the Llangollen with its famous aqueduct at Pontcysyllte. In Scotland you can walk from Glasgow to Edinbugh along the towing paths of the Forth & Clyde and Union canals or explore the Great Glen via the Caledonian. Ireland's Grand Canal, from Dublin to the Shannon, is navigable and Robertstown, 24 miles (38.5km) west of Dublin, is a good centre. Exploration of the unnavigable Royal Canal is also worthwhile, and north of the border the Ballinamore & Ballyconnel Canal repays discovery.

Any season is good for canal walking. In holiday periods the most popular places – Stoke Bruerne, Foxton or Little Venice, for instance – may be crowded, but a few hundred yards along you may be on your own with only an angler or two in sight. The hedgerows and trees are at their best in spring and autumn; canal, path and hedge form corridors many miles long, sanctuaries for plants and birds. In winter few boats are moving and the locks are idle; the water seems deeper, more mysterious as you walk on through the stillness.

45	Grand Union Canal near Watford, Hertfordshire	7 miles (11km)
46	Leeds & Liverpool Canal, North Yorkshire	6 miles (9.6km)
47	Caldon Canal, Staffordshire	11 miles (17.5km)
48	Forth & Clyde in Glasgow, Strathclyde	4 miles (6km)
49	Leicestershire Line of the Grand Union Canal	7 miles (11km)
50	Stratford-upon-Avon Canal (Southern Section), Warwickshire	7 miles (11km)
51	Monmouthshire Canal (Western Branch), Gwent	4½ or 11½ miles (7 or 18km)
52	Crinan Canal, Strathclyde	10 or 18 miles (16 or 29 km)

Useful addresses:

British Waterways Board, Melbury House, Melbury Terrace, London NW1 6JX (01 262 6711)

Inland Waterways Association, 114 Regent's Park Road, London NW1 8UQ (01 586 2556)

Further reading:

Hadfield, Charles. *British Canals*, David & Charles, 7th ed.

Ordnance Survey Guide to the Waterways (vol 1 South, vol 2 Central, vol 3 North), Robert Nicholson Publications 1983.

Russell, Ronald. *Lost Canals and Waterways of Britain*, David & Charles 1982.

(I gratefully acknowledge the help of Tom Brock, Nikki Ross and Adrian and Sarah Russell with some of these walks.)

45 Grand·Union·Canal·
NEAR WATFORD

Time: 3 hours.

Start and finish: Car park on west side of Cassiobury Park at end of Gade Avenue, Watford. Boots or stout footwear needed. Also accessible from Watford Station (Metropolitan Line) via Cassiobury Park Avenue and Gade Avenue.

Approach: On the north side of Watford town centre the A411 and A412 meet at a large roundabout. Take the A412 west towards Rickmansworth and in less than ¼ mile (.4km) turn right into Cassiobury Park Avenue. Pass the Metropolitan Line station, then at the end of the road turn right into Gade Avenue and enter the free car park.

Attractions: A pleasant country walk alongside a well-used and historic canal, easily accessible from the north London area.

OS sheet: 166

The Grand Junction Canal (now the Grand Union) runs from the Thames at Brentford to a junction with the Oxford Canal at Braunston, Northampton-shire, a distance of 93½ miles (150km) with 102 locks. This Watford part of the canal was a diversion from the original plan, made to avoid building a long tunnel and a flight of locks. The canal company paid the Earl of Essex £15,000 for the land it needed in Cassiobury Park and this length of waterway

Grove Bridge in Cassiobury Park, built to the order of the Earl of Essex (British Waterways Board)

was completed in 1797. The canal was opened throughout in 1800.

At the entrance to the car park take a footpath heading slightly downhill towards a small wood. Take two right forks about 80yd (73m) apart and join the River Gade which accompanies the canal for most of the walk, acting as feeder and overflow channel. Follow the path upstream; across the river are old watercress beds, now overgrown, and the canal, as yet not in view. To the right Cassiobury Park stretches away. This 900 acre (364ha) park was once the seat of the Earl of Essex, but the mansion and grand entrance gates have been demolished and all that remain are a few outbuildings and the splendid avenues of tall trees lining the many footpaths. The park is now a pleasure ground for the people of Watford with paddling pools and a miniature railway, and the river is popular with young anglers.

At a junction of footpaths turn left to cross first the river and then the canal; this place is known locally as Two Bridges. The earl stipulated that the canal through his grounds had to curve gracefully like a river and to be crossed by bridges that were aesthetically pleasing. Judge for yourself how successfully these conditions were met. Turn right along the towing path, passing Watford Lock and the West Herts Golf Course as well as several brightly painted narrowboats. This is a beautifully landscaped stretch of canal and has been described by Hugh McKnight in *The Shell Book of Inland Waterways* as 'one of the loveliest sections of a canal so near a town anywhere in Britain'.

Cross the Gade, now on the west side of the canal, by a low double-humped bridge. By the first of the two Cassiobury locks is a pretty Victorian cottage rescued and restored in 1970 when about to be demolished following extensive vandalism. New weirs have been constructed to cope with the extra run-off caused by the construction of the M25. Beyond the next lock, the towing path is carried across the canal by an iron bridge. Close to the next bridge is the attractive, isolated Grove Mill. There is a particularly sharp bend through the bridge which caused much trouble to boatmen in the days of horse-drawn boats.

Grove Bridge (164) is one of the canal's two fine ornamental bridges (the other is at Cosgrove in Northamptonshire), an enduring reminder of the requirements of the Earl of Essex, though seeming oddly out of place in the surrounding pastureland. Bridge 163 returns the path to the western side and you continue past Lady Capel's Lock; she was the daughter of the Earl of Essex and married the Earl of Clarendon, owner of Grove Park through which the canal now runs. By the M25 link-road bridge there are more new weirs and a milepost indicating 70 miles to Braunston. The next bridge takes the A41, heading for Aylesbury; then follows a straight stretch through two locks. The railway that took away so much of the canal's trade approaches from the right, while ahead is the tall spire of St Paul's, Langleybury.

At Bridge 162 turn right into the attractive canalside village of Hunton Bridge where there is good food and drink at the King's Head. From here either retrace your steps to Cassiobury Park or take a cross-country route back to the starting point. For the latter, return to the canal across the bridge and take the underpass beneath the main road. You now face St Paul's Church, a mid-Victorian confection well known for its hand-squared flintwork. Turn right and enter a small wood with a good variety of trees. Emerge by the entrance to St Paul's School with Langleybury House, built 1827–9 but now part of Langleybury School, ahead. Turn right to the road and continue up the hill, passing Home Farm, once part of the Langleybury Estate. Opposite the farm a grassy bank hides the M25 as it sweeps around the north of Watford.

The road walk through pastureland is pleasant enough. As you cross the A405 dual carriageway you should glimpse the canal to your left below the enormous roundabout. Continue, passing Heath Wood on your left, and bear left at the next junction into tree-shaded Grove Mill Lane. In about ¾ mile (1.2km) Whippendell Woods car park is reached. Take the path straight ahead which leads back into the Cassiobury Estate and across the golf course. Soon the tall trees give way to smaller trees and shrubs, and eventually the canal comes into view. Your path joins it at Two Bridges, a short distance from your car.

(opposite) *Elm Hill, Norwich* (Geoffrey N. Wright) (*see* page 168)

OVERLEAF
(left) *Landsdown Crescent, Bath* (Geoffrey N. Wright) (*see* page 153)
(top right) *York Minster* (Geoffrey N. Wright) (*see* page 149)
(middle right) *Leeds & Liverpool Canal near Williamson Bridge* (R. Russell) (*see* page 187)
(bottom right) *Path above the Gipping Valley, Suffolk* (Geoffrey N. Wright) (*see* page 259)

46 LEEDS·&·LIVERPOOL·CANAL

Time: 3 hours.
Start and finish: Gargrave, on the A65, 5 miles (8km) west of Skipton. Boots recommended, unless returning by the outward route.
Approach: Gargrave is a large, spacious village on the River Aire, bisected by the busy A65. Park in the centre or near the church if you plan to return via the Pennine Way.
Attractions: The route covers part of the finest scenic stretch of the 127 mile (204km) Leeds & Liverpool Canal, opened in 1816 and now the only surviving navigable trans-Pennine waterway. The return is along an easy length of the Pennine Way. Good views, several locks, and pubs at the beginning and halfway.
OS sheet: 103

Leave the village by walking along A65 heading west. The road crosses the canal just before the Anchor Inn. Don't cross the bridge but join the towing path on your left and follow it past three locks, beneath a railway viaduct and across an aqueduct above the Aire to Bridge 168 where the towing path changes sides. Now the path climbs gradually alongside the six Bank Newton locks; here it is wide, gravelled and dry, but it soon reverts to something more natural. Note the Yorkshire Dales boatyard, fitting harmoniously into its surroundings.

Between the fifth and sixth lock, the canal takes a sharp right-angled turn. At Bridge 165 the towing path again changes sides, for a few yards coinciding with a metalled lane. Rejoin the path through a handgate. The canal is tree-lined hereabouts but soon emerges into open country, the canal and path winding around several small hills following the contours. It is tempting to take short cuts across the narrow valleys, but you miss the changing perspectives if you do. A transmission mast is a useful landmark; it is visible from all angles as the canal winds its serpentine way. There is a remote feeling to this area of moorland and valleys, and you are approaching the highest stretch of navigable waterway in Britain.

The canal finally decides that it should be heading southwards at a tree-lined cutting by Bridge 163. For a few hundred yards the path is due south and straight. The next bridge, 162, is Williamson Bridge; beyond there are moorings and it is interesting to see the variety of craft that use the canal. Look out for a Pennine Way fingerpost on your left, as that indicates your return route.

Maryhill Locks, Glasgow Branch of the Forth & Clyde Canal (British Waterways (Board) (*see* page 194)

The canal near Williamson Bridge (R. Russell)

Now you become aware of the sound of traffic. Ahead is the odd Double Bridge, with one arch constructed on top of the original one when the road it carries, the busy A59, was realigned. On the far side of the bridge, steps lead up to the road; a few yards to the west is the handsome Cross Keys, a public phone and a village shop. This is the hamlet of East Marton.

It is possible to continue alongside the canal – to Liverpool, if you wish; but more practicably through another splendid stretch of Pennine countryside to the three Greenberfield locks and the canal's summit level, a further 2¾ miles (4.6km). This would mean returning by retracing your route to East Marton or alternatively walking back some distance along roads from the outskirts of Barnoldswick. It might be better to return to Gargrave and drive to Greenberfield, just off B6252 a mile (1.6km) north-westward from the centre of Barnoldswick, and walk the towing path from there.

At East Marton's Double Bridge regain the towing path, face about and head north. This part of the path coincides with the Pennine Way, which leaves it by Williamson Bridge. Follow the Way along a lane, then across stiles and through fields, muddy after rain, passing to the right of a small wood. Make sure you are between two barns, one of them ruined. Continue on a muddy track along the east side of a rounded hill, and look out for a single post ahead. Having reached the post you will see a farm to your left. Continue until you join the hard track leading to the farm, and follow this beneath the railway until it debouches onto Marton Street on the south side of Gargrave. Turn right to a T-junction by the church; then left for the centre of the village.

47 CALDON·CANAL

Time: 4½ hours.

Start and finish: Froghall Wharf, a few hundred yards along the minor road to Foxt, north off the A52 at Froghall. There is a car park opposite the picnic site. Boots optional.

Approach: Froghall is on the A52 Derby to Stoke-on-Trent road, 10½ miles (17km) east of Stoke. From the south, use A522 to Cheadle, forking right onto A521 which joins A52 on the outskirts of Froghall. From the north use A520/A522 to A52 4 miles (6km) from Froghall. There is a signpost to Froghall Wharf.

Attractions: A walk through a beautiful wooded valley with the canal and River Churnet close together, sometimes sharing the same channel. There are two flint mills on the route and you may see a horse-drawn boat. Best in spring and autumn.

OS sheets: 119 (Froghall to Black Lion) and 118

The 17 mile (27km) Caldon Canal branches off the Trent & Mersey Canal at Hanley, winds through industrial Stoke-on-Trent and emerges into pleasant countryside. It then turns south-east into the Churnet valley. At Hazelhurst Junction there is a 2½ mile (4km) branch to Leek; there was also a 13 mile (21km) extension from Froghall to Uttoxeter, closed in 1845. For many years the Caldon was busy with limestone traffic from Froghall, continuing into the present century. With diminishing trade the canal's condition deteriorated and, by the early 1960s, much of it was unnavigable. The efforts of the Caldon Canal Society aroused local interest and British Waterways Board reopened the canal throughout in 1974. There is a good firm towing path along its full length.

Froghall has long been an industrial centre and there is evidence of past activity in the bank of limekilns by the car park. The immediate area has recently been landscaped and the restored canal warehouse now includes a café and small craft shop; it is also the starting point for *Birdswood*, a horse-drawn passenger boat that offers 2½ hour public trips on Thursday and Sunday afternoons in the season. Cross the road by the warehouse to join the towing path which brings you in a few yards to the portal of the short and small-bore Froghall Tunnel. The path leads round the hillside; cross the B5053 Ipstones road and resume the towing path alongside Thomas Bolton's copper works. Soon you are clear of the works; the canal, very narrow here, is terraced along the lower slopes of a densely wooded hillside while below, on the left, is a single-track railway – there is still a train once a day – and the River Churnet. A recently restored milepost shows the distance from Etruria, where the Caldon leaves the Trent & Mersey Canal, and Uttoxeter, to where the Caldon Canal was extended in 1811. In 1845, however, the extension was closed and the railway built over much of the bed (there is a description of the remains of the extension in Ronald Russell's *Lost Canals and Waterways of Britain* (David & Charles, 1982).

Just over a mile (1.6km) from Froghall is Cherry Eye Bridge, of stone with a pointed arch possibly unique among canal bridges. Its name comes from the long-derelict Old Cherry Eye mine, high in the nearby woods; boats were once loaded with ore from the mine at a wharf close to the bridge. Note the rope grooves in the wooden bridge-guards.

At the next bridge the towing path is carried across and you walk below the woodland past a petrifying stream flowing down the hillside. The flint mill beside the lock – Flint Mill Lock, no 17 – is operated by water power, although not by waterwheel, grinding sand for the pottery industry. Next comes London Bridge, a reminder of the days when a mining company from London was working nearby. There is a cottage-pottery by a lane beside the towing path, with Keats's famous line 'A thing of beauty is a joy for ever' inscribed on the lintels. Canal and railway are now very close together; a retaining wall hems in the canal where there used to be a station and the derelict waiting room is still cantilevered over the water.

Very shortly the railway crosses the canal and a neat little bridge with floodgates is reached. Beyond the bridge, canal and river share the same channel for the next ¾ mile (1.2km). To the left the river continues its course, tumbling over a weir by the site of the seventeenth-century ironworks that gave this place, Consall Forge, its name. There are a few cottages, and the Black Lion stands above the unguarded railway line on the right. Here the towing path is carried across to the far side and you continue forward beneath a large bank of limekilns, once connected by horse tramroad to the Potteries; some of the lines can be traced. There is no public road to Consall Forge but it is often busy with walkers in summer. It is a fascinating and beautiful area.

Walk on through the wooded valley alongside the canalised river, sometimes flowing quite rapidly. At Oakmeadow Ford Lock, Churnet and canal divide and the path crosses to the eastern side. The valley now opens out. You pass a sturdy lift-bridge and in a further mile (1.6km) reach the first public road-bridge since Froghall – Basford Bridge, with the Boat Inn on the canal-side. A few yards away is a fine bridge over the Churnet and a restored railway station, the North Staffordshire Steam Railway Centre.

Another ½ mile (.8km) brings you past two locks to Cheddleton. Moored here is a splendidly restored narrow boat, and below the towing path is Cheddleton flint mill, now a museum of industrial archaeology. There are in fact two mills, once powered by the Churnet and used for grinding flint for the pottery industry. The buildings are open on weekend afternoons, but there are several clearly labelled outside exhibits to inspect. There is also a large working paper mill by the canal.

You are now 5½ miles (9km) from Froghall. The valley is so beautiful that the return walk along the towing path doubles the enjoyment. If there is time, however, a further 2 miles (3km) brings you to the pretty Hollybush Inn at Denford, Hazelhurst Aqueduct taking the short Leek branch of the canal over the main line, three locks and Hazelhurst Junction where the Leek Branch begins. There is an excellent walk of nearly 3 miles (5km) along the branch to the outskirts of Leek where, on the north side of the town centre, is the Brindley mill and museum with strong associations with the life and work of the first of the great canal engineers.

Leaflets describing walks in this fascinating district are obtainable from Staffordshire Moorlands District Council, Stockwell Street, Leek ST13 6HQ. The extraordinary pleasure grounds of Alton Towers are some 5 miles (8km) lower down the Churnet valley from Froghall.

48 FORTH·&·CLYDE·CANAL· IN·GLASGOW

Time: 2½ hours.

Start and finish: Start at Temple Bridge, where the Bearsden Road (A809) crosses the canal, ½ mile (.8km) from its junction with A82. Finish at Spiers Wharf, Port Dundas. Boots not needed; the towing path has recently been upgraded.

Approach: If using the M8, turn off at the junction with A82 and in 3 miles (5km) turn onto A739 heading north. From the north, join A739 and head south for Glasgow.

Attractions: A fascinating stretch of urban canal leading at a high level towards the centre of Glasgow along the Glasgow branch. Although not navigable, the canal is in water and the structures are mostly in good condition. The walk takes you across the massive Kelvin Aqueduct, up the five Maryhill locks and along the branch to the Victorian industrial splendour of Spiers Wharf.

OS sheet: 64

The Forth & Clyde was built as a ship canal from Grangemouth on the Firth of Forth to Bowling Basin on the Clyde. It was opened throughout in 1790, and in 1822 a connection was made at Falkirk with the Edinburgh & Glasgow Union Canal. For over a hundred years it was a busy and successful water route, especially valuable in the development of heavy industry and the timber trade, and with much passenger traffic. But as the canalside industries declined or moved away, the canal's fortunes decayed. Then, in 1963, the navigation rights were abandoned and a bridge on the realigned Glasgow–Stirling A80 road was built across the canal at low level, to save the money a lifting-bridge would have cost. This effectively ended through navigation. Since then, more road-bridges have cut through the waterway and some sections of canal have been filled in. However, in recent years with the change of public attitude the importance of the canal as an amenity has been recognised; it is hoped not only that no further damage will be done, but that repair and restoration will take place – indeed, this has already begun, with the full involvement of British Waterways Board and the regional and district councils.

Join the towing path at Temple Bridge and head eastwards. Pass two locks, a new canalside pub and cross over two railway tunnels. The next bridge, like many others, has been culverted, but happily all new bridges are constructed to give full navigational headroom to prevent any further obstructions to traffic. The canal then swings to cross the River Kelvin by the handsome four-arched Kelvin Aqueduct, 70ft (21m) high and 400ft (122m) in length. Opened in 1790 and a wonder of its time, this was the largest of its kind in Britain and the first of the four great Scottish aqueducts; the others, taking the Union Canal over the Almond, Avon and the Water of Leith, were built in 1822. The Kelvin Walkway, which follows the river to the Botanic Gardens, Glasgow University and the Kelvingrove Art Gallery and Museum, passes beneath the canal here.

Shortly the five Maryhill locks are reached, like the aqueduct now scheduled as Ancient Monuments, taking the Forth & Clyde up to its summit level. Halfway up the flight is the Kelvin dry dock with a slipway beside it, where boats were built and repaired. The dock could be emptied through sluices into one of the basins between the two locks below. These wide basins, or pounds, enabled boats to pass and also acted as reservoirs for the locks. A pub, the White House, stands by the top lock. From the aqueduct to the top lock is an industrial site of great importance, and Strathclyde Regional Council has recently undertaken a costly improvement programme to upgrade the area.

Soon the Maryhill Road Aqueduct, rebuilt in 1881, carries the canal across the busy Maryhill Road. In a further 500yd (450m) is the Stockingfield Aqueduct over Lochburn Road. This remains as it was originally built by Robert Whitworth, John Smeaton's successor as the canal's chief engineer. On the far side is Stockingfield Junction where the main line of the Forth & Clyde heads away eastwards while the Glasgow Branch makes for the city centre. Keep on the towing path following the branch. For the main line you have to descend from the aqueduct at this point.

Under Glasgow District Council initiative, extensive towing-path improvements and landscaping have recently been carried out on this canal corridor so near to the city centre. You advance on a high level with fine views across the city, and soon note a spillway for controlling the water level by draining off the surplus. At Ruchill Street, nearly ½ mile (.8km) along, the canal is unfortunately culverted, thus frustrating navigation along the length of the branch. Boats, however, are able to reach this point from the centre of Kirkintilloch, 8 miles (13km) distant. On the towing-path side is Ruchill parish church, its adjacent hall designed by Charles Rennie Mackintosh at the end of the nineteenth century, and opposite are the Glasgow Lead and Colour Works, once served by a canal wharf. The Glasgow Rubber Works which you then pass also had their own wharf. The tall chimney on the towing-path side is the laundry chimney of the East Park Children's Home.

The path continues across Bilsland Drive Aqueduct and parallel to Maryhill Road to a bridge across Firhill Road, passing the recently renovated Murano Street Tenements on the left. Nearby is Queen's Cross Church, also designed by Charles Rennie Mackintosh. The canal swings round Firhill timber basins, originating in 1788 and now used for sailing and canoeing. The Partick Thistle football ground, Firhill Stadium, lies on the right.

Further on, an overgrown cut on the left leads to an old quarry, now partly infilled and landscaped. In a few minutes you arrive at Hamiltonhill Basin (the Old Basin), terminus of the branch between 1777 and 1790, overlooked by the British Waterways Board's new office building. A small inlet in the bank in front of the offices is all that is left to indicate that this was once a shipyard owned by Sir William Burrell, whose collection of art treasures is in the new Burrell Gallery, Pollok Park, Glasgow. The footbridge here was once a lifting-bridge, of which there were several on the canal, but the bridge-keeper's picturesque bothy has been demolished.

Cross the Possil Road Aqueduct and pass through an area of industrial dereliction, served in more flourishing days by the canal. Then, round a bend, is the splendid range of industrial buildings fronting North Spiers Wharf, Port Dundas, built between 1851 and 1870. These comprised a sugar refinery and grain mills; now they are bonded warehouses of the whisky industry. The smaller building at the end of the range was the Forth & Clyde Canal company offices, built in 1812. From here passenger boats used to leave for Edinburgh, and from 1893 until 1939 this was the starting point for the famous pleasure steamers *Fairy Queen*, *Gypsy Queen* and *May Queen*, which cruised to Craigmarloch near Kilsyth.

Today this is where the Glasgow Branch of the canal ends, but you may continue to the Port Dundas basins, the terminus from 1791 until the canal's closure in 1963 but now isolated from the rest of the canal. The basins are reached by crossing Craighall Road and turning first left; clustered round them are several canal-associated buildings. Once there was a junction with the Monkland Canal. Now the latter is interred beneath the motorway in pipes feeding on average over two million gallons of water a day into the Forth & Clyde. Buses from nearby Garscube Road (services 21 and 60) will return you to the canal at Maryhill locks.

Brief descriptions of further walks on the canal, incorporating visits to the Antonine Wall, can be found in *The Forth & Clyde Canal Guidebook*, published in 1985 by Strathkelvin District Libraries and Museums in association with the Forth & Clyde Canal Society, (address below). The towing path is walkable throughout the whole length and passenger boats, including a restaurant boat, are based at the Stables Restaurant, Kirkintilloch, 8 miles (13km) from central Glasgow. British Waterways Board has appointed a project officer to develop and promote leisure and recreation activities on the canal and he should be contacted (see below) for further information.

Useful addresses:
Forth & Clyde Canal Society, (Secretary Mark Eden-Bushel), 32 Clouston Street, Glasgow G20 8QU
Tom Brock, Forth & Clyde Canal Project Officer, BWB, Canal House, The Old Basin, Applecross St, Glasgow G4 9SP (041 332 6936).

Warehouses at Spiers Wharf, Port Dundas (British Waterways Board)

49 GRAND·UNION·CANAL
LEICESTER LINE

Time: 3½ hours, including visit to site of Foxton Inclined Plane.

Start and finish: Car park near top of Foxton locks, 3 miles (5km) from Market Harborough. Boots not necessary except after rain.

Approach: The simplest approach is from the A427 Rugby to Corby road 2 miles (3.2km) west of Market Harborough. Take the minor road northwards at Lubenham, signposted Foxton, and turn left at a T-junction in 1½ miles (2km). The Foxton locks car park is signposted to the left.

Attractions: Two famous canal features close to each other – the Foxton flight of ten narrow locks and the site of the Foxton Inclined Plane, now being restored. This is a towing-path walk through gentle Leicestershire countryside to Saddington Tunnel.

OS sheet: 141

Follow the path beneath the trees to the canalside and the neat new foot-bridge. Cross the bridge and in a few yards you come to the top of Foxton locks. There are ten of these in two groups of five with a passing place for boats halfway down; they were built as part of a 22 mile (35km) canal linking the Leicester line, leading to the Trent, with the Grand Junction Canal to London. They were opened in 1814 and take the canal down 75ft (23m). You should be lucky enough to see a boat working through, either on the outward or return journey – quite a complicated procedure as each lock in a group of five opens directly into the one below. The house by the top lock is the lock-keeper's and he may well be supervising matters. As you descend you will see large rectangular ponds on the far side of the locks, although only the lower ones are clear and full of water. These ponds act as reservoirs for the locks, taking the overflow and replenishing them. Refreshments and souvenirs are available by the bottom lock, and there is a boatyard – boats can be hired from here – and a chandlery. The canal to the right at the foot of the locks takes a 5 mile (8km) winding course to Market Harborough.

Walk to the bridge ahead, which carries you and the towing path across the canal. The path now goes through the middle of the view enjoyed from the top of the locks. It is a firm grassy path with a good hedge alongside; canal hedges, generally speaking, are sacrosanct, which is more than can be said for those hedges dividing farmers' fields of which so many hundreds of miles have recently been lost. The canal winds along the 330ft (100m) contour crossed by a number of bridges, most of them accommodation bridges taking farm tracks, and no two identical. Many have been rebuilt and carry their date, but none of these fit so securely into the landscape as the unpretentious red-

The Foxton Flight (R. Russell)

brick examples originally built for the canal. To the left is Gumley Wood, with the village church spire and the tower of the Hall visible above the trees.

By Bridge 65 was Debdale Wharf, opened for trading in 1797, where Derbyshire coal was once sold for 11d (less than 5p) a hundredweight. A boatyard is now tucked inconspicuously away in a basin just through the bridge. The canal now swings towards the west, with hills rising on the far side. On the towing-path side the land falls gently away; the little stream through the fields below merges with the River Welland and finds its outfall in the Wash. This canal avoids villages; Smeeton Westerby lurks ½ mile (.8km) away, visible through gaps in the hedge.

Shortly after Bridge 71 there is a little feeder stream on the opposite side, bringing water from Saddington Reservoir a mile (1.6km) away. Cross an aqueduct over a farm track; soon the canal straightens out and beneath a bridge ahead can be glimpsed Saddington Tunnel – there is a point from which you can see right through the tunnel to the pool of light at the further portal. The bridge carries the Smeeton Westerby–Saddington road; pass beneath it and in a few minutes you are at the tunnel itself.

At 880yd (805m) Saddington is the twelfth longest tunnel still in use on the English canals. It was opened in 1797. There is no towing path through it; the boat horses used to be led along a horse path across the tunnel top and this pleasant track can be followed to the far portal if you wish. The tunnel is reputedly haunted by a headless ghost.

From Bridge 72 there is a choice of return routes. Either take the road north to Smeeton Westerby and follow a track opposite and just past the pub, across fields to the bridge above Debdale Wharf regaining the towing path there; or make south for Saddington village, passing through the village and taking the little road around the reservoir to Gumley and the top of Foxton locks. Nothing much is gained by either of these routes and it may be preferable simply to return by the outward path as the canal's surveyors certainly chose the pleasantest route through the countryside.

Back at the bottom lock of the Foxton flight, cross to the opposite side – noting the many canal relics around the pub – to a bridge over a short canal arm. Here, recently cleared out and now used as moorings, is the basin at the foot of the Foxton Inclined Plane. Walk up the hill to examine the remains of the incline now being restored by a voluntary trust; it was opened in 1900 as a means of bypassing the flight of narrow locks, both saving time and enabling wider boats to be used. Two caissons – long, narrow tanks capable of containing a 70ft barge – ran on rails embedded in a concrete slope, counterbalanced and aided by a steam engine at the top. Old photographs of the incline at work are in the pub nearby, and there are explanatory notices on the site. The upper part of the slope has been excavated and a museum is being built on the site of the engine house. The incline, however, though reasonably efficient, proved too costly to operate. Although the other locks between London and the Trent were wide, the Watford flight 20 miles (32km) south were, like Foxton, narrow, and the canal company was not encouraged to bypass them in a similar way. The incline stopped working in 1911 and was dismantled in the 1920s. However, inclines on a similar principle operate successfully in other countries and, had electrical power been developed in time, Foxton might have survived.

From the top of the incline you can follow the towing path of the abandoned canal arm that connected the incline with the main line. The latter is soon regained near the bridge and the path taking you back to the car.

Booklets on the story of Foxton and the inclined plane can be obtained from the shop by the bottom lock.

50 STRATFORD-UPON-AVON·
CANAL   SOUTHERN SECTION

Time: 3 hours.
Start and finish: Car park at Navigation Inn by aqueduct over the A34
Birmingham to Stratford-upon-Avon road at Wootton Wawen. Boots or
stout footwear needed.
Approach: Wootton Wawen is 2 miles (3km) south of Henley-in-Arden and
6 miles (9.6km) north of Stratford-upon-Avon. The aqueduct crosses the
road ½ mile (.8km) east of the church just before the Navigation Inn. There
is a large car park by the inn and space for parking in the village itself.
Attractions: A walk alongside a remote section of one of England's loveliest
canals. There are two cast-iron aqueducts, one of them among the longest in
England, Mary Arden's house (she was Shakespeare's mother) and a pub at
the halfway mark. Wootton Wawen has some fine buildings and the oldest
church in the county.
OS sheet: 151

The Southern Section of the Stratford-upon-Avon Canal runs from a junction
with the Northern Section and the Grand Union Canal at Lapworth to a
basin in Stratford in front of the Shakespeare Memorial Theatre, a distance
of 13 miles (21km). It was opened throughout in 1816, fell out of use in the
1920s and became wholly derelict. However, an attempt to abandon it failed
and in 1960 the canal was leased to the National Trust. Between 1961 and
1964 it was restored by a combination of volunteers, armed services and
prison labour, under the leadership of David Hutchings. In July 1964 it was
reopened by the Queen Mother as part of the Inland Waterways Association
National Rally at Stratford. The National Trust then took over the freehold,
but with the increase in boat traffic following the reopening of the Upper
Avon Navigation in 1974 maintenance costs rose considerably. Now the
National Trust would like to hand it over to a more suitable authority, but to
date nothing has been settled. A South Stratford Canal Preservation Trust
has been formed to campaign for its retention as a navigable waterway.

Wootton Wawen Aqueduct – note the inscription on the southern side –
gives 15ft (4.6m) clearance over the road, but lorries still manage to ram it
from time to time. The towing path can be reached by a narrow path climbing
up opposite the inn. If you miss this, turn along the lane heading north on
the far side of the aqueduct from the pub and in a few yards turn right on a
track leading to a bridge over the canal. Don't try to reach the towing path
from the boatyard behind the inn; it's on the other side.

The aqueduct, like the longer one to be crossed later, has its towing path below water level enabling examination of the construction of the iron trough. The path goes past a makeshift bridge, through a wooded cutting and then across the canal at one of the South Stratford's characteristic split or divided bridges. The split took the towing lines in the days of horse-drawn boats; notice the rope marks in the ironwork. These bridges do not span the towing path as most canal bridges do. Notice also one of the old diamond-shaped bridge signs denoting the weights which the bridge could bear; these used to be common by canal bridges but now very few remain. Soon a conventional brick bridge is reached, the brickwork worn and crumbling, and then an isolated lock, known as Odd Lock. Note the rather harsh brickwork patching and the worn coping stones. There is an efficient overflow weir on the opposite side.

The canal is now heading due south. In a few minutes you arrive at Bearley (or Edstone) Aqueduct, 475ft (145m) long, carrying the canal over the railway line (built beneath the aqueduct and opened in 1860, taking away much of the canal trade), a stream and the old road from Warwick. The iron trough is supported on thirteen brick piers; scramble down to the road from the far side to examine them.

The next 2 miles (3km) seem especially remote. The path may well be overgrown – there is only a small staff to look after the canal – but it is firm underfoot. You pass only one house, on the opposite side, and two split bridges. Hawthorn trees line the canal on both sides almost all the way, but

Iron split bridge

the countryside can be enjoyed through the occasional gap. This once was the Forest of Arden and there is still some fine woodland hereabouts. The railway, however, is close by and from time to time the sound of a passing train intrudes.

Towards the end of this stretch, pass a house on the left. The outbuildings line the towing path, and opposite note the good stone piling; there's little of this along the canal. There used to be lime and cement works here, served by a horse-drawn railway that crossed the canal by a bridge of which the abutments survive. Next as you round a bend are the retaining wall and moorings built by volunteers of the Stratford Canal Society, funded by a grant from Shell UK Ltd. Ahead is Featherbed Lane Bridge.

Leave the canal and turn right into the village, passing Mary Arden's house – an early sixteenth-century farmhouse now owned by the Shakespeare Birthplace Trust and open to visitors. At a T-junction in the middle of Wilmcote village, turn right and in a few yards look out for a public-footpath fingerpost. Follow this along the left edge of a field to an iron gate, then along the right-hand edge of the next field to another iron gate. The route is waymarked most of the way. Keep to the left side of a ploughed field and then of a grass field, and go through a gap in the far side onto a lane. Turn right into the hamlet of Newnham, and right again when the lane reaches a minor road. This soon leads to a T-junction a few yards from the Bearley Aqueduct. Regain the towing path and retrace the first 1¼ miles (2km) of the walk to Wootton Wawen, its aqueduct and the Navigation Inn.

To extend exploration of the Southern Stratford, walk northwards from Wootton Wawen through Preston Bagot (2 miles, 3km) to Lowsonford (another 2 miles, 3km) and the pleasant Fleur de Lys inn. Note the unique 'barrel-roofed' lock cottages on the way. From Lowsonford to Kingswood the path forms a nature trail. From Wilmcote you can continue into Stratford, passing sixteen locks as you descend. Better still, hire a boat for a week and explore this beautiful canal thoroughly; despite first appearances it is in quite good condition for boating and there should be no problems. Perhaps you will be encouraged to join the Preservation Trust and give practical support to its future wellbeing. The story and the fight for its preservation are told in *Save the Stratford Canal* by Guy Johnson (David & Charles, 1983).

51 Monmouthshire·Canal·
WESTERN BRANCH

Time: 2 hours, or 4 hours.
Start and finish: Crindau Bridge, Newport. Stout footwear needed, but boots not essential.
Approach: Crindau Bridge is on the west side of A4042 immediately south of Junction 26 on M4, on the northern edge of Newport. Park in one of the side streets off Malpas Road (A4042).
Attractions: A towing-path walk with contrasting urban and rural scenery. On the route is the Cefn (or Rogerstone) flight of fourteen locks, a major feature of industrial archaeology. These became disused after 1930, but were partially restored and a Canal Centre opened on the site in 1976. An exploratory trail has been set out and a small museum/information centre is open between April and October (every day in the height of summer, otherwise closed Tuesday and Wednesday).
OS sheet: 171

The main line of the Monmouthshire Canal was opened in 1796 and the Western Branch two years later. The canal's main purpose was to bring iron and coal down the valleys to docks on the Usk at Newport for export via the Bristol Channel, and it was connected to the mines by a series of tramroads, many traces of which remain. Trade on the whole canal was finished by 1939 and by 1962 both main line and branch were officially abandoned. Some sections have been recently cleared for canoeing and fishing and the towing path is walkable throughout, except where the canal has been eradicated in Newport and above Cwmcarn. In its heyday it carried nearly a million tons of freight a year. The main line runs from Newport to Pontymoile where it connects with the Brecon & Abergavenny Canal. This, one of the most beautiful of all inland waterways, is open and much used by pleasure craft. The Western (or Crumlin) Branch of the Monmouthshire follows generally the Ebbw valley from Malpas Junction to Pontywaun. The top few miles have been filled in.

If you have plenty of time, begin at Crindau Bridge by heading south towards Newport, through a pleasant tree-lined approach to the town. In ¼ mile (.4km) is the short Barrack Hill Tunnel, where the canal surprisingly vanishes. From here the water has been channelled underground to the Usk and the course of the canal has been obliterated.

Return to the starting point and walk westward parallel to the motorway. By Bridge 25 is Malpas Junction where the main line heads north beneath the M4 to join the Brecon & Abergavenny 11 miles (17.5km) away at Pontymoile.

Lock and cottage on the Cefn Flight

Follow the towing path along a pleasant rural stretch of well-watered canal, passing five locks and three bridges. This area is known as Allt-yr-yn and there are fine views to north and west. Gradually you approach the motorway again and pass the site of an old brickworks by Cefn Bottom Lock before ducking beneath the M4 by an underpass to emerge by the foot of the Cefn flight.

The fourteen Cefn locks lift the canal 168ft (51m) in just over ½ mile (.8km). They are not a true staircase – where one lock leads directly into the next sharing a single gate – but are mostly in pairs with a very short pound between each lock in a pair. There is a complex system of side ponds, channels, weirs and adits; one lock has been widened out with a boat-size shelf at one side. There is a waymarked trail around the locks and an explanatory leaflet is obtainable from the Canal Centre at the top.

The basin above the top lock has been cleared and landscaped with a picnic area and car park nearby. For the short walk, return down the flight by the waymarked trail. To extend the outing, carry on towards Risca. Much of the canal has been cleared as a local community project and is in water with good views across the Ebbw valley. It follows the contour past Rogerstone and the power station, with quarries close by for limestone and millstone grit. It is now near the A467 Risca–Newport road, so to return by bus leave the canal by any of the bridges and step down to the road.

The canal continues through Crosskeys; then it is crossed by the A467 and a short distance further on it ends. When built it ended at Crumlin, 3 miles

(5km) further up the valley; now the Navigation Inn is its memorial there, in the same way as the Viaduct Inn recalls the extraordinary latticework steel construction that took the railway across the valley 200ft (60km) below.

If walking back to your car, take in the fourteen-locks trail which adds only a few hundred yards to your journey. To vary the route, take the lane from the Canal Centre car park to the reservoirs and follow the waymark arrows through a farm to the motorway. An underpass returns you to the canal just over ½ mile (.8km) from your starting point.

If you are staying in the area, try to visit the canal junction at Pontymoile, the Brecon & Abergavenny wharf at Llanfoist and the Llangynidr locks in their beautiful woodland setting. The 3 mile (5km) walk from Llangynidr Bottom Lock to Talybont is highly recommended. A detailed towpath guide is available: *Brecknock & Abergavenny and Monmouthshire Canals* by R. Alan Stevens (Goose & Son, 1974).

52 CRINAN·CANAL

Time: 7 hours, or 4 hours. Allow 1 hour for the diversion.

Start and finish: For the longer walk, Ardrishaig, 2 miles (3km) south of Lochgilphead on the A83. The canal terminal is by the pier at the southern end of the village. For the shorter walk, Cairnbaan bridge, 200yd west on B841 from the junction with A816. Boots not necessary for the canal walk but recommended for the optional 2 mile (3.2km) forest diversion through Knapdale Forest.

Approach: Ardrishaig is 80 miles (129km) from Glasgow and 38 miles (61km) from Oban. Cairnbaan is 4 miles (6km) north of Ardrishaig. Parking at both places is easy. However, there is no public transport back from Crinan.

Attractions: The canal is well used in the summer months and some splendid and lavish yachts may be on view. The views, especially between Bellanoch and Crinan, are superb. Crinan itself is beautifully situated with usually a remarkable variety of craft packed into the basin. Refreshments are available at Cairnbaan and Crinan.

OS sheet: 55

The Crinan Canal was opened in 1801 to provide a safe route between the Clyde and the Western Highlands and Islands, shortening the distance by 85 miles (137km). It was much used by fishing vessels although their numbers have sadly diminished. In late July, on the first weekend of the Glasgow Fair, the canal forms part of the route of the three-day Tobermory Race when well over 100 yachts pass through in procession.

The canal connects with Loch Gilp via a sea-lock guarded by a breakwater and lighthouse. Join the towing path by the basin beside a swing bridge. Three locks lift the canal 24ft (7m) as you head northwards with hills rising on the left. In 2 miles (3km) you reach Oakfield Bridge on the outskirts of Lochgilphead and the site of the old wharf and coal store for the locality. Lochgilphead, ½ mile (.8km) by road, is a busy little town of 2,500 people – the largest settlement on OS sheet 55.

The canal now swings gradually north-west. A mile further on, the wood on the right conceals a number of cup-and-ring-marked rocks, evidence of Bronze Age settlement. To see these, leave the canal where it moves away from the main road, follow the road for 300 yards and take the track to Achnabreck Farm; the rocks are in the wood above the farm.

Cairnbaan, 2 miles (3km) from Oakfield Bridge, is named after a Bronze Age burial mound – the white cairn – a few yards south of the lock before the swing bridge. The inn here has been recently extended. Good locally made pottery and jewellery can be seen at a craft shop on the canalside.

Traversing bridge

At Cairnbaan four locks take the canal up to its summit level, 64ft above sea level. From here to Crinan the canal runs along the northern edge of Knapdale Forest. For the forest diversion cross to the south side and turn past the forest office and workshops, following yellow markers along paths taking you past an old quarry and up to the Dunardry triangulation point at 703ft, from where there are splendid views across Knapdale. Waymarked paths bring you in a circuit back to the starting point. Reservoirs supplying the canal lie deeper in the forest and can be reached by forest paths.

There are fine views from the summit level. To the south wooded hills rise steeply, while northward lies Moine Mhor, a strange stretch of drained marsh with the River Add winding a serpentine course through its midst. The rocky outcrop of Dunadd dominates the plain; this was the site of a fort, the capital of the kingdom of Dalriada, founded by Scots in the fifth century AD on their arrival from Ireland. Do not try to reach Dunadd by walking from the canal; it is accessible from a minor road off the A816, 3 miles (5km) north of Cairnbaan.

The summit level is less than ¾ mile (1.2km) long. Five locks, the Dunardry flight, take the canal down 45ft (14m). The passenger steamer *Linnet*, purpose built for the Crinan Canal, used to be berthed below Lock 9 in winter. She plied the canal from 1866 to 1929, carrying up to 270 passengers and completing the end to end voyage in 1hr 40min. Note the rolling or traversing bridge in the middle of the flight, wound back by the bridge-keeper when vessels need to pass.

There follows a mile of easy walking to Bellanoch Bridge, carrying the

B8025 across the canal. This road crosses the Add estuary by Islandadd Bridge and heads across the Mhor towards Kilmartin with its nearby stone circles and cairns. The towing path now is on a narrow embankment separating the canal from the estuary below. Bellanoch has a school, a church, a handful of houses and good views towards Loch Crinan, and here the canal widens into a basin or lagoon known as Bellanoch Bay where yachts are often moored.

In just over ½ mile (.8km) the canal turns sharply north-eastward. Soon you reach a bridge with an attractive bridge-keeper's cottage alongside; here the road crosses and unites with the towing path and steps lead down to the old station of the Crinan ferry. This final length of canal was cut through granite: the waterway is narrow and the bends sharp. The views to north and north-west open out as you begin to round the headland and approach Lock 14, most of which was excavated from the living rock. Then you arrive at the beautifully sited Crinan Basin. A lighthouse guards the entrance to the canal, entered by a sea-lock from Loch Crinan.

It's well worth spending half an hour or so exploring the basin and the immediate surroundings, admiring the yachts and fishing boats and, if there is time, walking past the hotel to the old harbour. A path from the harbour follows the shore-line for nearly a mile (1.6km) to the Sailor's Grave near Ardnoe Point. Thence you can climb some 700ft (213m) to a viewpoint overlooking the Sound of Jura with a scattering of small islands to the north. A yellow-marked path will return you to the harbour in some 30 minutes, or follow the green markings for a longer forest walk to Fort Dounie with a choice of return routes either to the harbour or to Kilmahumaig, ½ mile (.8km) along the road from Crinan Basin. Allow about 3½ hours for the longer walk.

Further reading:
A useful guide, *Knapdale Forest Walks*, can be obtained from the Forestry Commission, The Forest Office, Cairnbaan, Argyll. For the history of the canal, its engineers, construction and commercial past, an illustrated booklet, *The Crinan Canal*, is available from the Inland Waterways Association, 114 Regent's Park Road, London NW1 8UQ.

Writers·and·Artists

The walks in this section are not spartan affairs. They are almost all set in much-lived-in environments and are all short enough to allow plenty of extra time in a day for food stops, gazing at the sights and studying the particular writer's or artist's preserved habitation. So normal gear for the determined walker is not necessary. For most walks, good shoes are sufficient. An umbrella can stand service in place of some of the normal protective clothing, and if you feel qualms at walking into, say, The Wakes at Selborne with muddy footwear, simply take them off and pad around in your socks. The curators will surely prefer this.

Associating a walk with some writer or artist is hardly an innovation. Literary pilgrimages, in particular, have a respectable tradition and with good reason. Once you have tried one, you will find that your appreciation of the writer is substantially improved. This stems partly from the fact that regional differences in Britain used to be remarkably strong and could exert a powerful influence upon literary output. You get an immediate feel for the very distinctive Brontë background when you visit Haworth and its parsonage, and a walk over the nearby moors adds atmospheric depth and meaning for some of the great novels, particularly *Wuthering Heights*. Painters, too, can reflect their environments. Read a biography of Constable before you set out, and a walk around Flatford, Dedham and East Bergholt can greatly bolster understanding of both the man and his work. Cookham is as solidly linked with Stanley Spencer as Selborne with Gilbert White. Dylan Thomas has to be South Wales, just as Sir Walter Scott is a champion of the Borders.

The local impact is not, of course, always so clear. Shakespeare is not limited to Stratford-upon-Avon in any obvious way, though he remained remarkably loyal to the place. Turner took all Britain for his canvas – a truly peripatetic artist, rambling when he was young up to twenty-five miles (40km) a day sketching and painting. But even with such unconfined genius it is possible, in a walk, to enhance some facet of an interesting background. A ramble around the Greta can be justified by the sheer greatness of the associated Cotman, even though the artist lived in the area for no more than a few weeks.

Top Withins – the supposed site of Wuthering Heights *on Haworth Moor* (Geoffrey N. Wright) (*see* page 213)

In effect, there is a balance in this section between walks where regional influence is obvious and strong and those where the connections are more incidental. For reasons of space a good many obvious choices have been omitted: the peregrinations of the Wordsworths; Hardy country around Dorchester; Lawrence Sterne and Shandy Hall; Coleridge and the Quantocks; Blackmore and the Doone Valley; Graham Sutherland and Pembrokeshire; John Singer Sargent and Broadway and Fladbury, for instance.

The list of possibilities is indeed extensive. The British are the fortunate inheritors of a vast literature and a rich artistry which they tend to underestimate. The roots of this culture are still largely recognisable to those who look for them in our incredibly rich and varied landscape, the accumulation of centuries hardly touched by war. Castle and country house, church and village, the inimitable pub, are all still there in profusion, all linking us to our past. Rambling in the shadow of the great can be doubly rewarding, in both greater understanding of individual genius and appreciation of the diversity of our countryside. And there is the bonus of contributing in a minor way to the conservation of the best in our traditions, and of resisting the pressures of this age towards uniformity.

53	Brontë Country, West Yorkshire	7½ miles (12km)
54	Jane Austen and Gilbert White, Hampshire	9 miles (14km) or less
55	Dylan Thomas and Laugharne, Dyfed	8 miles (13km) or less
56	Robert Burns and Alloway, Strathclyde	8½ miles (14km)
57	Sir Walter Scott and the Tweed, Borders	7 miles (11km)
58	Constable Country, Essex	7 miles (11km)
59	Cotman and the Greta, County Durham	8½ miles (14km)
60	Stanley Spencer and Cookham, Berkshire	8 miles (13km) or less
61	Turner and Ivon Hitchens, West Sussex	7 miles (11km)

53 BRONTË·COUNTRY

Time: Around 3 hours. It would be worthwhile adding a visit to the Brontë Parsonage Museum. This is open year round, except in February, from 11am to 5.30pm, 4.30pm in winter. Boots are advisable, and be prepared for inclement weather. The walk is through sheep country, and dogs must be under control.

Start and finish: The Brontë Parsonage Museum in Haworth. This is well signposted and there are a number of car parks nearby.

Approach: Haworth is 8 miles (13km) west of Bradford and 3 miles (5km) south-west of Keighley.

Attractions: This must be one of the best-known literary landscapes in the world. The restricted life in the parsonage proved a forcing house of the genius of the three sisters, and the memory of their extraordinary lives has turned Haworth from a quiet and obscure textile village into a thriving tourist centre. The walk follows trails, now exceedingly well trodden, associated with the Brontës and their works. It should add to appreciation of such novels as Charlotte's *Jane Eyre* and Emily Jane's *Wuthering Heights*, for the sisters' writings reflected their own experiences and the wild and stern environment around them.

OS sheets: 103 and 104

From the parsonage, Georgian and dating from 1778, walk down towards the church. Patrick Brontë became rector here in 1819, and he and all his family, save his daughter Anne, are buried in Haworth. His wife died of cancer two years after moving to the parsonage and no daughter lived to be older than forty. His only son, Branwell, failed his early promise as a painter and died of drink and drugs. You may well wish to linger in the churchyard as you walk through it. Follow the yellow-marked Brontë Way signs.

After a flagstone path, turn right past a farmhouse, cross the road and follow a path up the side of Pennistone Hill to the Pennistone Hill Country Park rangers' base. Climb the hill to the left for a good panoramic view, then drop down right, still following the signs, to the Brontë Falls and Top Withins. Cross the road, leading right down to Lower Laithe Reservoir, and continue along a good macadam track which later deteriorates, with drystone walling on the right and a couple of solid stone farmhouses, sadly deserted.

Just before the Brontë bridge, turn up left to the right of the Brontë waterfall. It is a mild scramble, and don't expect too much of the waterfall; it is often no more than a trickle. At the top the path swings right of Harbour Lodge, which is before you, and around the foot of Harbour Hill, with Oxenhope Stoop Hill to the left. Keeping the beds of rushes and the stream to the left, drop down to the South Dean Beck, having covered a fine stretch of wild, empty moorland. Having negotiated the stream, work up left and join the well-beaten track to Top Withins. A few hundred yards before it, at some ruined farm buildings, you join the Pennine Way – the first of England's long walks, opened in 1965 and running 270 miles (435km) from Edale in Derbyshire to Kirk Yetholme in Roxburghshire. Top Withins is mostly ruin, though there is shelter against bad weather and some seats. The plaque, placed there by the Brontë Society, tells of its association with Heathcliff's home, Wuthering Heights.

Now retrace your steps and bear left along the Pennine Way. This is one of the better sections, with good firm walking and excellent views. Upper Heights and Lower Heights farms are passed on the left; then the Pennine Way drops left down to Ponden Reservoir and Ponden Hall, the model for Emily Brontë's Thrushcross Grange. You can appreciate the contrast which she draws between the warm comforts of the low-lying Hall and the windy harshness of Top Withins. Continue on, bearing right at the road to reach the pleasant stone-built village of Stanbury.

At the end of the village, take the first road right, marked Worth Valley Railway. This did not exist in Brontë times, not even in old Rector Patrick's, who outlived all his children and died in his mid-eighties. The railway came to Haworth in 1867; it was closed in 1962 and is now run by a preservation society based on Keighley. It featured in the film *The Railway Children*. Judge how quiet Haworth must have been before rail and motor vehicles.

The road goes over the Staithes Reservoir dam. On the far side turn sharp left by the Sladen Valley Filtration Works. When you reach Haworth cemetery, walk left along the road until the junction at West Lane. A wall stile on the right will lead back to the parsonage.

Deserted farmhouse on the path to Withins (Bob Brash)

54 JANE·AUSTEN·AND· GILBERT·WHITE

Time: Allow about 4 hours, or shorten it by an hour by driving to the church at Upper Farringdon and parking there, after seeing Jane Austen's house at Chawton. A full day could happily be spent visiting both the house at Chawton and Gilbert White's house, The Wakes, at Selborne. But check opening times. April to October the Chawton house is open 11am to 4.30pm; The Wakes, Selborne, from 12 noon to 5.30pm, except Mondays. Boots are not necessary, though sections between Upper Farringdon and Selborne can become very muddy in wet weather.

Start and finish: Chawton. There is no public car park in the village, but you should find a spot either in High Street or in the cul de sac opposite Jane Austen's house.

Approach: Chawton lies south of Alton near the junction of A31 and A32.

Attractions: The walk is a literary double-bill, starting with scenes well known to Jane Austen then rambling through pleasant rolling Hampshire countryside beloved of that doyen of field naturalists, Gilbert White. Though he lived most of his life at Selborne, he was curate at Upper Farringdon for twenty-three years. He must have known much of the walk like the back of his hand.

OS sheet: 186

You may like to start by visiting the house where Jane Austen lived with her widowed mother and sister, Cassandra, from 1809 until shortly before her death in 1817 – in the last throes of Addison's disease she was moved to Winchester for better medical treatment. It was a quiet existence. Cassandra was the housekeeper and Mrs Austen looked after the garden. Jane played the piano before making breakfast at nine, and her other chores included looking after the tea and sugar stores, and making mead and wines. But it was the period of her most successful authorship, seeing the publication of *Sense and Sensibility*, *Pride and Prejudice*, *Mansfield Park* and *Emma*. *Northanger Abbey* and *Persuasion* followed after her death. The house has a very interesting collection of memorabilia.

After leaving it, turn down the cul de sac opposite. To the left is St Nicholas's Church. Here Jane Austen worshipped and her mother and sister lie buried. Behind the church is Chawton House, which is private and cannot be visited. It was inherited by Jane Austen's brother, Edward, from his cousin, Thomas Knight, under the condition that Edward changed his name from Austen to Knight. The estate included the house Jane lived in.

Jane Austen's house in the High Street at Chawton (Bob Brash); (opposite) *View of Selbourne from the top of the Hanger* (Bob Brash)

At the end of the cul de sac, a small footpath leads to the busy A32. Keeping the same direction and on the left of the road, watch for a signpost pointing half-left after 400yd (366m). Follow the fence on the left to a good track, where turn right and continue for over ½ mile (.8km) through lovely Hampshire countryside and splendid avenues of yew and pine before dropping down to Upper Farringdon. A path left, at the end of a children's playing ground, takes the rambler to Upper Farringdon church. All Saints has interesting Norman columns and font, and a thirteenth-century tower.

Turn right down the road, past the village hall, to a T-junction where turn left in the direction of Selborne and Liss. Opposite a charming topiary swan, turn right into a shaded walk which can get very muddy in wet weather. Continue upwards until you reach an open field with a barn to the right. Turn sharp left along the hedgerow and continue for a good ½ mile (.8km) to the woods. After a time the walk is between two hedgerows and acrobatics may be necessary to dodge the mud after bad weather, but the views are good. Once in the trees, watch for a gate on the right at the top of a field. Cross the field towards the bottom of the wood on the left and there, with luck, you will find a further overgrown gate. Struggle through the wood in the same direction to a gate, this time in good repair, looking out over a broad sweep of open field. This is the trickiest part of the walk for the right of way is not clear on the ground. Aim diagonally left at a gate at the far edge of the field and half-way along the wood.

218 · Jane Austen and Gilbert White

Once at the gate, turn left along the road until the edge of the wood, then right onto a good track. At the top, turn left through a single gate and walk along the top of the field with the hedgerow on your right until you reach the woods of Selborne Common – National Trust property – also on your right. Turn into the woods, keeping to the right-hand track. This bridle track can get churned up in wet weather, but there is plenty of room to dodge the mud. Continue, with fields visible through the wood on the right, until two oak four-direction signposts are reached. Take the footpath pointing left from the second post. This leads ¾ mile (1.2km) through splendid deciduous woodland to a circle of magnificent beeches – and the glimpse of a house ahead. The path bears left. At a T-junction turn right and then left along a smaller path, and reach the walk along the top of Selborne Hanger. Through the trees on the right there are views of the village. Eventually, descend to the right down a flight of log steps. Follow the fence at the bottom right. After a short descent, cross the field left and reach the road.

Bear right along the road for 300yd (275m) or so, to The Wakes where Gilbert White was born in 1720 and where he died in 1793. Here he wrote *The Natural History and Antiquities of Selborne*, the meticulous account of his local environment which has proved his lasting memorial. The house contains a fascinating account of his work and times, and after walking over the common and the hanger you should be in the mood to appreciate it. There is the unexpected bonus of the upper floor devoted to the travels of the Oates family and particularly of Captain L. E. G. Oates, who heroically walked out of the tent to certain death in an antarctic blizzard in the vain hope that he would enable his friends in the 1912 Scott expedition to live.

Retracing your steps, you will see St Mary's Church across the green on the right. Gilbert White lies buried here in the simplest of graves. There is, however, a marvellous modern stained-glass window in his honour, depicting St Francis and the birds; the detail is quite remarkable. Outside there is a splendid old yew, allegedly 1,300 years old. One wonders – the church only reveals Norman ancestry.

Return to the point where you left the field on coming down from the hanger, and continue along the road to Newton Valance. There are pretty thatched cottages on the left. Go up a track just past the last house on the right, and continue on up the hill through an iron gate, with the hedge on your left. Bearing left, cross the field diagonally to a stile in the far right corner. Continue between two hedges to the top of the hill and onto the road. Leave the road immediately by turning right up Bush Down, along a track between trees and the field. As the hedgerow drops away to the left, continue straight on over the fields to the right of a new hedge. Cross the wooden fence at the bottom of the field and turn left along the hedgerow. It can be very nettle-choked in summer! With some relief, reach the very quiet metalled road leading left to Upper Farringdon. Take the right fork past the Rose and Crown and turn left to Farringdon church at the T-junction. From the church, retrace your steps to Chawton.

55 Dylan·Thomas·and· Laugharne

Time: Up to 3½ hours but, if you lack the time, the walk can be cut to 2½ or 6 miles (4 or 9km). In addition you will probably wish to visit Dylan Thomas's last home, the Boat House, and to see his grave in St Martin's churchyard. Good shoes are all that is necessary.

Start and finish: The car park by the castle at Laugharne.

Approach: Laugharne lies south-west of Carmarthen in South Wales. From there take the A40 to St Clears, then the A4066 to Laugharne.

Attractions: Apart from the associations with Dylan Thomas, the walk offers some splendid views over the estuaries of the Rivers Taf and Tywi and the gentle rolling countryside of this part of South Wales. Laugharne itself is an attractive old town, proud of a unique corporative structure which dates back to 1307, the time of Edward I.

OS sheets: 158 and 159

Leave the car park by the path round the foot of the castle. This was founded by Rhys ap Gruffyd in the twelfth century, but the present structure dates from a century later, at the time of Norman occupation. The peripatetic Turner did a watercolour of it in a storm, with a dismasted ship at anchor offshore and figures salvaging flotsam and jetsam – a good deal of artistic licence, you may think. Dylan Thomas lived for a time prewar at Sea View on the town-ward side of the castle, and used to write in the gazebo on the castle wall. The path goes to the Boat House, but first passes Dylan Thomas's work shed, actually built as a garage for the first car to come to Laugharne sixty-odd years ago. Here he wrote some of his finest work, including the bulk of *Under Milk Wood* – the model for Llareggub is generally regarded as Laugharne.

Descend steps to the house itself; Dylan Thomas never owned any property, and the house was rented to him by Margaret Taylor, the wife of the historian A. J. P. Taylor. He lived there with Caitlin, his wife and their three children until his death from alcoholic poisoning in New York in 1953. The house is now owned by the Carmarthen District Council. There are fine views over the estuary. There are seldom signs of much activity offshore, and it is hard to imagine that Laugharne used to be a great producer of cockles – over 10,000cwt (508,000kg) a year in the mid-twenties.

Continue up the path past the house. Cross over a track swinging down to the shore on your right. At a stile the ramble changes from pleasant woodland walking to open field with a hedgerow separating you from the estuary. Reach the empty and deteriorating Delacorse farmhouse and follow the farm track up the hill. Take the metalled road left and follow this quiet country lane down until St Martin's Church appears on the right. Steep steps to the right of the lane lead into the old churchyard. The church itself is worth a visit. It was established by the local Norman lord, Gui de Brienne, standard-bearer to Edward III at the battle of Crécy in 1346. But most of it is fifteenth century and it was much restored in Victorian times. The oldest object is a tenth-century Celtic cross. On the wall is a replica of the tablet commemorating Dylan Thomas in Westminster Abbey; his grave, marked by a simple wooden cross, is in the new section of the graveyard, reached by a footbridge over the lane.

Continue through the graveyard to the lich-gate and left down the main road back to the centre of Laugharne. It has considerable architectural charm. Pass the tiny, quaint Town Hall built in 1746 and with the clock which Dylan Thomas alleged told the time backwards, and two haunts of his – Brown's Hotel and the Cross House Inn. You have now walked about 2½ miles (4km) and may chose to stop. Otherwise, walk across the car park and take the path along the foreshore, past Laugharne's well-disguised sewage works and then under the cliffs which border the eastern edge of Sir John's Hill. It is necessary to be wary of the tide, but you can keep clear of the mud with some clever footwork and the distance until you reach the meadowland beyond the hill is quite short. The path keeps close to the cliff on your right round to Salt House, where you can expect a canine welcome. Steps by the house lead up to the path back to Laugharne, so again you can call it a day.

If you wish to stretch your legs for a further 3½ miles (5.6km), turn left at the house and follow the hedge to an overgrown concrete bridge over a wide drainage ditch. Turn right on the other side and quickly descend left into the field, with another drainage ditch to the right. The way leads almost directly to East House Farm – at one point, at a track, cross over to the other side of the ditch. Circling the farm on your right, turn right onto the metalled road. On the left are Burrows Dunes fenced off by the Ministry of Defence. A good mile (1.6km) brings you to a metalled road back to the foot of Sir John's Hill. Opposite the entrance to the stone quarry, turn right into a track which leads back to Salt House.

The steps by the house lead to a path up the wooded slope. Near the top, just past a ruined cottage, chose whether to continue around the hill through the woods, or turn left up to the top where there is an open meadow with a splendid view over the dunes and out to sea. Pendine Sands are to the right; here the world land-speed record was five times broken between 1924 and 1927 by Malcolm Campbell and Parry Thomas. Walk to the left of the hill-top farm and take the farm track downhill back to town. Just before the houses by the main road, there is a track to the right which leads through a gate down to the foreshore, where the car park is on the left.

The Castle at Laugharne (Bob Brash)

56 Robert·Burns·and· Alloway

Looking across the Doon to the Burns Memorial at Alloway

Time: Up to 4 hours. But you can make it a very full day by visiting all the various Burns sites around Alloway. Good shoes are necessary.
Start and finish: The car park by the Burns's Cottage.
Approach: Alloway is south of Ayr on the B7024. It is well signposted.
Attractions: The walk starts from the place where Burns was born and goes south along the coast to splendid shoreline walking around the Heads of Ayr and then back to Burns heritage at Alloway.
OS sheet: 70

You may wish to start by going into Burns's birthplace, the 'auld clay biggin', which his father William built by himself in order to marry Agnes Brown whom he met at Maybole some miles to the south. Robert was born on 25 January 1759, a date commemorated every year by Scots around the world as Burns Night. And the cottage has indeed become an international literary shrine. Robert in fact left it when he was seven; the family moved to a farm at Mount Oliphant, a mile (1.6km) or so to the east.

Return to the car park, then leave it by Greenfield Avenue in the direction of Doonfoot. First the golf course, then Belleisle Park is on your right. When the A719 is reached, turn left across the bridge and then very shortly right into Scaur o'Doon Road. This leads to the mouth of the River Doon with fine views out to sea and the mountains of Arran on the skyline.

Bear left on grassy walking along the foreshore and after ¾ mile (1.2km) reach a small promontory with the ruins of a castle on top. It is only a mild scramble up to the castle and the view is rewarding. Continue along the foreshore. Wet sand, when you can find it, gives the best walking. Pass Butlin's holiday camp on the left, set back some way from the beach. Eventually the foot of Bower Hill is reached. There is no problem about walking round the foot of it when the tide is out, and you should be all right, perhaps with a bit of scrambling, even if not. The cliffs have a fairly gentle slope at the base. Not many walk this way and you may well have a very splendid bit of unspoilt coastline to yourself. Halfway along the cliffs a path leading up through the bracken will take you, if you are feeling energetic, to the top for a truly extensive view. Having rounded the Heads of Ayr, Bracken Bay is reached. This is definitely low-tide walking; so use your judgement and turn back if necessary, consoling yourself that, once past the bay, the best of the walk is over.

As you walk around the shore of the bay, you pass a small waterfall splashing over the cliff to your left and reach some trees. The path leads up through a mini-ravine to open fields and the remains of a disused railway on the right. Keep the track on your right until a bridge is reached. Pass under it and climb up left onto the old track itself. The map now shows the path as taking you all the way along the disused track to Alloway and that would have rounded off a splendid walk; unfortunately the track is later wired off and completely overgrown. So, after walking along it some way, turn off right at a camp site and walk up to the main road. Turn left in the direction of Alloway. After passing Butlin's holiday camp on the left, you again reach the old railway track. It is now usable; drop down right to it at the entrance to Burton Farm. To the right is a good view of Newark Hill and the Scottish baronial mansion owned by the whisky distillers, Walkers. Eventually the old railway leads to the bridge over the Doon. To the right there is a pleasant view of the road bridge, partly obscuring the Auld Brig beyond.

Having passed through a quite long and gloomy tunnel, turn right, up the cutting at the far end. There on the right is the ruin and graveyard of the Auld Kirk, where Burns's parents lie buried. Further on you see, perhaps with some astonishment, the copy of a Grecian monument to Lysicrates which serves as the memorial to Burns. The road to its right leads down to the Auld Brig and a very pretty section of the Doon: 'Ye banks and braes o' bonnie Doon, How can ye bloom sae fresh and fair.' Returning to the railway bridge, you pass the Land o' Burns on your right – another temptation. Once over the bridge it is 400yd (366m) to the car park.

57 Sir·Walter·Scott·and· the·Tweed

Time: Up to 3 hours. You may well wish to visit Melrose Abbey (open daily 9.30am to 7pm, except Sundays when it is 2pm to 7pm), the nearby Scottish National Trust Priorwood Garden, which specialises in plants for dried flowers, and of course Abbotsford (open daily 10am to 5pm except Sundays when it is 2pm to 5pm). So the outing can become a full day. Good shoes should be sufficient.

Start and finish: The free car park opposite Melrose Abbey.

Approach: Melrose Abbey is just north of the market square in Melrose and is well signposted.

Attractions: A visit to the area is a 'must' for those interested in the background of the great Scottish novelist and poet. Melrose, the base for the walk, can be regarded as the centre of 'Scott' country. Abbotsford, the Scottish baronial edifice which he built as his dream home, lies a couple of miles (3km) to the west. From his deathbed there he was taken to lie in Dryburgh Abbey 3 miles (5km) to the south-east. The border region figures strongly in his poetry and novels, and the vicinity of Melrose particularly in *The Monastery* – not a particularly successful work. Sir Walter apart, Melrose itself has a proud and ancient history. The Selgovae tribe had their main settlement on the Eildon Hills which dominate the town from the south; the Romans had a signal station there for two hundred years; there are even Arthurian connections. Saints Cuthbert and Boniface both worked at the monastery at Old Melrose, founded in the seventh century by monks from Lindisfarne and 2 miles (3km) to the east of the present abbey. This was established by Cistercians from Rievaulx in Yorkshire some five hundred years later. Much battered by the English over the years, the abbey was finally plundered and closed by Scottish Reformers.

OS sheet: 73

Leaving the rose-brown ruins of the abbey on the right, walk down the B6361 in the direction of Newstead. Pass the motor museum on your left and turn left down a farm track as the road swings sharply right. The track leads past a chain footbridge built in 1826 across the Tweed, and along the bank with a fine view over the weir constructed by the Cistercians to service the abbey with water. It continues up some steps. To your left can be seen the relatively modern parish church; until the beginning of the last century the church was in the ruins of the abbey. On the far side of the river is Gattonside where the Cistercians, always great stockbreeders and gardeners, had orchards and gardens. Gattonside is still noted for its fruit. The path goes straight on past garden walls, to a road.

A kissing-gate to your right leads to a pleasantly open bank along the river. A good ½ mile (.8km) brings you to the bridge over the B6360. Cross it, take the minor road marked Lowood Stables, and when you get to them in another ½ mile turn down sharply right, through the buildings, back to the river. After some pleasant walking along the bank, pass under a disused railway bridge. The track down to the right has its attractions, but it is perhaps better to keep high, passing Tweedbank Farm on your left. Drop down to the right of some broad open grassland, and meet a good track which leads to the busy A6091 bridge. Cross and the path descends almost to the river. To your right is the original Abbot's Ford, just this side of the bridge. Follow the track up left from the ford to reach the car park to Sir Walter's house itself.

Sir Walter bought an old farmhouse, Cartleyhole, with 110 acres (44ha) here in 1811. Since the land had originally belonged to Melrose Abbey and the ford was nearby, he changed the name to Abbotsford. Over the next six years the farm was torn down and replaced by the present mansion, which Sir Walter turned into a real jackdaw's nest of a place. It is full of curious items which he collected: Napoleon's cloak clasp; Mary Queen of Scots' crucifix; Rob Roy's purse; Burns's tumbler and so on. You can see the desk where he wrote most of his novels and which was modelled on a desk which took his fancy when staying with John Morritt at Rokeby Hall. He was hospitable, and entertained many artists and writers, among them Turner who stayed some time in Abbotsford in 1831 working on illustrations for Sir Walter's poems.

Leave the car park by the little lane leading upwards to the left of the telephone booth. After a couple of right-angle turns, pass Bauchlin Cottages on the left. Turn right uphill at the next junction for an excellent view of the heather-covered Eildons. The most northerly hill has traces of the 2,000 year old Selgovae fortress, and it was here that the Romans had their signal station. The middle Eildon is however the highest – just over 1,300ft (396m).

Turn left at the next junction, and the road descends gently downhill, with good views on all sides. Pass Huntlyburn House on your right and, hidden beyond it, Chiefswood, which Sir Walter had built for his daughter Sophia on her marriage. Once under the disused railway bridge, you are in Darnick. Before settling on Abbotsford, Sir Walter tried but failed to buy the old tower here. Turn right past the bridge and follow the road back to Melrose. The town is worth a loiter. It was once a royal burgh and has great traditions. The Freemasons here reckon to have the oldest Lodge north of the border; the locals enthuse over seven-a-side rugby, and The George and Abbotsford is the model for The George in *The Monastery*.

58 CONSTABLE·COUNTRY

Time: Up to 3 hours. But there are plenty of reasons to linger on the way. In particular, the Truman Heavy Horse Centre is open from 10.30am to 4.30pm during the summer, and the Sir Alfred Munnings Art Museum at Castle House, Dedham, is open 6 May to 6 October on Wednesday and Sunday, and during August also on Thursday and Saturday, from 2pm to 5pm. It allows an interesting, comprehensive appreciation of his life and work. Good shoes should be sufficient.

Start and finish: The car park at Flatford.

Approach: Flatford lies just south of East Bergholt, which is about a mile (1.6km) east of the A12 between Colchester and Ipswich.

Attractions: The walk is through countryside and villages which would have been well known to John Constable (1776–1837). He was born at East Bergholt, the son of a prosperous corn merchant who had been fortunate enough to inherit various properties, including the Flatford watermill, from an uncle. He bought the corn mill at Dedham. John was destined to follow him and only with difficulty broke away to follow his artistic ambitions. He went to London when he was twenty, but his links with East Bergholt remained strong. Well into his thirties, he declared his love for Maria Bicknell, the granddaughter of the Reverend Dr Durand Rhudde, Rector of East Bergholt, who resisted the marriage because of John's apparent lack of prospects, for seven years. Recognition indeed came slowly, and substantially in Paris first before London. He was elected a Royal Academician only at the age of fifty-two. In 1836, in keeping with his deep affection for the area, he bought Old House Farm at East Bergholt, but did not live to enjoy it.

Sir Alfred Munnings (1878–1959) bought Castle House at Dedham in 1919 and lived there for the remainder of his life. He is particularly remembered for his equestrian pictures and for the pungent views on some aspects of modern art which he expressed when President of the Royal Academy. It was his wish that the house and its collection should be left to the nation.

OS sheets: 168 and 155

From the car park, walk to Flatford Mill and Willy Lott's cottage. Neither can be visited, since they are occupied by the Flatford Mill Field Centre, which has research facilities and runs courses in the field sciences and other subjects such as art and photography. The view is, of course, immortalised by Constable. Return to Bridge Cottage, now owned by the National Trust, and turn left to cross the bridge over the Stour. Turn left along the bank, past Flatford Lock. Descend right from the far end of the concrete sluice, then immediately left over a concrete cattle bridge. Half-right across a field leads to a concrete farm

Willy Lott's cottage at Flatford (Bob Brash)

track. Pass the farm buildings on the right and turn through a gate into a lane which leads to Manningtree Road. Turn left, and where the road bears left take a good track to the right across fields to East Lane. Turn right on the road, and shortly to the left pass the Truman Heavy Horse Centre. At the end of the road, on the left, stands Castle House, the Sir Alfred Munnings Art Museum.

Cross the road ahead half-right to Cooper's Lane, and turn down the track on the right between two cottages. This leads to stables and the path goes off to the right over a stile. Continue down the meadow, with the stable on your left to a stile and footbridge, then half-right across a field to further stiles and kissing-gates until you reach the Duchy playing fields at Dedham. There is a fine weaver's house with a splendid courtyard to your right. Dedham church, St Mary's, facing, is a fine, well-proportioned edifice, dating back to the fifteenth century and well worth a visit. The Pilgrim Fathers are commemorated in a pew dedicated to the people of Dedham, Massachusetts in the United States. The timber roof is excellent and the richly decorated stonework beneath the tower is superb. Dedham itself enjoys a charming variety of architectural styles, and has won the Essex best-kept-village trophy on several occasions. You may, therefore, like to wander up and down the High Street, and perhaps drop into the Arts and Crafts Centre, an interesting, ambitious, development of a church building. Constable knew Dedham well; he went to Dedham Grammar School.

Weaver's house at Dedham (Bob Brash)

Walk down Mill Lane, opposite the church, to the bridge across the Stour. Pass Dedham Mill, now being converted to private dwellings, on your left. Once over the Stour, turn right along its bank. The river makes a sharp left turn, and, where it veers right again, leave it left up a good track which leads to a planked bridge. Take the left fork in the track and walk up to the East Bergholt–Flatford road. Turn left along the road to reach St Mary's, built between 1350 and 1550, with its unfinished tower and extraordinary bell cage at the rear. John Constable's parents lie in the churchyard, and there are memorials to Maria, his wife, and her grandfather, the formidable Dr Rhudde.

Leave the church on your right, and enter the village itself. A plaque on the wall, right, shows where John Constable was born. The small shop by the gate belonged to John Dunthorne, Constable's life-long friend who did much to arouse his youthful artistic talent. Further along, on the other side of the road, is the Stour Garden Centre, the grounds in fact of the late Randolph Churchill's home. Continue up Gaston Street and turn right into Chaplin Road. At the first little cul de sac to the right there is a good path, left, which leads across fields, with excellent views of 'Constable' country to the right, to Gandish Road. Here, turn left to Burnt Oak Corner and straight on, along Flatford Lane, back to the car park.

59 COTMAN·AND·THE·GRETA

Time: Up to 4 hours. Boots are necessary. The path becomes quite rocky at times.

Start and finish: The Dairy Bridge over the Greta.

Approach: The bridge is just south off the A66, south-east of Barnard Castle in County Durham. It should not be too difficult to park along the road or near the Morritt Arms Hotel.

Attractions: This deserves to become a classic river ramble. The walk is along both sides of the River Greta, through Brignall Banks and down to the confluence of the Greta and the River Tees. It is an area of great beauty and of especial interest to the field naturalist. Further, it is steeped in history. The Dairy Bridge stands at a river crossing much used since Roman times, and protected then by a fort. The bridge was built in 1773 by John Morritt, owner of nearby Rokeby Hall. His son, John, was a cultured patron of the arts. He tried to acquire some of the Parthenon marbles and in 1814 bought the 'Venus' by Velasquez, still known as the 'Rokeby Venus'. He counted Sir Walter Scott among his many friends and guests and the area inspired Scott's *The Outlaw*: 'O Brignall Banks are wild and fair, and Greta Woods are green . . .' John Sell Cotman, introduced to Morritt by the Cholmeley family of Bransby Hall near York, came to Rokeby Hall in 1805. He moved quickly to one of the several coaching inns by the bridge, and was inspired to paint some of his finest watercolours, paintings which count among the greatest in our British artistic heritage. The most famous, that of Greta Bridge itself, is in the British Museum. Some regard Cotman as our finest watercolourist.

OS sheet: 92

Just over the bridge, in the direction of the Morritt Arms Hotel, climb over the wall on your left at a footpath sign; there are obliging stone steps on the other side. To the right are the grass-covered ramparts of the Roman fort, occupied from the second to fourth century and covering a 2½ acre (1ha) rectangle. To the left are the brown waters of the Greta, often obscured by trees. Unfortunately this section is private and some scenes used by Cotman, notably the Devil's Elbow and the Scotchman's Stone, are not accessible without permission. There are fine views on the right and after a time Brignall church becomes visible in the distance. The wood clears on the left and you drop down to the river and the romantic ruin of old St Mary's Church. It was presumably built here to be out of the way of northern marauders, and was abandoned in last century for the church on the hill. The 'new' St Mary's was built in 1833–4, but burials continued in the graveyard by the river for another fifty years.

A stile leads back into self-regenerating woodland of considerable interest to the naturalist; then it's out into the open again with a splendid sweep of hill coming down to the river. The walk gradually becomes hemmed in by cliffs which rise to 20 and 30ft (6 and 9m). A sweep up a wooded slope leads to a stile and open fields with Moor House Farm on the right. The path leads onto a macadam farm track which runs down left to the river again, with fine views across the valley to Barningham Moor. At the bottom, Brignall Mill is reached, a Grade 2 listed property which still retains the old mill machinery. Walk left around the mill and onto the steel footbridge. There are roughish sections ahead and you may prefer at this stage to retrace your steps.

Over the bridge, turn left, and after ½ mile (.8km) a wooden bridge is reached crossing a small tributary from the right. Over it, turn up right and the path brings you to open fields and, bearing left, to the remains of Scargill Castle – not much more than a fifteenth-century gatehouse with its archway blocked up. Turn left along the road; there are fine views. Drop down into the wooded valley of the Gilbeck. The path now goes off left before the bridge and roughly halfway up the slope from the stream. It can be difficult to find. Make your way down to the confluence with the Greta and cross the Gilbeck. The path, again at times obscure, works its way half-right up the wooded slope and runs some yards below the fence. Eventually pass a barn in the field on your right and, after walking through a fine stand of pine, cross a gate into an open field, with the path running to the left of Crook's House. A farm track leads onto the road at Wilson House. Continue by road back to the Greta bridge.

The Gatehouse – all that remains of Scargill Castle

Just before the Dairy Bridge on the right there is a stone stile in the wall. The field here gives the best view back to the bridge and you may judge the artistic licence (or inspiration) which Cotman exercised. The bridge very much reflects its architectural period; it was built in 1773, at a cost of £850. It has a graceful single arch of 80ft (24m) with a balustraded parapet. Cotman makes it seem much wider, and he also widens the river and rearranges the rocks, clearly interested in developing a pattern of colours and shapes.

The path goes under the A66 bridge and to the right of the woods on the skyline. Just over the summit, leave the wall on your left and continue straight on following the line of some trees to a track which sweeps left down to and around Mortham Tower, a beautiful old house with a fourteenth-century peel tower. The driveway leads down to a bridge over the Greta and on to the confluence with the Tees – a famous beauty spot, much painted by Cotman and others.

Again you may wish to retrace your steps, for the route forwards follows the road around the Rokeby Estate. There are only meagre glimpses of the Palladian structure built in the 1720s by Sir Thomas Robinson, son-in-law of the Duke of Carlisle. When you reach the A66, cross over. After 100yd (90m) as you walk left along it, there are steps up right to the old road, which leads back to the Dairy Bridge.

60 STANLEY·SPENCER·AND· COOKHAM

Time: Allow 3 to 3½ hours. If that is too much, halve the walk by joining it at Terry's Lane: (see page 234) reached by walking down High Street, past the War Memorial and on over the causeway for a further 400yd (366m). You may wish to start with a visit to the Stanley Spencer Gallery, open from Easter to October daily from 10.30am to 1pm and 2pm to 6pm and in the winter on Saturday and Sunday from 11am to 1pm and 2pm to 5pm. Apart from seeing a selection of his art, you learn something of the topography which dictated his almost obsessional link with Cookham. Good shoes should be quite sufficient.

Start and finish: The public car park at Cookham.

Approach: Cookham lies just north of Maidenhead. If you take the A4094 from Maidenhead to Cookham, the car park is on the left, just before the Stanley Spencer Gallery and High Street.

Attractions: Cookham is a pleasant village, largely preserved from development by its surrounding commons. Apart from the greatly increased traffic, it must still be much as it was in Stanley Spencer's day. He lived there for all but nineteen of his sixty-eight years (1891–1959). He loved the place and used its scenes and people as materials for his religious and other fantasies. Although his talent was recognised early, while he was still a student at the Slade, he remained throughout his life rather down at heel and frequently short of money. The tattered old pram which he used to carry his materials, on show at the Gallery, is typical of the man. Small, and by nature frugal and something of a recluse, he expressed his strength of feeling not only in his paintings but in voluminous private writing. As a result, his life and art are particularly well documented; the setting for each of his paintings is more or less known. The most important single commission in his life was the interior of the Burghclere Chapel, some 40 miles (64km) west of Cookham, devoted to his army experience in Macedonia in World War I. But Cookham is the backdrop for much of the work of this very great British artist.

OS sheet: 175

After leaving the Gallery, which in earlier days was the Wesleyan Chapel where Stanley Spencer's mother used to worship, stroll down High Street. A few houses down on the left is Lindworth, where he settled for some years from 1932. Further on to the left is Fernlea, where he was born and spent his final months before dying of cancer at the Canadian War Memorial Hospital at nearby Cliveden. Fernlea appears in his 'Christ Carrying the Cross', and

Holy Trinity Church, Cookham (Bob Brash)

the little passage between it and The Nest is the scene for his 'St Francis and the Birds', with his father in his dressing-gown representing the saint. The War Memorial at the end of High Street appears in two important paintings – the 'Unveiling of the War Memorial' and 'Village in Heaven'. It is intriguing to see how the vision of the painter transmutes the ordinary.

Returning to the Gallery, turn right down Sutton Road and then shortly left into the quiet of Mill Lane. At a 'private' road sign, take the footpath, right, to the Thames. The path turns right along the bank. This is one of the best stretches of the river, and only approachable on land by path. Opposite are the magnificent woods of Cliveden, given to the National Trust in 1942 by Lord Astor; Stanley Spencer once dined there with Lord Astor with his pyjamas under his dinner suit.

Walk along the bank for a mile (1.6km) and, just after a little bridge, turn right before the first house into a path which leads to Islet Road. Continue along this, past pleasant suburban houses and turn left at Sheephouse Farm. This is the most tedious part of the walk. Keep on and then turn right into Summerleaze Road. Where it makes a sharp left, take the signposted path to the left of the gravel works. Cross a footpath over a stream, continue over the field, over a track and again over the field on the marked path.

Then make a somewhat zigzag course: left at the triple signpost, right at the next post, with the water on your left; right away from the water at the next post and left along the track. Where the track bears left, continue straight ahead, with the hedge on your right. Cross the brook on your right and take the stile immediately left. Ignore the stile to your left and continue straight over the field to a stile at the opposite end. It is then a straight walk along the edge of fields, some of them covered with poppies at the end of June. Widbrook Common stretches away on your right. It is richly treed, lush arable, Thames flat land. After half a mile (.8km) you come to the Cookham–Cookham Rise road, with Moor Hall, the headquarters of the Institute of Marketing a little further on to your left.

Cross the road and turn up Terry's Lane. Just past the last house on the left, there is a short cut across the field. At the top cross the road and take the track opposite, leading to a stile and a path along the top of the golf course. There is a splendid view across the Thames to the Cliveden woods. Cross the bridge over the railway and continue straight on over the fairways to the house seen on the skyline. Here, at the top of the hill, cross two stiles and take the path signposted right. This leads to National Trust land and a fine view over the Thames, somewhat spoilt by gravel works. You can drop down the quite steep hill before you to the stile seen below. There is an easier, but difficult to find, diagonal route down to the right.

Continue on past the stile until you turn right at some riverside bungalows and again reach the bank of the Thames. Keep firmly along the bank with first Cockmarsh and its tumuli, then houses and a pub, on your right, until you reach Cookham church and the bridge. These were the scenes for some of Spencer's most famous paintings. Swan upping, directed by the Queen's Swan Keeper and Waterman and carried out by the City Companies of Dyers and Vintners, takes place here every year in July and was recorded in one of his early canvases. His regatta series, and especially the immense unfinished 'Christ Preaching at Cookham Regatta' on view at the Gallery, are all placed here. Walk through Holy Trinity churchyard; the church, with its twelfth-century nave is well worth a visit. But again it is all commemorated by Stanley Spencer, notably in his 'The Resurrection, Cookham', which can be seen at the Tate Gallery. From the churchyard it is a short walk back to the Gallery and the car park.

61 Petworth·Turner·and· Ivon·Hitchens

Time: Up to 3 hours, with extra for a visit to Petworth House, owned by the National Trust and one of the loveliest great estates south of London. The opening hours are 2pm to 6pm on Wednesday, Thursday, Saturday and Sunday. Good shoes should be sufficient.

Start and finish: The public car park at Petworth.

Approach: Petworth stands on the junction of A272 and A285, just north of the River Rother. The car park is well indicated as you enter the town.

Attractions: The walk goes from Petworth, which has strongish Turner associations, across the River Rother to Lavington Common, where Ivon Hitchens made his home early in World War II. Turner first came to Petworth in 1809, and became a frequent visitor after the death of his father. A lonely bachelor, he enjoyed the warmth and gaiety of Petworth House under its amiable owner, George O'Brien, third Earl of Egremont. The earl, a great patron of the arts, had a happy if complex life. Rumour had it that he fathered no less than forty-three children and that most of them lived at Petworth. He married his wife only after she had had six children. As a result of the friendship with Turner, numbers of the latter's paintings can be seen in the

Rotherbridge Farm near Petworth (Bob Brash)

very fine art collection. Ivon Hitchens (1893–1979) was influenced by Turner in his early days, and like Turner developed his own very personal approach to landscape art. From 1940 he remained largely secluded at his house, Greenleaves, tucked away on Lavington Common. The richness and colours of the local landscape were main ingredients in his artistic abstractions.

OS sheet: 197

Start or finish the walk by a stroll around Petworth. It is a charming small country town, filled with antique shops. Perhaps walk up Lombard Street to the much reconstructed St Mary's Church. In it, in the north-west corner, is a statue of the third earl. Don't be put off by the rather muddled aspect of Petworth House from this angle: it well repays a visit.

From the car park make your way to the A272 in the direction of Midhurst. Just past Cricket Lodge, one of the entrances to Petworth Park, on the right, turn left onto a public footpath leading across a broad field to a large coppice. There is a good view across the shallow Rother valley to the South Downs beyond. Bear right at the coppice, and follow the track as it bends left. Turn right at a cottage and follow the path to Rotherbridge Farm. Do not take the bridge across the river, but rather the track to the right. It leads through three gates to another footbridge. Turn left along the far bank and, where the river bears left, turn up right along a fence. This takes you across a disused railway bridge, into woods and along the edge of a field, to a good track where you turn right. Pass Cathanger Farm on your right and to the left are the woods and bracken of Lavington Common.

Turn left when at the crossroads and walk to the National Trust car park on the left. Ivon Hitchens's old house is further on, on the right-hand side, really hidden in the woods just beyond the entrance to Westerlands Stud – it is private. Take the path to the right of the car park. This leads straight on to a splendid heather and pine walk over Lavington and Duncton Commons, until the A285 is met at Heathend. Turn left along it, cross the bridge over the disused railway track and turn down a quiet country lane, past Kilsham Farm on the left and back to the Rother at Rotherbridge Farm. Leaving the farm on the left, take the path left into a shady cleft cut out of the rock. This leads up to a sandy track, turn right and follow the track straight on leaving the coppice on your right. This leads back to the A285. From here it is a short walk left back to the car park.

Bradgate House and Park looking north, Charnwood Forest (Bradgate Park Trust) (*see* page 332) *Pencaithland churchyard* (Geoffrey N. Wright) (*see* page 265)

LOWLANDS

It was that princely yet most mystical of walkers, Richard Jefferies, who wrote, 'They only know a country who are acquainted with its footpaths. By the roads, indeed, the outside may be seen, but the footpaths go through the heart of the land.' This is as true now as it was a century and more ago when Jefferies found beauty, peace and wonder in the quiet landscapes around his Wiltshire home, when each walk brought 'a fresh footpath, a fresh flower, a fresh delight'.

Statistically, lowland landscapes cover over half of England, and within this area there must be a high proportion of the 120,000 miles (over 193,000km) of public rights of way. Upland paths, probably because of their more dramatic and challenging nature, together with some of the newly created long-distance footpaths, may attract more attention; but it is the thousands of miles of lowland footpaths which have the deeper roots, bearing the imprint – or footprints – of generations of the common man. Prior to this century they were important means of communication linking farm to hamlet, hamlet to village, village to market town; they led to the church, the mill, the inn, the crossroads, the bridge over the stream – to any place regularly visited by country dwellers. Now they are rarely visited by either town or country people.

These historic footpaths of lowland country may not present the hairy-chested challenge of high places, but they offer rewards every bit as satisfying, albeit in a different key. On the purely physical level they are, for the most part, less demanding in having considerably fewer ups and downs. Along the lowland paths you are less likely to have to resort to using a compass when the clouds come down, although you should still carry one for when you are lost in a wood, or are confronted by fields of corn, one no different from another, and with no visible sign of a footpath.

While you may find shoes or trainers suffice as footwear, I would still advise comfortable walking boots for the better protection of the ankles. Shorts are unsuitable for lowland walking for it is on such walks that you discover the hostility of vegetation – bramble and briar, nettle and thistle – as well as the too-frequent habit of some farmers and landowners to resort to barbed wire and the occasional electric fence across a path.

Tree felling in the New Forest (Leigh Hatts) (*see* page 342)
Old Scotney Castle, Kent (Geoffrey N. Wright) (*see* page 245)

Usually, but not always, I have walked alone, happy with the intimate landscapes of fields and copses, quiet streams and welcoming stiles which, no matter how rustic and shaky, are such reassuring pointers on the way. The mixed and varied landscapes have presented new scenes every few hundred yards, each with its new sights and sensations. Because on a lowland path there is a degree less need to concentrate on every footstep, there is more scope for looking around, observing, listening. Wayside flowers and butterflies, bird song, rustle of leaves, kiss of grass walked through, wind-waved corn, bare winter branches against the sky, clouds which mimic mountains on far horizons. Indeed, skies provide the drama on many lowland walks.

Lowland walking, be it through pastoral or arable landscape, can be incredibly lonely. Be prepared not to meet another human soul along your way. Nor, except at certain times and seasons, are you likely to meet anyone working in the fields with whom to exchange a word. Any farm worker seen will probably be on a distant tractor. Even the villages and hamlets are quiet; only at weekends and during school holidays are there signs of life. I have rarely seen village children on country paths. Do they now mostly learn about wildlife only 'from the box'? Nor have I met country folk walking on the paths of their parish, unless exercising their dogs.

Obviously, therefore, a vast number of paths are little used. Being little used they become overgrown or obstructed, and when that happens they are likely to be used even less. Although the Countryside Commission has designated 'recreational paths', identifying a few here and there, surely all country footpaths are recreational, their quiet delights awaiting exploration and rediscovery by walkers sharing Jefferies' belief that, 'there never was a footpath yet which did not pass something of interest'. But it was the Northamptonshire poet John Clare who best expressed the joy of lowland walking:

> Making oft remarking stops
> Watching tiny nameless things.

62	Somerset Levels	7 miles (11km)
63	Lamberhurst, Kent	5 miles (8km)
64	Frensham Little Pond and the Devil's Jumps, Surrey	7 miles (11km)
65	Midhurst and Heyshott, West Sussex	6 miles (9.6km)
66	Elmley Castle and Bredon Hill, Hereford and Worcester	6 miles (9.6km)
67	Derwent Valley, Causey Arch and Tanfield, Tyne and Wear/County Durham	9 miles (14km)
68	Gipping Valley, Suffolk	7 miles (11km)
69	Eden Valley, Cumbria	8½ miles (14km)
70	East Lothian, Lothian	10 miles (16km) or less

Derwent Valley, the old railway track (Geoffrey N. Wright) (*see* page 257)

62 SOMERSET·LEVELS

Time: Some 3 or 3½ hours should be sufficient.

Start and finish: The bridge over the Westport Canal near the village of Hambridge.

Approach: The village of Hambridge is on the B3168 between Ilminster and Langport. From it, take the lane signposted to Kingsbury Episcopi and Martock. In a few hundred yards there is plenty of room to park by the bridge over the Westport Canal. This canal was opened in 1840 as part of the Parrett Navigation, largely to carry goods en route from Dorset to the Bristol Channel. By 1880 it was disused.

Attractions: There are few areas in Britain where one can walk 7 miles (11km) without crossing a contour line. This walk in deepest Somerset does that, and succeeds in having great charm and interest without dependence on beauty spots or any of the pegs on which a walk is usually hung.

OS sheet: 193

Cross the stile on the north side of the road, to walk along the towpath of this delightful canal arm. Rural stretches of canals have great appeal; they are quiet, secretive, their graceful curves lend surprise, and the inherence of vegetation and overhanging trees pleases with its intimacy. Moorhens jerk earnestly along, an indignant heron springs into flight, while all around is a dazzle of azure dragonflies.

Having passed two picturesque bridges in about a mile (1.6km), the canal's confluence with the River Isle is reached. In comparison with the usually turbid waters of lowland Somerset, this bonny river is almost limpid, and supports a fine crop of waterlilies. Maintain your course down its right bank. If the field you circumvent has been tilled, vast quantities of freshwater mussel shells will have been revealed. Presently a lane is reached where you climb the stile, cross the bridge and follow the left bank along a good hard track. Here you suddenly realise that the river on your right is higher than the South Moor to your left, always a rather disturbing thought. A row of willows fringing the river gives a Constable air to the scene, while cattle keeping cool in the water epitomise summer in deep England. Below is a small rhine, or ditch, which is richer in plant and insect life than the main river.

Presently, reach a bridge over the river, leading to an electric sluice set among the usual trees planted by public bodies to disguise the cubic joys of municipal architecture; nothing wrong with the trees themselves, they just have a suburban air. Walk across the sluice, to attain the left bank of the River Parrett. This point, where Isle and Parrett meet, demonstrates how much toil has gone into taming these lowland rivers; the high banks and

Westport Canal near Hambridge (Geoffrey N. Wright)

levées, the old sluices, having been hard work to construct. Also, the current is faster here, encouraging different species of flora and fauna. Across the levels to the north stands Muchelney church; now the skies seem bigger, there is a growing impression of distance and flatness.

As you now stride out, along the dyke which is the west bank of the Parrett, the eminence of Hamdon Hill rises directly ahead. This is pleasant, unhindered walking, the turf kept short by sheep, and the views kept long by the slight elevation above the surrounding country. At this low level a distant feature may be a mere 2 miles (3km) away, yet appear to be twice that; such tricks of perspective induce a mood of imagination rather than wonder.

At length, however, the hamlet of Thorney is reached, where you turn right on arrival at the road, past Thorney Manor. This is a pleasant, if unremarkable community; there are nicely proportioned houses, and the chirp of sparrows is restful in the sunny somnolence. After ¼ mile (.4km), turn right along a 'drove' or lane, this being the second to have branched off. Heavy rain and heavy tractors can render this lane rather sticky.

As is commonly the case on drained erstwhile marshland, the trackways over this moor are straight, and the next mile (1.6km) is just that. This is not synonymous with lack of interest; there is much to observe, notably for the botanist. The bird of these moors, the lapwing, with its joyous flight and unfettered cries is the very spirit of space and fresh air. The little rhines with their yellow flags and sedges, the meadow and grazing land, the little osier copses, all provide subtly different habitats to please different birds.

At length reach a T-junction of earthy tracks; turn left, and for ⅓ mile (.5km) walk towards the higher land that carries the orchards of Lambrook. Then turn right along another drove, which this time has hedges. This is a lovely ½ mile (.8km), the way becoming progressively overgrown with all the luxuriance of vegetation of which Somerset in summer is capable. Huge creamy heads of meadowsweet, heady scented, tend to shade the red campion, later to be out-topped by teasels. There is all the encouragement you need to pause before reaching the road, cars and modern life; pause, savour the peace, the avid growth about you, the rank real smell of wild plants and the incredible variety and multitude of insects.

Distant prospects are denied by trees, so naturally the immediate scene becomes more vivid. Encouraged by the song of reed buntings, and maybe the splash and quack of duck taking flight, there is no difficulty in feeling that little has changed here since the Dark Ages. When you debouch upon the metalled road, and a car passes, the shock is quite real.

The walk is now nearly completed; on turning right at the road, a few minutes along its willow-bordered easiness brings you to the canal bridge, and your vehicle in its ample parking space. A fitting conclusion is to enjoy a cup of tea sitting by the tranquil canal, savouring the episodes of a most delightful ramble.

63 LAMBERHURST

Time: Allow 2 to 3 hours as there are hilly sections and the way can be muddy in places.
Start and finish: Lamberhurst, where there is a car park behind the Chequers Inn.
Approach: Lamberhurst is on the A21, east of Tunbridge Wells.
Attractions: This fine walk is through various types of man-made Wealden landscape, with the option of seeing a picturesque garden of the 1840s.
OS sheet: 188

The gentle green-banked valley of the River Teise washes past Lamberhurst, where even the busy A21 does not wholly mar the charms of a delightful village whose main street is lined with tiled and weather-boarded Wealden houses, as well as a few fine half-timbered ones. Leave its exploration until after the walk which, starting from the car park, makes its way eastwards across a cricket pitch and football field towards quiet farmland beyond a gap in a hedge. Cross a stile in the next field-corner and head obliquely for the lower corner of an oakwood, where a good path climbs quite steeply by the left side of the wood to the corner of a field at the top.

A kissing-gate by an oak should merit appropriate action as you pause and look northwards across the gentle valley towards Lamberhurst church and Court Lodge nearby. This point will be crossed again on the return part of the walk. Now, however, go through the gate, encouraged by a sign 'To Kilndown and Lamberhurst Down'. Go diagonally across a knoll crowned by Scots pines, a few oaks and a pheasant-rearing pen, to a stile, then follow a field boundary on the left down the hill to a wooden gate at a road. Turn left along this road and in 80yd (73m) cross a waymarked stile on the right onto a pleasant path, passing more Scots pines, to a footbridge across a small stream which is really the River Bewl. Continue, over stiles, into the wood ahead, and follow the main path winding upwards through hazel, birch and oak with plenty of evidence of coppicing (timber for Wealden iron-furnaces, perhaps) and the joy, in season, of bracken, foxgloves and bluebells. The darkening track through mature trees at the top of the wood offers welcome shade on a warm day, but in the open again the way becomes steeper.

Turn left along the cart track at the top (FP sign on sawn trunk) and right on the road towards the church at Kilndown, whose name recalls the old industry of the area. The Globe and Rainbow inn nearby provides bar snacks, and a seat and table by the village pond and hall are quite welcome after an hour's walking and climbing. Retracing steps slightly, turn along the lane signposted 'Public Footpath to Lamberhurst and Scotney Castle'; the familiar oak-leaves logo being a reminder that all land around here is part of the National Trust's Scotney Castle Estate. Hence the good identification of paths and provision of stiles.

A dark, shady track leads south-westwards for almost a mile (1.6km), one glorious stretch through a glade of beechen green eventually bending right and losing height, becoming more muddy, and passing an area where recent felling has cleared the trees. Beyond a clearing, with the track firm and stony, and flanked by rhododendrons, turn right at a cross-track – a waymarked sawn trunk indicating the way to Lamberhurst. After entering parkland at a white gate, with splendid oaks, a copper beech and a monkey puzzle, the track recrosses the River Bewl and passes through another white gate.

Ignore the route swinging right, ahead, but bear left between trees, climbing gently across parkland (signposted Footpath) to a small iron gate on the edge of woodland, above and to the north-west. This gives access to Scotney Castle drive, so if it is intended to visit Scotney Castle's famous, romantic, early Victorian landscaped gardens, together with the small, ruined four-

Looking across the River Teise Valley to St Mary's Church (Geoffrey N. Wright)

teenth-century moated castle, turn right along the drive to the entrance (National Trust: admission fee. Open April to October, afternoons except Monday and Tuesday.) Otherwise, cross the road, climb steps into more woodland, and pass a line of chestnuts on the brow of the next clearing. The crest ahead with its Scots pines, oaks and pheasant-pen, is recognised from earlier in the walk.

So it is back to the kissing-gate, this time continuing ahead by a hedgerow, descending to a gate and slanting left down the hill to the River Teise, while aiming steadily for the church on the far side of the valley. Cross two foot-bridges in quick succession and climb towards the church, a nineteenth-century restoration of a fourteenth-century building, with memorials to the Hussey family of Scotney Castle. A tombstone in the churchyard com-memorates a couple aged 96 and 101, with the apparently inappropriate inscription: 'Surely, I come quickly.'

From the porch, leave the churchyard and cross the golf course, walking westwards to the main road where a raised path on the left keeps you a little away from the traffic noise as you descend to the welcoming warmth of red-tiled houses and the car park behind the Chequers.

64 FRENSHAM·LITTLE·POND· AND·THE·DEVIL'S·JUMPS

Time: Allow 3 to 4 hours. This is riding country; the bridleways are extensively used, but being sandy are clean for walking, though progress along them is necessarily slower than on firmer paths.

Start and finish: The National Trust car park at Frensham Little Pond.

Approach: The starting point is 1 mile (1.6km) east of the Farnham–Hindhead road immediately south of Millbridge.

Attractions: This walk is largely over sandy heathlands with rewarding views. It continues over Kettlebury and Yagden hills to Stockbridge Pond and Tilford, with riverside and woodland to finish. There are no stiles and the steep path up the Devil's Jumps can be avoided.

OS sheet: 186

From the car park aim for the north-eastern corner of pinewood-girdled Frensham Little Pond (National Trust), and follow the path down its eastern edge. In a few hundred yards, where the way forks, keep to the lakeside path, now much narrower. Beyond the lake's southern limit, continue southwards between wire fences, with a field on the left and woods on the right. In about ½ mile (.8km), go over a cross-track and almost immediately turn right onto a bridleway near a house. At a minor road turn left, and in a few yards, opposite another house, take another bridleway which leads onto heathland.

Ahead, the three peaks of the Devil's Jumps command the immediate skyline – an odd-looking trio associated with legends of Thor and the Devil. Cobbett likened them to 'three rather squat sugar-loaves'; after climbing them you may be less sweetly disposed. Before them, however, the path reaches a small, secluded lake reflecting its attendant pines and rhododendrons; a short detour along a lakeside path is worth the small effort involved, and soon the original wide sandy track is regained. When this reaches a cross-track, the way to the highest of the Devil's Jumps goes straight ahead, and a short, steep climb takes you, panting slightly, to the crest and its sweeping panorama from Hindhead to the Hog's Back. Descend the same way, and turn right on the cross-track.

If the climb is to be avoided, turn left on the cross-track, heading eastwards on a good bridleway with two skyline houses a useful guide. The track does not go to them but emerges, after a short climb, onto the minor road at Rushmoor. Turn left (northwards) by the Post Office and bus stop, and opposite a garage take the track by a Ministry of Defence notice, leading to Hankley Common. Cross a small stream, pass a large clearing beneath tele-

Frensham Little Pond (John Whatmore)

graph wires, and take a wide path which leads uphill to pine trees, across a small depression, and up to the crest of Kettlebury Hill ahead. This is the last climb of this walk, and an excellent place for a rest, for views, and for the silence of surrounding heathland. All this is part of Hankley Common, 745 acres (300ha) of largely scrubland on the coarse sands of the Lower Greensand.

Turn left on Kettlebury Hill to make good progress northwards, keeping right at a fork near a pillbox. After a mile (1.6km) along this splendid upland ridge, with trees to the left and open views to the right, bear left at a meeting of tracks strangely called the Lion's Mouth, and lose height. At the bottom of the slope continue between wire fences, forking left again towards a golf course. At a wooden hut near the eleventh tee, the path turns right along the foot of Yagden Hill, with the golf course on the left beyond gorse and young birches. At a three-way fork keep left, descending slightly, over a cross-track, left again and down to Stockbridge Pond and its small car park. A lane by the pond takes you to the road a short way south of Tilford.

Cricket on the village green at Tilford with the Barley Mow beyond

Immediately opposite is the most direct route back to Frensham Little Pond, 1¼ miles (2km) away; but far more worthwhile, and only about a mile (1.6km) further, is a visit to Tilford and a short stretch of riverside as contrast after all the sandy heathland.

Turn northwards and follow the road into Tilford, which is far more village green than village, and all the better for it. The triangular green slopes down to the River Wey, whose two arms meet in the short distance between two medieval bridges probably built by the monks of Waverley Abbey. Somewhat older is the great tree known as the King's Oak at the northern corner of the green; its 26ft (8m) girth impressed Cobbett no end. The Barley Mow, of about 1700, is a famous focal point and worthy pub; but on summer Saturdays even it plays second fiddle to cricket on the famous green. What other village team enjoys a pavilion (really the village institute) designed by Lutyens in 1893?

Before the bridge, beyond the north-west corner of the green, turn left onto a public footpath, passing delightful Malt House, and continuing along a grassy path towards the river. This track soon enters a wood where it eventually joins a track from the left and, after a paddock and a group of buildings, swings left and quickly right, joining the previously mentioned bridleway. Then it's over a small watersplash, back to Frensham car park.

65 MIDHURST·AND·HEYSHOTT

Time: 3 hours should be ample for this ramble over pasture and arable, wood-lands and heath along the scarp-foot zone below the South Downs.

Start and finish: Midhurst – the public car park off North Street.

Approach: Midhurst is on the A286 Chichester–Haslemere road, 12 miles (19km) north of Chichester.

Attractions: Few walks start with such an historic highlight as this, for the impressive ruins of Cowdray House exercise an almost magnetic attraction at the end of the causeway running eastwards from the car park. Take your fill of their consistent Tudor dignity, the outcome of sixty years of building under three owners between 1495 and 1540.

OS sheet: 197

From the ruins of Cowdray House turn right along a riverside path and sub-sequently left at a public footpath sign between two buildings, over a small bridge, then climb up the side of a field with a ditch and trees on the right. At the top of the pasture is a stile – a place from which to look back and appreciate the widening, civilised landscapes of the gentle Rother valley to the north.

Among the group of farm buildings ahead is a particularly good granary, two-storeyed, of mellow brick and tile. Cross a stile to the right of the build-ings, and join a road downhill to Coster's Cottages at the north-eastern end of West Lavington. The way ahead is signposted 'Bridle Path to Heyshott, Graffham', and is a good track by a stream. About 20yd (18m) before this track turns sharp right, look for a shady bridlepath cutting steeply up the hill on the left, which reveals itself as a hoof-pitted hollow way, muddy and slippery in wet weather. Over the crest it descends less steeply, with views opening out southwards to the Downs, where the chalk-pit above Cocking is particularly prominent.

After joining an obvious bridleway coming from the left, turn right to follow a dusty, sandy track between hedges, with pastures each side and open views. At a T-junction turn right onto another good bridleway, crossing the disused Midhurst–Pulborough railway and its steep-sided cutting, and enter-ing conifer woodland. Ignore the temptation of a direct course ahead in favour of another signposted bridleway immediately branching off to the left. Along this, spruce eventually yields to young oak and silver birch. Continue across all subsequent tracks, including a fire-break beneath electricity power-lines, across a small stream, and emerge on the more open landscapes of Ambersham Common, characterised by sandy heath with gorse, heather, bracken, birch and a few pines. Although only about 200ft (60m) high, the

Cowdray House (Geoffrey N. Wright)

views southwards to the Downs and northwards towards Midhurst and the wooded hills beyond, embrace within a small compass the deep-loved essence of Sussex landscape. Rising slightly, the track continues south-eastwards to a road. Turn left, and at the crossroads in 200yd (183m) turn right and follow this road southwards past Hoyle, and in one mile (1.6km) turn very sharp right into Heyshott village.

Flint and brick, and a little half-timbering, in unspectacular harmony, grouped around a humble thirteenth-century church, make up Heyshott, birthplace of that uncompromising Victorian free-trader, Richard Cobden. With your back to the South Downs, follow the road northwards for ½ mile (.8km) to Heyshott Green, with its reedy pond, spacious cricket pitch and houses hiding between well-kept hedges. Continue over the crossroads, north-westwards, to a signpost 'Footpath to Midhurst'. Bear left at a group of houses and keep left at a modern barn, looking for a wooden stile, with the path beyond crossing a meadow diagonally to a distant wooden gate. Through

this, an inviting grassy path with a hedge on the left and a fence on the right leads towards a beechwood on the hill ahead.

These are landscapes without drama; even under the brightest sun, colours are muted and soft, and a backwards glance to the Downs confirms their calm, cloud-dappled contours. Ahead, the path leads to the wood, where beech gives way to oak and the dull, dark leaves of rhododendrons, gloomy for so much of the year. Emerging at the car park for Duncton House, continue down the drive which gradually starts to climb. At the top of the hill by Pendean Lodge at a road junction, a narrow footpath straight ahead identified by a sign adjoining a small iron gate, leads once more into woodland, but soon joins a road near the Royal Oak inn. Traffic noises indicate the presence of a main road 100yd (90m) away on the far side of the pub, and a path goes off to the left past the inn, entering woodland, and soon emerging at the A286. Turn right down the road and keep straight ahead at the bypass junction, entering Midhurst by South Pond. South Street runs uphill with subtle and intimate views as it performs a dog-leg by the Spread Eagle and Old Market House, swinging into North Street and the car park lower down.

66 Elmley·Castle·and· Bredon·Hill

Time: 3 hours should be allowed as there is a considerable gain of height.
Start and finish: Elmley Castle. There is car parking near the church.
Approach: Elmley Castle is 2 miles (3km) south of the A44 and 4 miles (6km) from both Evesham and Pershore.
Attractions: The walk involves about 600ft (183m) of climbing with the reward of one of the great views of Midland England. It is ideal for an afternoon in late summer when hedgerow blackberries provide the ideal reason for taking it all very leisurely. Part of the walk is along the Wychavon Way.
OS sheet: 150

It may seem like stretching a point to include in a chapter on Lowland Walks one which involves reaching a height of 850ft (260m); but the climbing is gentle, the effort minimal and, on a clear day, the views over the Vale of Evesham show the quintessential landscape of the south Midlands Plain.

Bredon Hill rules over this land of Tudor villages, orchards, pasture and cornfields, marred nowhere by a hint of industrialisation. The base of the hill is girdled with villages, and Elmley Castle, on its north-eastern flanks, takes its name from the medieval castle of Robert le Despencer, later a Beachamp home, refortified in the fourteenth century. The walk passes close to the grass-covered fragments which remain on the wooded slopes of Bredon.

From the village take the road signposted to Ashton-under-Hill, and in ½ mile (.8km) turn right (signposted Public Bridleway and Wychavon Way waymark, a castellated W). A good track climbs steadily but not steeply ahead, south-westwards, with a splendid blackberry hedge on the left. Passing through a small gate, it continues into thin woodland with ash and hazel signifying the limestone basis of the soil, and suggesting its affinity with the Cotswolds across the Vale.

The waymarked track steepens, with glimpses across open space between the trees of grass-grown ramparts and, a dozen miles (20km) away to the north-east, Meon Hill and Lark Stoke Hill beyond Chipping Campden. As the path gains height and passes through another small gate, ash and hawthorn give way to young sycamore. A blue bridleway sign points the direction across a grassy ride and into beechwoods, some trees being very venerable. A good track leads ahead to the edge of the woodland, emerging onto the open crest beyond a non-existent gate. Green canopy yields to the sky's blue dome and, if you have chosen the right day with the breeze in the west or north-west, clear visibility and an exhilarating sense of freedom. Ignore the track

The track on Bredon Hill (Geoffrey N. Wright)

ahead, but turn left and follow the Wychavon waymark.

Now comes a mile (1.6km) of sheer delight, first along the edge of woodland, subsequently on Bredon's broad, smiling breast, far above the spread counterpane of Housman's 'coloured counties'. Edge Hill, North Cotswold and the Malverns dance delicately across the skyline of the Vale; in the blue distance can be identified the Sugar Loaf and the Black Mountains, with the silvery Severn estuary separating Somerset's hills from those of Gwent. The joy of walking along the grassy track far above the plain reaches a poetic intensity, sharpening the senses, enriching the heart's experience.

The path gradually loses height as it swings right. A few yards after passing a waymark on a gate, turn left through the next gate, through a field to another gate, its descent towards Ashton-under-Hill identified by yellow waymarks at stiles in hedge-gaps. Eventually it joins a farm track in sight of the church, where you aim for the tower, subsequently leaving the churchyard by the lich-gate at its southern entrance, near the fifteenth-century village cross. Walk northwards through the village, past the Star, where lunches and bar snacks may be obtained and, near the end of the main street, where the road bends right, turn left up Wood Lane. At the end of its small cul de sac of modern houses, continue ahead onto a field path with a hedge and fence on its left.

The path continues through a cornfield, over a stile, into rough pasture enriched by wild flowers and butterflies. Stoop and scramble through a gap in the next hedge, emerging into another cornfield, aiming for a gate on its farther edge. Obliquely cross the next cornfield beyond this gate. The next hedge is negotiated at a short stretch of wooden fence by some large trees, with the easier prospect of grass-covered ridge-and-furrow pasture beyond. Climb slightly to the right of the crest of a low hill to reach the minor road near Kersoe. Turn left and head north-westwards for Elmley Castle, a much easier mile (1.6km) away than the similar distance just negotiated from Ashton to Kersoe. Arable and pasture so often present more problems in route-finding than tracks in wild upland country, but the satisfaction of meeting their challenge is no less great.

67 Derwent·Valley·Causey· Arch·and·Tanfield

Time: Between 4 and 5 hours should be allowed.
Start and finish: Rowlands Gill picnic area.
Approach: The picnic area by the B6314 is immediately west of the River Derwent, 4 miles (6km) south-west of Blaydon and is reached by the A694.
Attractions: The ramble is through pastoral valley and wooded landscape. There are strong overtones of former industries, with part of the walk along a disused railway and an old colliery waggonway.
OS sheet: 88

Enjoyable at any time of year, this walk, because of the many woodland stretches through which it passes, is at its most colourful in late October or early November. For the first part it largely follows, north-eastwards, the track-bed of the former Derwent Valley Railway, an 11 mile (17.5km) branch line from Scotswood Bridge Junction to Blackhill near Consett, which operated from 1867 to 1962. A slight detour on the main A694 is necessary at the Derwent Park public recreation area, part of which is a caravan and camp site. Continue on the road past the Rowlands Gill Garage, and in 200yd (182m) pick up the old railway by the official Derwent Walk sign (blue and brown waymarks).

For the next 1½ miles (2km) the walk traverses wooded cuttings, mainly between stands of silver birch, golden in the autumn sunlight, with frequent 'window' views across the Derwent Valley to the mature woods of the great Gibside estate, landscaped by Sir George Bowes from 1729 onwards. The tall statue to British Liberty was erected in 1757, but apart from the elegant Mausoleum Chapel, most of the buildings are ruinous. From the nine high arches of Lockhaugh Viaduct the views are more open, with young plants and trees starting to colonise old spoil heaps of colliery waste.

Where the walk enters more mature woodland it is worth making a short detour (signposted) to Old Hollinside Manor, a ruined fourteenth-century fortified tower above a steep, holly-rich hillside. From it another path descends northwards to the Derwent Walk, and at the junction with the old line take the track signposted 'Clockburn Wood', climbing steeply south-eastwards through woods. Clockburn Lonnen, as this ancient hollow way is called, was once part of a drove road from Scotland to England and parts of it show signs of a metalled surface.

Beyond a gate it opens out, with wide views northwards, on an easier gradient. Continue straight across Fellside Road, with Whickham's housing estates spreading over hillsides to the east, and in ¼ mile (.4km) a stile on the right (yellow waymark) indicates a field path to Cuthbert's Hill with its wind-blown trees. Contour round the foot of the hill to Riding Barns (farm), over a stile, and left along a lane between the farm and The Garth. At the second hedge on the right, a waymark shows the path following field boundaries, over stiles, to the A692 at Marley Hill. Cross this main road and take the lane to Longfield House Farm, working round the northern and western sides of the farm buildings. Look for more stiles and waymarks to join a field path descending to the Bowes Railway, a relatively late waggonway (c1850–60) linking nearby Byermoor Colliery with George Stephenson's waggonway between Kibblesworth and Jarrow.

Cross the old track and descend a field southwards to a gate (no waymark) at its bottom corner. Beyond, and now in County Durham, a rough grassy track invites you into attractive, broad-leaved woodland, curving round to join the gentle valley of the Bobgins Burn, leaving the trees for open pasture, and aiming for a pair of wooden power poles ahead. Turn right on a minor road, cross the burn, and immediately turn left, following the footpath signs to Causey Arch, crossing and recrossing Causey Burn four times in quick succession, as the stream winds and changes direction in its journey through a thickly wooded gorge where sandstone crags offer good scope for rock climbing. In Durham, these steep-sided ravines are called 'denes', which, as new coal pits in the county were developed in the eighteenth century, proved difficult obstacles in the transport of coal to the Tyne.

Causey Arch, built 1725–6 by a local mason, is the world's oldest surviving railway bridge, constructed to carry the Tanfield Waggonway from Tanfield Colliery; but because of a pit explosion, it was never used after the 1780s. Now restored, it soars, a single span of 100ft (30m) across the gorge, 80ft (24m) high – a dramatic highlight of this walk. Climb the right-hand side, detour across it to see a typical waggon and a stretch of rebuilt, wooden-railed waggonway, as well as a magnificent view of the arch itself. Retrace steps, and follow the line of the waggonway from woodland, and as field paths, south-westwards to Tanfield village, a mile (1.6km) away, aiming for the church. From the west side of the churchyard turn right onto a surfaced path which enters a field by the vicarage.

Follow hedgerows alongside fields ahead, with the well-defined path passing through pleasant, open arable landscapes, past a shelter-belt, and eventually emerging by a golf course near cottages at Crookgate Bank with their very productive gardens. Cross the main A692 onto a tarmac path ahead, descending to Burnopfield. Follow the B6314 (signposted Rowlands Gill), where a roadside path takes you the last 1¼ miles (2km) to the starting point, and it's downhill all the way! If time and energy allow, divert to see Gibside Chapel (National Trust) in its parkland setting (open, small charge, April to October, Wed, Sat, Sun afternoons). Its classical elegance sets a contrasting seal on a walk of great variety, sustained interest, memories, and masonry of old industrial landscapes where men toiled hard yet built with skill and care.

68 GIPPING·VALLEY

Time: Allow at least 3 hours, but preferably 4. There are no steep gradients.
Start and finish: Barham picnic site.
Approach: Barham picnic site is 5 miles (8km) north-west of Ipswich, off the A140 Stowmarket road. There is no direct access from the A45.
Attractions: This is a walk along the riverside paths of mid-Suffolk, through woodland and intensively farmed arable land. It is sufficiently undulating, and with copses and shelter belts, to maintain intimacy and interest.
OS sheet: 155

Although the Gipping Valley Countryside and Recreation Project was set up by a group of local authorities in 1978, and the initial work involved reopening the former towpath alongside the River Gipping – an early navigation improved in the late eighteenth century – and waymarked walks were created, the first few hundred yards of this walk are made complicated by the presence of gravel pits and a main railway line. However, some green waymarks do help.

Leave the picnic site by the side gate along Pesthouse Lane, heading south-east for the railway along a track, liable to be muddy in wet weather, between willow-fringed gravel pits popular with anglers. Turn left along the path at the foot of the embankment, cross a stile and soon reach the river. Turn right under a railway bridge and walk to a lane which crosses the river, turning right again past the first house onto a short drive. Almost immediately look for a very narrow opening on the right, which goes by the side of a private garage. If you miss this turning you will reach the church at Great Blakenham in 200yd (182m). Recognising your error, retrace your steps and try again for the semi-hidden path which soon reaches the river, after which you can relax and start to enjoy the scenery. This is dominated by the tall chimneys of nearby cement works, which undeniably are an eyesore, but on the last part of the walk serve as a useful beacon identifying the proximity of the Barham picnic site.

A succession of stiles is a reassurance of the continuing riverside path, with the river on the right. Beyond it gravel pits are being reclaimed, and the railway is never far away. Rough land gives way to pastures where Canada geese graze. The riverside scenery steadily improves as Sharmford Mere comes into view across the river, backed by broad-leaved woodland beyond the main road. Continue to keep the river on the right, as the path follows its winding course through pleasant pastures to Baylham Mill.

Most good lowland walks have accents and highlights along the way and the white, weather-boarded Baylham Mill is certainly one – an eighteenth-century building, probably with an older core, with its working gear intact, though not functioning. The mill also has the only remaining lock gates on the Gipping. Turn right, cross the river and follow a lane, its metalled surface cracked and mossy, its battle lost against the enfolding tide of hawthorn, blackberry, bracken and nettle. Only an occasional walker comes this way now.

Soon, the A45 is reached, with a footpath sign on the far side, 100yd (90m) away, the immediate goal. Cross the busy carriageway with care, and go through a gate into Sheepwalk, now mixed woodland of the Shrublands Estate, but whose name surely indicates its former use as open pasture. A plethora of waymarks points the way ahead, across two rides, turning left at the third, then right at the next ride to the woodland edge, with a cornfield beyond.

The path goes northwards across this field to a footpath sign directly opposite. On my first visit, ripening corn periodically obscured the track. However, the distant path was reached, leading into a hollowed ride through bracken and trees. The next cornfield before the Needham road showed a good path as a clear swathe.

Right on the road for a mile (1.6km) to the Three Cocked Hat near Coddenham. This is not a pub but a small, triangular green with a few trees. Right again here, left at the next junction, and in 50yd (45m), take the path indicated by a green metal sign. A good woodland track starts encouragingly and then encounters a house built across it. Presumably the path is diverted; if so it is not visible. I crossed a hedge on the left and followed this along to Brick Kiln Farm. Go through one gate, right through a second, then left parallel to a hedge on the left, aiming for a thatched cottage two fields away. A gate to the left of the building has the encouragement of a waymark and stile leading to Bulls Wood.

At the far end of Bulls Wood another cornfield is encountered. Turn left along the field edge, and in a few yards follow tractor wheel-marks and plunge across the field to a small cottage, picking up, with relief, a good track to Barham Green. Keep right, along the road to Pond Farm, but just before the building take the path signposted on the right, past an allotment, following a hedgerow, crossing a plank bridge on the left. Turn right immediately past the next hedge, and follow a headland track between two fields into Broomwalk Plantation. By now, the cement works' chimneys will have raised your spirits, and it's downhill all the way, following waymark signs across a bridleway, past some poultry houses to Pesthouse Lane which leads back to the picnic site.

High summer may not be the best season for this walk unless you enjoy the challenge of corn. A crisp winter's day allows plenty of daylight time for its completion, and frozen ground is always good to walk on.

Baylham Mill (Geoffrey N. Wright)

69 EDEN·VALLEY

Time: 4 to 5 hours.

Start and finish: Little Salkeld, although alternative starting points could be Eden Bridge, Kirkoswald or Glassonby. There is some parking space in the village of Little Salkeld from where the walk is made in a clockwise direction.

Approach: Little Salkeld is 6 miles (9.6km) north-east of Penrith. Turn off the A686 at Langwathby.

Attractions: The walk includes pleasant countryside of the lower Eden Valley, with river, farmland, parkland, woodland and varied scenery. There are sandstone caves, prehistoric stone circles and an interesting church. Wild flowers are a feature in late spring.

OS sheets: 90, 91 and 86

From Little Salkeld, a signpost indicates 'Footpath to Lacey Caves and Eden Bridge'. Take this, and initially the route follows a tarmac or concrete farm track leading northwards above and parallel to the railway (Leeds–Carlisle line) and well above the river, allowing wide views westwards to the village of Great Salkeld and the distant mountains of northern Lakeland.

In about a mile (1.6km) the buildings associated with a former gypsum mine (Long Meg) are reached and the path, still signposted to Lacey Caves,

Lacey Caves

descends, hairpinning, towards the river, entering delightful woodland with a rich carpet of flowers in spring. Following the former track of a narrow-gauge line serving the mines, with a view to a weir on the river, the path continues to the caves. These have been hewn out of red sandstone in the side of a cliff about 20ft (6m) above the river, and have rooms linked by short galleries – a fine viewpoint and a good place to shelter.

The path continues as a short flight of steps behind the caves, and descends again through a young plantation to a stile with a yellow waymark sign by it (look out for these on this part of the way). Continuing through pastures above the river, the path heads for another stile and a larch plantation beyond, where the route is again waymarked and leads to the Glassonby–Kirkoswald road at the bridge over Hazelrigg Beck. Some 150yd (137m) north along the road a sign indicates 'Public footpath to Eden Bridge'. At first this keeps to the western edge of an arable field to a stile at a wooden fence, giving access to what in wet weather could be a muddy section just above the river. Beyond a field gate the path enters pasture, and diverges slightly from the river keeping close to a barbed-wire fence on the right (east), aiming for two iron gates, close together, and following a flood bank above a slow stream by trees on the left. Beyond a line of hawthorns it turns through another gate and heads for the eastern end of Eden Bridge, a handsome structure in red sandstone.

Follow the road into Kirkoswald, turn right and immediately left at the top of the first hill (signposted Park Head). In 150yd (137m) a signpost to the right indicates 'Public footpath to Glassonby'. This passes to the west of the former moat and meagre ruins of Kirkoswald Castle, goes through a gate, and heads south-eastwards through a broad valley pasture. The track is not very distinct, but a distant iron gate round a slight bend indicates the way ahead. Pass a small marsh with rushes and willows on the left, then go through another gate, when the track climbs slightly between two grassy hills with a wood ahead, to a shooting hut with a gate near it. Continue beyond this gate and keep the wood, mainly coniferous, on the right. Cut across a corner of the pasture which adjoins it and climb slightly, bearing right, still close to the wood, to a gate from which the buildings of Old Parks Farm are now in view ahead. Go through the farmyard, turn right by the house, and continue along the surfaced farm road to join the Gamblesby road. Turn right down the hill, across Glassonby Beck, and climb into Glassonby village, following the signpost pointing southwards to Hunsonby.

In about ¼ mile (.4km) a lane on the right (west) leads to Addingham church (late seventeenth century), formerly the parish church serving the villages of Glassonby, Hunsonby and Little Salkeld. Happily, it is normally open during daylight hours – a useful and quiet place in which to pause awhile before continuing on the final stage of this walk. The path southwards through the large churchyard leads to a field which is a tree nursery; the grassy track neatly bisects this, then crosses a road where a waymark points the path ahead. This soon slants slightly right and gradually descends south-westwards towards the now-visible stone circle of Long Meg and her Daughters. This Bronze Age site of 59 large stones, 27 of them still standing upright, is in the form of an oval, 360ft by 305ft (116 × 93m), with Long Meg herself outside the south-western periphery – a 12ft (3.6m) monolith whose flat surface reveals spiral carvings.

The track joins a farm road on the south-east edge of the site, which is followed for a short distance to where it makes a sharp left turn, away from the broad cart track which is followed to the village of Little Salkeld. Where this widens and joins the road, turn right and a short descent soon leads into the middle of the village, and the starting point of the walk.

Long Meg and her Daughters

70 EAST·LOTHIAN

Time: There are no steep gradients, so 5 hours should be ample.
Start and finish: Woodhall picnic site, where there is a free car park.
Approach: Woodhall picnic site is 1 mile (1.6km) west of Wester Pencaitland on the A6093 Dalkeith–Haddington road.
Attractions: The walk uses field paths, part of the old Pencaitland Railway and a short stretch of road, through arable and pastoral landscapes with two interesting villages.
OS sheet: 66

Although East Lothian is one of the great farming counties of Scotland, and pioneered many agricultural developments in the eighteenth century, it also had an early coal industry. The history of the Pencaitland Railway is more closely related to mining than to a passenger service. Some 6½ miles (10km) of its track, from Saltoun station to Crossgatehall, which passes through farmland not normally accessible, has been bought by East Lothian District Council for public use as a walkway and bridleway. This walk uses the stretch between Ormiston and Saltoun, which was opened in 1901 by the Gifford & Garvald Light Railway Co, ceased passenger use in 1933, and goods use in 1964 following the closure of all coal mines in the area. The picnic site and car park are on the site of the old Woodhall Colliery.

Leaving the site and crossing the main road, follow the old railway northwards, first in a cutting then across the Tyne Water onto an embankment with sewage works on the right. Where the track crosses Hillview Road, east of Ormiston, the original metals have been retained. Leave the line here and take a path heading due east, along the headland between two arable fields. When I walked it a breeze whispered across the growing barley, moving the grasses into an ever-changing pattern of greens. The path continues between wire fences through a small plantation, over a stile at the end, to join and then accompany a burn coming in from the left.

Clear-flowing water alternates with stretches of still water luxuriant with weeds, rushes and kingcups, with the path keeping to the edge of pasture where the natural curiosity of grazing stirks attracts them to the water. Passing Loanfoot (house) to the left, with the path now on the edge of arable again and the burn more overgrown, Winton House comes into view ahead. Where the path meets a farm track coming in from woodland to the left, zigzag right for 50yd (45m) to pick up a broader burn on the south side of a field, with the path keeping to the embankment adjoining . Winton House, high above the river, looks very impressive, although the show-front of this early seventeenth-century house faces north. Twisted chimneys and ogee-capped towers help to make an arresting skyline.

At the narrowing corner of the field, cross a fence and join a woodland drive, curving south, to meet the road near the bridge between the twin Pencaitland villages. Detour east for 200yd (180m) to see the sixteenth/seventeenth-century parish church in Easter Pencaitland, and browse round its churchyard. Return to Wester Pencaitland, turn south by the 1695 Mercat Cross, glancing at the former early nineteenth-century school with the stone figure of a pupil above a porch. Follow the Saltoun Road southwards to the end of the village, turn right near the 30mph sign, along Huntlaw Road, to the railway bridge ahead; and join the old line heading south, almost immediately passing a small concrete monument marking the site of Huntlaw Pit (1807).

The line gradually climbs in a cutting for about a mile (1.6km), eventually opening out near Lempock Wells Farm with its extensive outbuildings. Good views here embrace the Lammermuir Hills ahead and the distinctive hump of Traprain Law away to the east. After the track has passed beneath a road bridge it becomes pleasantly grassy and even richer in flowers than before. Eventually a white gate ahead marks the end of the public access part of the line, by the dilapidated corrugated iron shed that was Saltoun station.

Turn right (south-west) and, climbing steadily, follow a minor road past the turn to Preston Bank and Glenkinchie. In another ½ mile (.8km), at the highest point in the walk (550ft, 167m), take the former Lampland Quarry road north-west, gradually losing height, to Templehall, a farm group by the Kinchie Burn. Go ahead past the row of cottages and turn left on the minor road; then north down B6371 for ½ mile (.8km) to the House of Muir. By the first cottage on the right take the unsurfaced track which heads north-east towards Fountainhall. This climbs slightly, and where it joins Big Wood on the left, after a short double bend, seek the path which cuts off to the north near the seventh roadside tree. This very pleasant path skirts an arable field, but keeps close to woodland on its right as it gradually descends northwards, with good open views to the north revealing the contrasts of East Lothian landscape. Ormiston's new estates spread outwards, engulfing one of Scotland's most famous planned villages, built as a result of the pioneering zeal of John Cockburn between 1735 and 1740 to improve agriculture and encourage industry – mainly a brewery, distillery and linen mill – on his estate.

The path passes a neat modern memorial in a field to a local farmer and his wife, and soon joins a broad track leading to the modern roadside row of houses at Wolfstar, with the Woodhall picnic site ¼ mile (.4km) east along the main road.

The church at Easter Pencaitland (Geoffrey N. Wright)

DOWNLANDS

The term 'downs', which comes from an old English word, *dun*, a hill, is used to describe the round grass-covered chalk hills which occur in Surrey, Sussex, Kent, Hampshire, Dorset and Berkshire. Similar chalk hills in Lincolnshire and Yorkshire are called 'wolds', and though they are geological cousins, to the rambler such northern hills present a landscape of quite different mood which lacks the soft character of their southern counterparts. Here we are concerned with the true downs; lovers of the wilder northern landscapes will find routes a-plenty in other chapters.

Fortunate is he who has trodden the springy turf of the English downs, those delicate grasslands with their steep slopes and waterless valleys. To wander these skybound places is to walk on the roof of England with huge cloudscapes where one can watch the advance of a gathering storm or observe the clouds forming in the morning warmth and decaying as the day wears on. Up in these lonely landscapes, it is not difficult to imagine that this is England as it was centuries ago. This is a settled land, a place inhabited by English kings, lords and peasants. Despite the intrusion of the plough, this is still our homeland as it was, largely as it has always been, and it is a scene in which to delight.

These limy conditions provide life for many rare wild flowers, particularly orchids which thrive among the fescue grass. Each summer the rambler-naturalist meets the fauna and flora as old friends: rare or common, each species has a place in the order of downland life, while always present is the background song of the skylark, for if any creature calls to mind the feel of these romantic downlands it is the song of that small brown bird. Man, too, leaves his mark: ancient burial mounds pimple the summits reminding us how long these lands have known human habitation. Caesar's legions trod their slopes, so no doubt did other armies, now long forgotten, after the Romans left. We still wonder at the white horses and giant figures carved in the turf. Were they of deep religious significance? Surely many were.

Because chalk does not retain moisture, these lovely upland slopes are largely free of trees, though trees often cling to life in the valleys, forming clumps known as hangers. For centuries sheep have ensured that the rough scrub which would have sprung up has been kept at bay; but agricultural patterns change and tractors can now take the plough onto all but the steepest slopes. Nevertheless, there is a delicate balance between man and nature which must not be allowed to be disturbed, for once an area of down-land is lost, it can never be restored. We owe it to those who follow to see that we pass on that heritage.

The South Downs Way above Arundel (John Whatmore)

71	Hampshire Downs	11 miles (17.5km)
72	Salisbury Plain, Wiltshire	10 miles (16km)
73	Downs above Arundel, West Sussex	13 miles (21km)
74	North Downs, Surrey	6 miles (9.6km)
75	Dorset Downs	3, 6 or 9 miles (5, 9.6 or 14km)
76	Lambourn Downs, Berkshire	6 miles (9.6km)
77	Marlborough Downs, Wiltshire	10 miles (16km)
78	Ridgeway Wanderings, Berkshire	12 miles (19km)
79	The Seven Sisters, East Sussex	7 or 13 miles (11 or 21km)

71 HAMPSHIRE·DOWNS

Time: At least 4½ hours, more if long pauses are envisaged at the top of hills. Allow at least half a day to explore Winchester.
Start and finish: Winchester city centre. Boots are not necessary in good weather.
Approach: Winchester is easily reached by train, bus or car. There are plenty of parking places, and the city council has earmarked some of them as 'tourist car parks' where vehicles can be left all day.
Attractions: A walk with sweeping views in all directions where it sometimes seems that the walker is striding along the very roof of southern England. The distant views from Cheesefoot Head must surely be the finest in Hampshire, but the walk also includes a stroll beside the River Itchen as it winds away from Winchester, which is arguably the most interesting city in southern England.
OS sheet: 185

Some cities create difficulties for the walker anxious to reach open country; too often there are miles of uninteresting suburbs between him and his goal, but Winchester is not one of these. It is a town that delights in its river – a clear, sparkling brook that divides into a bewildering number of channels. The list of places of interest in Winchester is far too long to go into here, but do not miss the Cathedral and its close, the Great Hall and Round Table and the City Mill. There is an information centre in the main street.

Leave the centre of the city by walking down the shopping precinct in an easterly direction to the statue of King Alfred (AD 871–99), king of the West Saxons who drove the Danish invaders from Wessex and who is buried at Winchester which was his capital. Pass (or visit) the City Mill on the left and here cross the road and take the path alongside the river, walking downstream (south). The remains of the city's Roman walls are on the right. Remain as close as possible to the river, leaving it only where the path is forced to divert to avoid buildings and private gardens. As the path passes through a meadow, the buildings of Winchester College with its playing fields will be seen on the right. Banks of daffodils make this a pretty spot in spring.

Continue to a minor road and here go left onto the road opposite a brick and flint house called Meadow View. The road crosses several branches of the Itchen and in a few minutes the roar of traffic on the A33 can be heard. Just before that road would be reached, turn right along a path running beside the river and after ½ mile (.8km), at a small weir, a prominent redbrick railway tunnel comes into view quite suddenly. Pass through it, under the A33 and

Calstock seen from Calstock Bridge (Leigh Hatts) (*see page 348*)

Stone carving in Winchester

climb St Catherine's Hill by a clear path. The purpose of this steep but short climb is to see the view of Winchester spread out below. Walk right around the summit and descend by the path on the east side. This soon connects to a waymarked path passing through two gates. Take this path, going left through wooded country and in ½ mile (.8km) a road is reached marked on the Ordnance Survey sheet as Roman Road.

Do not go quite as far as the road, for just alongside it is a fingerposted foot-path going south-east, and this is your route. The path runs straight as an arrow for nearly 2 miles (3km), dipping first through wooded country then climbing over high downland. The views to the west are particularly good, and at times of gathering rainstorms the black clouds can be seen moving in, dispersing grey curtains of rain. As one walks this ridge one cannot help but feel that this is a great place to be, though the effect may be somewhat diminished by the sound of gunfire from the army's ranges nearby.

The path descends over Hazeley Down and reaches a minor road west of Morestead. Turn left on the road towards that village and continue for ½ mile (.8km) to a crossroads. The village is away to the right but there is no need to visit it unless one needs provisions. Continue over the crossroads along a surfaced wide track. After ½ mile (.8km) there is a fork; take the left

Whittington Stone, Highgate Hill (Leigh Hatts) (*see* page 365)
Looking down Loch Ness from the path (Leigh Hatts) (*see* page 363)

arm. The trackway is now unsurfaced and fringes the firing ranges, but does not cross them. It climbs steadily and then bursts out into wide open country with typical downland views on all sides.

As one walks on, the views get more and more spectacular. This is Fawley Down, real 'Roof of England' country and the chalky way seems wonderfully remote, although only 3 miles (5km) from Winchester as the crow flies. There are 2 miles (3km) of this grand country until the A272 is reached. However tired one may be, it is with a sense of regret that such a wonderful section of the walk has been completed. But the point at which the path reaches the main road is Cheesefoot Head, justly famous as one of Hampshire's greatest viewpoints. Cross the road and admire the view to the north.

Cross back over the road and return for 50yd (45m) or so along the path you have just used, making a right turn at the first stile onto a bridleway which roughly parallels the main road, going north-west. The summit of Telegraph Hill is soon reached and the way can be seen twisting downhill with Winchester in the background. Follow the path to the boundary of the firing range and there turn right down a lane beside a house called Little Golders. This takes the rambler down to the village of Chilcomb. Walk through the pretty village, and as the road swings sharply left there is a footpath on the right marked by a fingerpost.

Take this to its junction with the A33 (¾mile, 1.2km), cross the main road and continue along the pleasant suburban road back into Winchester, arriving at the statue of King Alfred.

72 SALISBURY·PLAIN

Time: Allow 4 hours for the walk to give plenty of time to enjoy the extensive views. If a visit is also made to Stonehenge, a full day could pleasantly be spent.

Start and finish: Free car park beside Stonehenge (admission charge). Boots are not necessary except in winter when snow sweeps across this high plain.

Approach: By road from Salisbury to Andover. Stonehenge lies between the A303 and A344, 3 miles (5km) west of Amesbury, and is well signposted.

Attractions: As the route starts and finishes at Stonehenge, this gives the rambler the opportunity to visit one of Britain's best known and most romantic landmarks. This is a hilly walk that includes plenty of typical windswept upland scenery with the bonus of dipping into the valley for a ramble along the banks of the upper Avon and visiting some delightful villages.

OS sheet: 184

An estimated 750,000 tourists a year visit this lonely starting point. Construction of Stonehenge began about 3000BC and falls into three fairly distinct periods lasting about 900 years. There are many theories about the purpose of the huge edifice and the people who built it, but one thing is certain – it was not constructed by the Druids. No work was done on Stonehenge after 1300BC, and the Druids, who were a Celtic priesthood, could not have been active there before 250BC. They may have used the circles for their rites but it would have appeared to them as a mystic ruin, just as it does to us today. Those who wish to pursue the fascinating theories of the origins of Stonehenge will find plenty of literature on sale at the site.

Leave the car park by turning right (north-west) onto the road and in 100yd (90m) turn left onto a broad track. This has a stony surface with wide grass verges and is the sort of path that is good in any weather. You are, from the start, on high upland country with burial mounds scattered around and a 360 degree horizon. After a little more than ¼ mile (.4km), cross the A303, continuing on the track for another ¼ mile until a National Trust fingerpost is reached saying 'Old Sarum 7m'. Turn left at this point, cross the stile, and follow the path along the edge of a field. There is a good view of Stonehenge away to the left, all the better now that you are too far away to see the wire and barriers surrounding it. Soon a wide grassy track is reached crossing the field path at right angles. Bear right onto this track and continue for a mile (1.6km) to Springbottom Farm where the track becomes surfaced and climbs steeply up Lake Down. Pause at the top to look behind at the sweeping views.

The way ahead has all the appearances of a lane but in fact is a right of way for walkers only, the only motor traffic is that which serves farms, so you will not be over-troubled by vehicles. In ½ mile (.8km) turn right at a road junction and arrive in the hamlet of Wilsford. Visit the church on the left-hand side of the road, in a particularly lovely setting.

Continue along the road maintaining southerly direction; it is no penance to be walking along this road instead of on wilder byways as it gives good views to the left of the River Avon 20ft (6m) or so below. When the author last walked this way, the trees alongside the river were being cut down, and while one never likes to see this happen there is no doubt that it improves the view from the road. In a few minutes you enter the village of Lake, with some topiary work on the right-hand side of the road just before Lake House is reached. This is one of the 'great houses' of this part of Wiltshire and was originally built in the very early seventeenth century, though later destroyed by fire and rebuilt. Continue out of the village, climbing steeply, and at the top of the hill, on the left, beside a thatched timber-built house, is a fingerpost marked 'Bridleway to Great Durnford'. Take this delightful little path which plunges down to the River Avon at a spot where there is a footbridge across the river to Great Durnford. Our route does not in fact cross the river so if you wish to see the village, cross the bridge and then retrace. Otherwise, take the footpath which leads up on the right (west) away from the river. This is a very pretty path in summer, and it soon emerges onto a byroad where turn left.

Follow this byroad for a mile (1.6km) to Upper Woodford. You are now looking for a track off to the right, but it is important to get the correct one as, although there are two, only one is a right of way. Ignore the first surfaced path at the start of the village alongside some cottages; the correct route is a few hundred yards further on and comes just after a village store but before the main part of the village. Turn right onto this surfaced track and after 200yd (180m) you will see that it is marked 'Private road, public footpath'.

The road soars up from the village into the downland with sweeping views all round. Skylarks sing continually here in summer and there are hares and rabbits everywhere. After a mile (1.6km), the surfaced track turns right at a sign saying 'Private road to Westfield Farm'. The right of way is the grassy track which continues ahead. Stay with it for a mile (1.6km), emerging through a field gate onto the A360 opposite a large farm called Druid's Lodge.

Turn right onto the main road for ¼ mile (.4km), and on the right is a broad track heading off north-east. The line of the track can easily be seen running across the downland. Stay with this track for nearly 2 miles (3km), enjoying the views all the way, until you find that you are back at the 'Old Sarum 7m' fingerpost. Continue straight on along the path that you took from the Stonehenge car park.

One of the advantages of this route has been that of treading routes that were old when the Romans first used them. There are plenty more old paths around Stonehenge and if time permits it is well worth exploring them, if only to see Stonehenge from different aspects.

73 Downs·above·Arundel

Time: 6 hours should be allowed for the full walk, but it is not difficult, with the aid of an Ordnance Survey map, to cut the walk short at a variety of points.

Start and finish: Arundel town centre.

Approach: Arundel is easily reached by car, and is situated 4 miles (6km) north of Littlehampton on the A27. There are bus services during the summer months from the nearby South Coast resorts, and there is a railway station with a good service to and from London. The station is ten minutes' walk from the town.

Attractions: Unlike many of the traditional downland walks in this section, this ramble begins along a river valley, passes through a couple of lowland villages, then ascends into the hills to continue along the South Downs Way. The views from the summits are excellent, often with Arundel Castle silhouetted against the skyline.

OS sheet: 197

Leave the town by walking down the main street with the castle behind you, and when the river is reached turn left into Mill Road where there is a sign to the wildfowl reserve. There is a clear footpath along the bank of the River Arun, take this and stay with the river. To the north, the South Downs rise, while to the walker's left is a good view of Arundel Castle. It is easy walking along the banked-up path and soon the Black Rabbit inn is reached. The path goes between the inn and the river, passing through the car park. Remain with the river path to South Stoke. This is a pretty spot with an interesting church and convenient seat in the churchyard for a picnic. (The author found two enterprising young boys selling plums at a cottage gate which gave the tea-and-sandwiches stop an added flavour.)

Retrace a few hundred yards to the river, cross it by the metal lattice bridge, and turn left onto the river bank. In 200yd (183m) turn right over a stile and through a wood. The path now crosses a small wood-and-metal bridge over a tributary of the Arun. Follow the path, crossing the stiles over meadowland to North Stoke. Turn right (north) at the start of the village, taking the lane to Amberley Station. (There are a few shops here, but the real village of Amberley is off the route a mile (1.6km) to the north.) Bear right along the rather busy road, pass under the railway bridge and climb the hill. Caution is needed here as there are sections of the road without a footpath and traffic can be heavy. However, in a few minutes the rambler turns right off the road onto a byway called High Titton, where there is a fingerpost indicating that this is part of the South Downs Way.

This is traditional high downs country with grand views opening out in all directions. On summer weekends one does not go far before meeting other walkers, happy to stop and exchange experiences of walking this most popular of long-distance paths. Stay with the Way to the point marked on the OS sheet as Springhead Hill (about a mile (1.6km) from our junction with the Way), then go right (south-west) following a very prominent track which descends steadily towards Arundel. Soon the castle appears in the valley. This true downland walking, with skylarks everywhere and plenty of signs of wildlife from common blue butterflies to hares. After 2 miles (3km), the route is off the high country and has reached a railway line just before the village of North Stoke. Do not go as far as the village, nor even cross the railway line, but immediately before the bridge over the line find a footpath, on the left. Take this and follow it around the edge of one wood and through another until the village of Burpham is reached. Take the track down to the river by the pub and stay with the river, passing under a railway bridge. The path here has been banked high above the waterway, a meander of the Arun.

The walker will soon recognise that he is now on the opposite bank of the river to that along which the walk began; and should he be completing the ramble during the evening he will probably see geese on their sundown flight, or in winter teal, wigeon or pochard, as there is a wildfowl reserve on the opposite bank. Remain with the riverside, the short distance back to Arundel.

74 NORTH·DOWNS

Time: Allow 2½ hours, including stops.

Start and finish: Car park on southern side of Leith Hill, Surrey, marked Wotton and Abinger Commons. Boots recommended after heavy rain, otherwise stout shoes are sufficient.

Approach: By car, turn off the Guildford to Dorking road 2 miles (3km) after Gomshall where there is a signpost to Leith Hill. The car park is three miles (5km) along the road, on the left, and is clearly marked.

Attractions: This walk includes the summit of Leith Hill, the highest point in south-east England. Unlike most in this section, the ramble passes through woodlands for much of its course with frequent distant views. It is particularly attractive when spring flowers are in bloom.

OS sheet: 187

Turn your back on the road and leave the car park in a north-easterly direction along a fairly distinct broad track. After a few hundred yards bear left up steeply rising ground following any of several small paths. In a few minutes the bulk of Leith Hill Tower will appear on the right, silhouetted against the sky. The National Trust, which now owns the tower, estimates that 100,000 people a year visit this spot. The hilltop is 965ft (294m) above sea level and so just misses becoming what is technically a mountain; however, the top of the tower is 1,029ft (314m) above sea level.

The tower was built in 1766 by Richard Hull, a prominent lawyer. A Latin inscription at the base says that he erected it for the enjoyment of himself and his neighbours. Six years after doing so he died, and was buried under the tower. The view from the top is superb as there is nothing to break the all-round horizon whose circumference is at least 200 miles (320km). Some rather fanciful claims have been made of the number of counties that are visible; but Eric Parker, doyen of Surrey writers, records that in 1844 ordnance surveyors counted the spires of forty-one London churches from the top.

Leaving the tower on your left, walk in an easterly direction along a prominent track and work to the right until a wide pathway is met after a few minutes. This trackway skirts the hill and gives more great views. Continue for perhaps a mile (1.6km) until one surprisingly meets a tiny cricket ground, complete with pavilion. Turn right at a fingerpost saying 'footpath', slightly backtracking, and then edge left almost at once to follow a path which descends along an almost sheer bank with views straight down onto the village of Coldharbour with, in the background, much of Sussex spread out to the south. This path brings you out to the road at Rowe Mount Cottage, Coldharbour.

Turn left onto the road and in 200yd (183m) a church is reached. It was built in 1848 and is typically Victorian, but among all the glass of that period is a window of 1942 depicting St Francis which is well worth entering the church for. Continue along the road through the village to the Plough inn. (Immediately before the Plough is a picturesque footpath, on the right, leading alongside cottage gardens to pass along the bottom of an ancient British settlement known as Anstiebury Hill. If this diversion is taken, retrace to Coldharbour.)

At the Plough, go left along a wide track marked with a Forestry Commission sign and continue, past cottages on the left, until after ¼ mile (.4km) a fork is reached where bear left. The route now passes through woods – largely beech, silver birch and conifers – with signs that there will be plenty of bluebells and bilberries at the right times of year. Pass an isolated cottage on the right and shortly afterwards a prominent bridleway is reached immediately after a Forestry Commission sign saying 'Bury Hill'. Turn left onto the bridleway. The path immediately becomes confused; the correct line is to keep a barbed-wire fence on your right-hand side, going west. The path soon descends steeply in a series of broad steps and is very muddy indeed after rain, but after a few hundred yards it meets a level-surfaced path at a spot where there are frequent small waterfalls and attractive streams. Continue (left) along the path and in 200yd (183m) go right at a T-junction, then left at the next where there is a riding centre. Now go left into the village of Broadmoor.

This is another pretty little Surrey village and a good place to pause. Next to Leith Cottage is a path on the right marked 'no horses'. Take this, climbing steeply with a good view of the village below and on the right. Continue, crossing two metalled roads. Just here a deer burst out of the undergrowth while the author was walking the route, and the countryside all about is rich in wildlife, particularly birds. Ignore the path which enters Severells Copse and continue straight on, descending until the large pool of Friday Street comes into view. Continue to the waterside and, keeping the lake on the left, follow the road around it.

The hamlet of Friday Street is one of Surrey's most famous attractions as the lake is encircled by tree-clad slopes making it rather Swiss in appearance. Indeed, it has been suggested that only the tinkle of cow bells is necessary to complete the illusion. There is also a car park here so the walk could begin and end here if more convenient. The lake is unlikely to be totally natural and is probably a hammer pond. From Elizabethan days, in places where iron ore was available, streams were dammed to form such ponds, the water outlet being controlled to provide water power to drive the bellows of the blast furnace, so producing pig iron.

Continue along the road, pass the Stephan Langton pub and the road soon becomes a track. Continue until a road is met where turn left onto the road and then in 100yd (91m) right onto a bridleway where there is a postbox set into a wall. Continue along this bridleway for about a mile (1.6km) until

again a road is met; turn left onto it. You are now ½ mile (.8km) from where
the the walk began. Either continue along the pleasant road as a change from
almost continual footpaths, or take one of the many woodland tracks that
parallel the road. The car park is on the left of the road.

Leith Hill Tower, the highest point in south-east England (John Whatmore)

75 DORSET·DOWNS

Time: The shortest of these variations should take no more than 1½ hours, while for the longer walks 3 and 5 hours should allow plenty of time for contemplation.

Start and finish: The car park on the north flank of Bulbarrow Hill.

Approach: Bulbarrow Hill is approximately 8 miles (13km) west of Blandford Forum or 6 miles (9.6km) south of Sturminster Newton. A little country-lane navigation is called for, but Bulbarrow is signposted, and there is a prominent radio mast at the summit close to which the car park will easily be found.

Attractions: The views from Bulbarrow Hill are superb. The starting and finishing point of the walks is 902ft (275m) above sea level, and below stretches the whole patchwork of the Blackmoor Vale, with Sherborne nestling 11 miles (17.5km) away and, on a really clear day, the blue smudge of the Quantock Hills more than 40 miles (64km) to the north-west.

OS sheet: 194

For all three versions of this walk, leave the car park by turning right along the lane in the direction of Ibberton. The views are stunning and no apology need be made for indulging in a little road walking. Wild raspberries grow in the hedgerows and an old stone barn along the road has been turned into a restaurant claiming to serve cream teas with the best view in Dorset. Continue for a little over a mile (1.6km) until a fingerpost indicates that a turn to the left goes to Ibberton. Take this tiny lane which plunges down the hillside and remain on it into the village. This is a charming, tucked-away spot which is so often missed. Swing right in the village, climbing up to the church along what is signposted as a 'halter path'. On no account miss a visit to the church, if only for the views from the churchyard. The building is a gem, built around 1400, and includes the arms of Elizabeth I in stained glass. An earthenware pitcher in the north aisle was used at Christmas by bellringers who carried it around local farms to be filled with cider and then drunk in the belfry.

Continue on the track past the church and rejoin the steep lane down which you came to the village. Turn left onto it and soon you will be back at the Ibberton fingerpost. Anyone who has had enough can now retrace along the road to the car park and enjoy those grand views for a second time, so completing the 3 mile (5km) walk.

Those wishing a longer ramble should take the bridleway (blue arrow on a farm gate) immediately beside the Ibberton fingerpost, going east along Coombe Bottom. It passes through sheep country and is easy, pastoral walking. Usually the track is well marked, but occasionally the true route becomes

The village of Ibberton (John Whatmore)

obscure. Keep the electricity pylons on your right for 1½ miles (2km), at which point the bridleway is alongside the pylons. Those wishing to keep the walk down to 6 miles (9.6km) should now duck under the power lines, taking the bridleway back west to Ibberton Hill. A glance at the OS sheet will prevent any confusion here. The return route is roughly parallel to the outward one and brings the rambler back onto the road by which he left the car park – again with those stunning views for the last ½ mile (.8km) back to the car.

For the 9 mile (14km) walk, do not duck under the power lines, but remain with the bridleway from Coombe Bottom for a further ½ mile (.8km) then pass under the power lines onto the bridleway going due south. Again, a glance at the OS sheet will avoid any confusion. Stay with this pleasant path to the village of Winterborne Houghton. The church is well worth a visit and has the distinction of having a bridleway actually passing through the church-yard. Continue along the village street, which is marked 'No through road', turn right at the end of the village and take the bridleway through Higher Houghton Farm and back to Bulbarrow Hill car park.

76 LAMBOURN·DOWNS

Time: This is essentially a short walk, ideal for a summer afternoon or in the dark days of winter. For most people, 2½ hours should be sufficient.
Start and finish: See route below.
Approach: Lambourn is 8 miles (13km) south-west of Wantage on the junction of the B4000 and B4001. It is a simple drive from either the Oxford or Newbury directions.
Attractions: Lambourn, an attractive spot, is one of the centres of the English racing scene, a place of weatherbeaten trainers, of shops selling saddles. John Betjeman wrote of 'feathery ash in leathery Lambourn', and this ramble passes not only through ash plantations but along pathways thick with wild roses in summer.
OS sheet: 174

From Lambourn church, drive north-west along the B4000 to Upper Lambourn where a minor road on the right is signposted to the Downs. Drive along this until the road ceases to be surfaced and then leave the car, continuing along the track on foot. As the path climbs, tempting glimpses of sweeping downs, crowned with coppices, are seen between the trees. Bear left at the intersection of paths marked on the OS sheet as Hangman's Stone. After heavy rain, this section is extremely muddy, but parallel tracks have been made to avoid the worst of the problem.

Soon the walker emerges onto the traditional high down scenery. Stay with the path to Crog Hill where turn off right onto a prominent path waymarked 'CR'. Continue along Long Barrow, then go right onto a surfaced lane. After ¾ mile (1.2km), where the road goes left at Postdown Farm, bear off right along a prominent track. In June, when the author last did this walk, the barley fields were splashed with scarlet poppies, and the wild flowers were a delight. Remain on this track and it will bring the rambler back to Hangman's Stone, and so back into Lambourn in plenty of time for a pint in one of its pubs.

Typical high downland scenery near Crog Hill (John Whatmore)

77 MARLBOROUGH·DOWNS

Time: A really cracking pace could be set on this walk by anyone so inclined, for there is surprisingly little rise and fall in the route; it holds onto its height almost throughout. About 4½ hours would be right for most people. Though there are muddy patches, boots are not needed.

Start and finish: There is no railway station at Marlborough and it is assumed that the rambler will have his car, so the start and finish of the route has been selected 2 miles (3km) out of the town at a convenient point on high ground.

Approach: Marlborough lies on the junction of the A4 and the A345 and so is easily and quickly reached by car.

Attractions: This walk covers typical downland with wide views taking in the best of the high country north of Marlborough and touching on one of the scenic villages along the River Og, a tributary of the Kennet. Marlborough itself is justly known as one of the most delightful towns in Wiltshire: the elegance of its main street, its interesting little shops and its college buildings make it an ideal place in which to spend a weekend.

OS sheet: 173

Drive out of Marlborough, leaving the high street by its northerly end and at the church bear left up the hill. In a few moments the main road (A345) bears right, while straight ahead is a lane signposted to Wootton Bassett. Take this and continue for nearly 2 miles (3km). Look for a prominent stony track on the right by a large chestnut tree and some modern cottages. This is the spot marked 'Old Eagle' on the OS sheet and is just before the turn to the hamlet of Rockley. A place can easily be found here in which to leave the car.

Take the track, and almost at once reach a signpost stating that it leads to Four Mile Clump. This is a track well used for exercising racehorses; jockeys are a friendly bunch and you are likely to get a cheery 'Good morning' from a string of riders. There are now no pathfinding problems as the way goes straight ahead with good views in all directions.

After 3 miles (5km) the track joins the Ridgeway path. There is now an optional diversion. The site of Barbury Castle – just the earthworks now remain – is ½ mile (.8km) away and well signposted. This is now a Country Park and an information centre provides details of the history and wildlife of the area. If this diversion is taken, retrace to the junction with the Ridgeway path.

The route now goes to the right (south-east) along Smeathe's Ridge, and the views get even better. This is dramatic walking with the chance of great skyscapes, and the main road in the distance carries lines of tiny cars, distancing modern life from the rambler on his lonely ridge.

The route along Smeathe's Ridge near Barbury Castle (John Whatmore)

The path becomes indistinct in places, so do not gain or lose height and watch for the next distant stile. Soon the path picks up again as a stony way: stay with it until a road is reached; bear right onto the road and in a few yards, turn right off it, at a Ridgeway path sign. You now temporarily lose the high downs scenery and pass under trees and through thick vegetation. The destination is Ogbourne St Andrew, but be careful not to follow the path left into the hamlet of Southend; the fingerposting is a little confusing here, but a few moments' thought with the map will show that the true route continues south over a rather overgrown path, finishing in the village.

After passing the church on your right, turn right onto a track beside Downsway Cottages. This broad track climbs up the downs, and where it turns left after ½ mile (.8km) take the footpath on the right. This may be a little difficult to spot if the ground is under crops. Follow it to its junction with a track marked on the OS sheet as a road used as a public path, go left on this and follow it back to the original route along which you began the walk. Take this for less than a mile (1.6km), and you are back with your car.

78 RIDGEWAY·WANDERINGS

Time: Nearly 5 hours should be allowed, to include a stop for tea along the Thames.

Start and finish: Streatley. There is a small car park at the start of the walk; parking in the town is difficult owing to the narrow streets and the heavy traffic which soon builds up in summer months. Boots are not usually needed.

Approach: Streatley lies on the A329, 10 miles (16km) west of Reading. The town, with its 'twin', Goring, on the opposite bank of the Thames, is a good place in which to stay the night, to enjoy a quiet dinner by the river or merely to take tea before beginning the walk.

Attractions: This route combines the high, windswept time-remote land along which runs the Ridgeway, that ancient Green Road, with the much gentler Thames valley. The Ridgeway is one of the oldest roads not only in Britain but in the whole of Europe, and many claim it to be *the* oldest. It was ancient when the Romans came to Britain; it was already there when Stonehenge was built, and it was trodden by people of the Old Stone Age before Britain was even an island. Though we can only guess at much of its early history, its effect on the development of this land of ours was immense.

OS sheet: 174

Leave the little town by walking up the B4009, going west away from the river, and climbing a 1 in 6 hill. Alternatively, drive up this hill to a point just before the golf club where there is a fingerpost indicating a public foot-path to the right of the road. There is room here for several cars to park off the road. Take this path, going due north, passing a sign saying 'Danger of flying golf balls'. Now stride out across the golf links, as the first of many good views opens out to the north. The footpath is signposted across the course. Leave the golfers behind by continuing with the path through a farmyard, and at a quiet and attractive metalled lane go left for ¾ mile (1.2km) to Warren Farm, where take the broad dirt track on the right.

This is the start of the Ridgeway path or, more accurately, the start to one of its sections. An information board at this point states that a voluntary code has been agreed with national organisations interested in the use of Green Ways for motor sports, under which the Way should not be used by motor vehicles on Sundays and Bank holidays between 1 May and 31 October. Motor vehicles have a legal right on our ancient Green Roads, but the noise they – especially motor cycles involved in trail riding – can cause on these quiet byways is something that many lovers of the Ridgeway have come to dread.

Walk along the Ridgeway path as it climbs up to where the skies are large

Moulsford Church (John Whatmore)

and the views open out all around. Pass Warren Farm – did the existence of large colonies of rabbits here form an important part of the food supply of the area at one time? When a crossing point of tracks is reached, bear right off the Ridgeway path. Although you have turned off the official Ridgeway, you remain in its characteristic countryside with sweeping views and cloudscapes in this area of 360 degree horizons. Skylarks and crows provide the main sound. After a mile (1.6km), at a crossing of tracks, turn right onto Fair Mile, a broad well-trodden track which goes across Cholsey Downs and descends to a junction with the A417.

Go right on the main road for a few hundred yards to the bottom of a hill where go left on a public footpath. Follow this, through countryside now quite different from the high lands so recently left behind, skirt a wood, and enter Moulsford. The field before the village was a blue haze of germander speedwell when the author walked it.

At the main road, turn left to visit the church, attractively set beside the River Thames. The colourful interior roof alone is worth the visit. Now retrace your steps into the village and go left beside the Beetle and Wedge Hotel – a beetle, apparently, being a mallet. You are now firmly under the influence of the Thames. Pleasure craft rule the scenery here; their colourfully dressed crews call to each other across the river, and stops at the many pubs along the river are the order of the day. Hotels along this stretch of the river are alive to the custom generated by the boating fraternity and many lay tables in their riverside gardens to provide refreshments.

The path now follows the Berkshire side of the river, clinging to it all the way. At times it goes under willows, at others it is fringed with wild flowers, and always there is something to see happening on the river. This is the country of Jerome K. Jerome's *Three Men in a Boat* and, one suspects, of Toad and Water Rat. Stay with the path for 2 miles (3km) until the tower of Streatley church appears above the trees, then turn away from the river bank and cross the stile leading back into the town.

79 THE·SEVEN·SISTERS

Time: Two versions of this walk are included here: the shorter should easily be completed in 3½ hours, while for the longer route allow at least 6 hours including a lunch stop.

Start and finish: The Forestry Commission car park a mile (1.6km) south of Litlington which is a little over a mile (1.6km) from Alfriston. No boots are needed.

Approach: The car park at Litlington is easily reached fom Seaford by driving along the A259 and then taking the first left after Exceat Bridge. Those coming from the London direction should avoid entering Alfriston village as there is no bridge over the Cuckmere River there. Instead, immediately north of Alfriston, turn left at the signpost to Litlington.

Attractions: This route, which includes part of the South Downs Way, passes along cliffs where the scenery is unsurpassed in south-east England. The walk along the Seven Sisters – actually there are eight of these dramatic white cliffs – soars up and down making this an energetic ramble. The route then turns inland but keeps to high ground, and there are frequent distant vistas. Both versions of the walk finish through Friston Forest.

OS sheet: 199

Leave the car park by the way you drove in and turn left along the road. Take the first left in a few hundred yards or so, and walk up a pretty lane to West-dean, a little tucked-away village with brick and flint cottages and a duck pond. It is a spot well worth lingering in. Leave it by the footpath at the south-west of the village, going west-south-west soon to reach the A259. Cross this road and continue south on a wide, surfaced track. Those who object to walking on a hard surface will find that there is a path off to the left roughly paralleling the broader way and passing close to Foxhole Farm. The route continues across open downland until the sea comes into view at Cliff End.

The route now becomes hilly as the coastal path soars and descends along the cliffs. However hard the going may seem, this is walking par excellence with, in summer, the green of the downs stretching away on the left and the blue sea to the right: in fact it is 3 miles (5 km) of delight. The coastal section of the walk ends at Birling Gap where there is a pub, coffee house and hotel. Leave by taking the wide, rough track going north-west up Went Hill where the thorn hedges are trimmed and bent by the winter gales. At the summit, the town of Eastdean comes into view below and on the right.

(Those making the shorter of these two walks should now bear left following the footpath signs to Friston. Throughout this walk the footpaths are well

The wide rough track going north-west up Went Hill (John Whatmore)

signposted and there should be little chance of becoming seriously lost. At Friston, cross the A259 by the church and pick up the footpath signs for Friston Place. The route passes through pleasant parkland-type scenery, through quaint gates set in old walls. At Friston Place, there is a prominent bridleway running west over Friston Hill. This is easy walking with plenty of wildlife and flowers on this south-facing hill. Indeed, just before Westdean is reached, a vineyard is seen on the right. On reaching Westdean, to avoid finishing the walk on the road along which the ramble was started, take the path going north at the western edge of the village and almost at once bear off left through the woods for the last ½ mile (.8km) back to the car park.)

Those favouring the longer of the two routes should bear right at the top of Went Hill, taking a prominent footpath directly down into Eastdean. The village is attractive despite the considerable amount of residential building to its north, and there is a village green. Bear right out of the village along Upper Street, turn right at the T-junction then take the first left into the suburbs at Summerdown Lane. While a suburb of 800 houses may not seem ideal walking country, this development does show that the suburbs we need in this modern life can be built attractively. The gardens are large and well laid out, and if there is such a thing as an ideal suburb, perhaps this is it. As the houses come to an end at the top of the rise, take the bridleway on the right signposted to Willingdon. Those who hate modern housing developments will now be pleased to see that true downland country has again been reached and sweeping views open up to the right. The walker is now on Willingdon Hill and mile after mile of distant views open out. At a prominent junction of bridleways, take the route signposted to Jevington and descend to that village. This is a splendid place for tea on a summer Sunday and its attractive church, almost hidden away from the rest of the village, is well worth a visit.

Leave Jevington by going south-west along a prominent track. Pass through Friston Forest following the broad track, and bear right at a gate where there is a signpost saying 'Forest Walk'. This will bring you to the western edge of the forest and to the car park.

OLD·RAILWAY·LINES

From 1948 when British Railways came into being, until about 1968, during which time the modernisation scheme of the mid-fifties had brought about the rapid demise of the steam railway, 6,000 miles (8,047km) of track disappeared. In the same period, half the total number of stations closed. The time of the accountant had arrived in the 1960s with Dr Beeching's plan, and when the axe fell the railways were never to be the same again.

Abandonment and decay always bring sadness, and the ever-shrinking network of the British railway system is sad indeed, but there is light at the end of the tunnel. Main lines will continue to the twenty-first century and even some branch lines, though these will be the victims of any further purges. Even so, a little philosophy still permits a bright picture, for what is lost to the rail traveller can be gained by the traveller and his dog, on foot.

A journey by rail is a glorious way to view the countryside if you are not bowling along at 100mph and more. A steady pace of something like 3mph along former branch lines, or the last main line to open and the first to close – the Great Central Railway – gives a much better appreciation and brings the other senses of hearing and smell into play.

Today there are some 8,000 miles (12,875km) of abandoned lines, most of them reverting to nature; but thankfully progressive planning by some county councils and other local authorities has rescued about 10 per cent from obliteration. A great deal more could be done to save these ready-made footpaths, the cost of retaining them being minimal. Landscaping is neither necessary nor desirable and should not even be considered. Surfacing can be a boon but is not vital. The important lesson to be learned now is to keep them for future generations, for they will otherwise perish and cannot be replaced. Meanwhile, those we have we can enjoy.

Retention of the railway features is vital, for the railway atmosphere prevails long after closure. Bridges, well built and in many cases defiant of neglect, embankments, cuttings, tunnels, platforms, buildings, signal posts, all trappings of the railway, can and should be saved. These are no ordinary footpaths; they are part of our national heritage and have been described as biological corridors, for they provide a haven for our dwindling wildlife from the merciless road traffic and the offensive over-use of insecticides in the fields. Species threatened with extinction are finding sanctuary in these lost green ways, but for how long?

The Neston Rock cutting in the Wirral Country Park (G. Hutt) (see page 298)

MEON VALLEY RAILWAY (WEST MEON - DROXFORD)
THE PUBLIC MAY MAKE TEMPORARY USE OF THIS
DISUSED RAILWAY LINE FOR WALKING OR HORSE
RIDING. NO LIABILITY IS ACCEPTED FOR INJURY
OR DAMAGE ARISING FROM SUCH USE.
PLEASE OBSERVE THE COUNTRY CODE.

One of the joys of railway walking is to observe the rare or the unusual, sometimes provided by man, but more often by nature – a bullfinch, a prancing hare or slinking fox, a stoat standing up to sniff the air, wild orchids, a mass of violets or primroses. Only the rabbit seems to be in need of control, and nature can provide that too. The worst types of undergrowth cannot be left to nature. Gorse and bramble in particular will soon form an impenetrable wall if left unchecked, as many a walker has found out the hard way.

In both urban and rural areas, obstructions are many and varied, even when the landowner has been identified and permission has been given to go through. Detours are nearly always possible around the obstacles, some of the commonest being missing bridges, cattle on the line, blocked drainage channels, new buildings and, of course, barbed wire. There are also some novel uses such as a miniature speedway track, gymkhana practice course, garden lawn, gypsy caravan site and the largest manure heap in the land. The problem is magnified when the land is purchased piecemeal, spoiling the continuity with part of a garden here, a rubbish tip there, a factory or a ploughed-up section.

By contrast, there are also many long open stretches, mostly owned by local authorities where walking for the well-shod is comfortable and for the most part unimpeded; but any restrictive notices must be heeded. Walking is often permitted, but few routes are public rights of way.

The explorer who wants to break fresh ground or discover if a certain station still exists, will inevitably confront the question of trespass at some stage. The only way to eliminate this risk is to trace the owner, often difficult or impossible, or take the tried and trusted official Railway Walks. The majority of these are a real pleasure, the exceptions being the landscaped ones which are of much lesser interest. These official walks are free from fences, encroaching brambles, gardeners and farmers; some of the preserved railway buildings are treasures and will remain, as they have been put to domestic use.

The Railway Ramblers Club, formed in 1978 and comprising several hundred members of kindred spirit, seeks to increase such routes and can offer organised walks, or information and advice, to members.

Lack of preparation will detract from the enjoyment of a walk and it is essential to check beforehand on transport arrangements. An Ordnance Survey map is a must and a feed-bag advisable especially in remoter areas, but travel as light as possible.

A railway walk is a transport of delight and the following are some examples. These and the other hundred plus throughout Britain await you.

80	The Wirral Way, Cheshire	12 miles (19km)
81	Kingswinford Branch Walk, West Midland	8 miles (13km)
82	The Speyside Way, Grampian	6½ or 16 miles (10 to 26km)
83	Wickham to West Meon, Hampshire˙	9 miles (14km)
84	Woodhall Spa to Horncastle, Lincolnshire	5 miles (8km)
85	Penmaenpool to Barmouth, Gwynedd	5 miles (8km)
86	Wadebridge to Padstow, Cornwall	6 miles (9.6km)

80 THE·WIRRAL·WAY

Time: 5 hours should be sufficient, plus time to dally at the many points of interest.

Start and finish: The walk can be joined at either end, or at one of the many intermediate access points along the way; but to appreciate the whole route of about 12 miles (19km) a start at West Kirby or Hooton is necessary.

Approach: West Kirby is served by fast and frequent electric trains from Liverpool over the lines of the former Wirral Railway. Hooton is similarly provided for with the addition of diesel train services from Helsby and Chester.

Attractions: The Wirral Country Park or Wirral Way is based on the disused railway trackbed which runs from Hooton station in the middle of the Wirral Peninsula to West Kirby on the extreme north-west tip of the tongue of land jutting out between the Rivers Dee and Mersey. In following the route of the railway the Wirral Way passes for the most part through open country affording fine views of both the Wirral and North Wales including, on a good day, the island of Anglesey.

OS sheets: 108 and 117

When one thinks of Merseyside one tends to recall stories of decaying docklands and crumbling inner-city areas such as Liverpool and Birkenhead. It is true that a physical decline has taken place in certain parts, but country-loving walkers can find a surprisingly rural haven no more than 8 miles (13km) from Birkenhead.

A few words of history are necessary to put the route into perspective. The Birkenhead Railway which ran between Birkenhead and Chester, and which was operated jointly by the Great Western Railway and the London North Western Railway, applied to Parliament for an Act to build a branch line from its station at Hooton to the fishing and colliery village of Parkgate situated on the banks of the River Dee. The railway was authorised on 17 June 1862, and construction commenced. The line opened for traffic in 1866. It was extended along the banks of the Dee from Parkgate to West Kirby in 1886 thus, in effect, creating a circular route Hooton to Hooton via West Kirby and Birkenhead. Stations were built on the extension at Heswall, Thurstaston, Caldy and Kirby Park. The terminus at West Kirby lay alongside the separate Wirral Railway's own West Kirby station. The line closed to passengers on 12 September 1956 and to freight on 7 May 1962.

Let us set off, then, to walk the route where the iron horse ran for over three-quarters of a century. Starting at Hooton one immediately realises that this walk is going to be different from any other country ramble. Set off along the platform formerly used by the branch-line trains. Nestling in the bushes

Hadlow Road Station, Willaston (Maurice Blencowe)

is the shuttered and boarded waiting room and the original maroon-enamelled British Railways style station nameboard. The route then leaves the station buildings and immediately plunges into countryside. For the first few yards the path is closely paralleled by the original trackbed, clearly identifiable by the remaining ballast stones. This joins the Wirral Way path and the remainder of the walk is over the actual trackbed although tender soles need have no fear, the ballast has been removed. The thick brambles and young trees close in from either side providing a quiet haven for butterflies and wild flowers. Here and there railway relics such as downed signal gantries and gradient posts add to the nostalgic mystery of the walk.

About 2 miles (3km) from Hooton the route emerges from the lush greenery to arrive at the gem of the Wirral Way – Hadlow Road railway station. This served the nearby village of Willaston and has been preserved as a museum representing a typical rural station. Inside the main building everything is as it was, as though time has stood still on a working day in the 1950s and the booking clerk has just popped out for a moment. Railway parcel-trollies and engine-cleaning tools are laid out on the platforms, old-fashioned advertising boards adorn the fences, and there is even a short stretch of single track between the platforms plus a signal box, semaphore signal and level-crossing gates. The whole site is quietly mysterious and evocative, and is kept meticulously clean. The museum is free and open to the public every day; it is well worthwhile as a long slow look back in time.

Pressing on through the countryside, the next main item of interest is the ½ mile (.8km) long Neston sandstone rock cutting – the only major railway engineering feature along the branch line. The damp eerie rock walls strewn with young trees and shrubs crowd in on the walker. Such gloomy dampness encourages plant and flower growth, and the cutting is used as a nature reserve. An interesting feature is the long moss-covered hump along the cutting floor. This is in fact a modern sewer pipe covered in concrete to which the moss has clung. The walker need not be afraid as the pipe is not unsightly; in fact it blends in well. Just beyond the cutting the route of the railway is blocked by housing development on Neston station site, but the way round is well signposted – via Station Close and Station Road!

The walker next passes under the in-use Wrexham to Bidston railway line and is directed, with a short detour back onto the old trackbed, to continue through fields on the outskirts of Neston. After a further ¼ mile (.4km), the observant walker will discern the tree-lined route of another trackbed joining the Wirral Way from the left. This was once the spur down to the long-gone Wirral Colliery right on the banks of the River Dee, good views of which now open up.

The walker next arrives at the site of Parkgate station. The original station of 1866 opened as a terminus; but with the opening of the line extension to West Kirby in 1886, the first station was rebuilt to permit through running of trains. Traces of the cobbled setts of the station approach road and broken brickwork from the station buildings, can still be seen.

Heading towards Heswall, the walker is afforded attractive views of the fields sweeping down to the River Dee with the Welsh hills beyond. At Heswall the trackbed has been built on for a ½ mile (.8km) or so, but the underbridge parapets and the station house can be made out at Station Road on the right.

Beyond Heswall the countryside really opens out to give fine views of Thurstaston Common to the right and the Dee and North Wales coastline to the left. Soon the busyness of the Thurstaston visitor centre appears in the distance. Based alongside the site of the old Thurstaston station, which has retained its platforms, the centre has displays and exhibitions depicting the history, geography, wildlife and plant life of the Wirral Country Park. Nearby are the famous Thurstaston cliffs dropping sheer into the Dee, and there are panoramic views of the River Dee estuary and out over the Irish Sea.

Another mile (1.6km) of countryside brings you to the edges of suburbia at Caldy on the outskirts of West Kirby, the end of the line. Here the trackbed narrows from the wide open spaces into the close confines of the built-up area, and this narrow but pleasant stretch emphasises an odd feature of the walk. The observant walker will have deduced that the many bridges which remain are all wide enough to take double track, but in fact the route was only ever laid as a single-track line.

At the busy sailing and holiday town of West Kirby, the Wirral Way ends conveniently at the bus and railway stations, the former having been built on the actual site of the rail terminus from Hooton.

81 KINGSWINFORD·BRANCH

Time: For the full-length walk, about 4 hours including a lunch stop.

Start and finish: Access is possible at most bridges within Wolverhampton (and indeed, all along the route), but the official start of the walk is at the Aldersley Stadium car park (grid reference 898007).

You can walk as far along the line as you wish, but the suggested end-points are either the site of Himley station (875911) where there are car-parking facilities, or the bridge which carries the old line over the A449 Wolverhampton–Kidderminster road (883907) where there are buses back to Wolverhampton. Boots are recommended but not essential.

Approach: The start of the walk is reached by turning northwards off the A41 Wolverhampton–Newport road at a crossroads 2 miles (3km) north-west of the centre of Wolverhampton. Follow the signs to the Aldersley (or Wolverhampton) Stadium where access to the old railway can be gained.

Attractions: The scenery along the route is pleasant rather than breathtaking, but the raison d'être of this walk is to provide an easy, gratifying and traffic-free passage out of a heavily built-up area into the open countryside with the added fascination of numerous railway relics along the way. Additionally, the embankments and cuttings as they gradually return to nature make ideal habitats for many species of flora and fauna, some rare, which can be observed at leisure.

OS sheet: 139

The Kingswinford Branch was built by the Great Western Railway Company between 1912 and 1925 as a branch of the Worcester & Wolverhampton main line. The line was single track, except at Tettenhall, Wombourne and Himley where there were passing loops. A passenger service on the line operated for just seven years between 1925 and 1932, although the line was well utilised for freight as a Wolverhampton bypass. The line was closed in 1965 after a working life of just forty years; which seems rather wasteful as you walk the line admiring the stations, bridges, embankments and cuttings and the effort which went into constructing them.

The walking surface alternates from gravel chippings to a hard-packed sandy consistency which tends to become waterlogged after several days of heavy rain. Initially, the path is well screened by trees as it passes between housing estates. This leafy corridor is much more pleasant than one would expect of such a densely populated area; on a warm summer's day, oak, sycamore, birch and willow trees take turns in providing welcome shade.

Just as you imagine that you are wandering through a wood in the heart of the countryside, Tettenhall station comes into view with both platforms and all station buildings still remaining. The station is being renovated, presumably ultimately to achieve the same standard of preservation as the station at Wombourne (see page 304). Even in its present condition, one can stand on the platforms and picture the trains pulling in and the hustle and bustle as passengers board and disembark. Until recently the Waiting Room and Ladies Room signs remained in their original positions. While exploring the old line in preparation for writing this piece, we met a pensioner standing on the down platform looking at the old station. To our delight, we discovered that the elderly gentleman, a Mr George Bradford, had actually worked as a porter on the line for two years in the 1930s and was able to recount his memories of the railway days. This meeting was, of course, somewhat melancholy as the line is no longer operational; but at least the Kingswinford Branch is being preserved in a different form, unlike so many other disused railways each of which have their own stories to tell.

The old railway runs parallel to the Staffordshire & Worcestershire Canal before eventually crossing it by way of a superb girder bridge (with cross supports) which is certainly worthy of a photograph. The avenue of trees is soon replaced by a long, deep cutting which is both attractive and soothing. This is a place where people can stroll in quiet contemplation with only the wind in the trees and the birds as companions. There is a sense of being cocooned in a peaceful, green tunnel as the sights, sounds and smells of what amounts to a linear nature reserve begin to imprint themselves on the consciousness. The vibrant purples of the vetches complement the orangy-yellow of bird's-foot trefoil, the tiny yellow pinpricks of hop trefoil and the pale shades of yellow rattle.

Continuing in this vein, the old line leaves the confines of Wolverhampton and runs on into open countryside. The walker, still in a deep

Tettenhall Station looking south (John Gibberd)

cutting, is unaware of this; but there is no hint of boredom and occasional bridges over the line, built sturdily in blue brick (caked with soot from long-gone steam locomotives), add to the relaxing atmosphere.

The line turns south and then south-east as it passes the platform at Lower Penn Halt and a public house where refreshments can be obtained. Along this stretch, the delicate white tracery of cow parsley, hogweed and ox-eye daisy appear and reappear as an edging of lace along the hem of the green undergrowth. The urgent song of the wren and the trills of the willow warbler contrast with the repetitive call of the yellowhammer. The eye is often attracted by flashes of colour as bullfinches fly from branch to branch, and a greater spotted woodpecker passes overhead. Butterflies will also be in evidence; wall browns and common blues respond to the warmth in the air and the sweetness in the flowers.

The cutting eventually ends and the walker is now presented with views on all sides – metamorphosis is complete. The scarp of Orton Hill can be seen to the east, while westwards there are views of distant hills. The old railway now running ruler-straight on a low embankment, thus provides a pleasant alternative to the lengthy cutting now left behind. Before long, the walker turns southwards again and the fully and tastefully restored station at Wombourne (870940) comes into view. Resplendent in its original GWR colours, it houses a permanent exhibition of the conversion of the old railway, provides accommodation for the warden and also incorporates a toilet block. Leaflets on various aspects of the walk can be obtained here. There are picnic tables dotted around the station and cars can be parked in the old goods yard.

Wombourne station is a good place to rest and take a photograph, but the walk is not over yet. Continuing through Wombourne, the old line passes beneath several splendid three-arched bridges and then turns south-east again to run through Himley Plantation. The platforms marking the site of Himley Station (875912) are soon reached where there are more picnic tables and a car park for those wishing to end their day's exploration at this point.

For those continuing onwards, the trackbed runs on a fairly high embankment with the pathway split down the middle by an oppressive and rather unnecessary wooden barrier, with the intention that walkers go on one side and horse riders on the other. This rather spoils the effect especially when the chances of getting trampled underfoot are negligible! As the line approaches the bridge over the A449 (883907) an attractive row of Corsican pines flanks the old railway on each side. These were planted at the same time as the railway was built, to placate a local landowner who objected to the sight and sound of steam trains crossing his territory. Beyond the A449, the walk actually continues to a dismantled bridge at 890906, although there is little of interest on this final stretch.

For anyone wishing to get away from it all, the Kingswinford Branch railway walk is an ideal day's (or afternoon's) outing, especially during spring and summer when the flora is at its best. Long after the foot ache has gone, the images of varied flowers and fresh green leaves will remain fixed in the memory.

82 THE·SPEYSIDE·WALK

Time: Two versions of this Dufftown to Ballindalloch walk are included, the first section to Aberlour should be completed in 3 hours, the longer section will take 7 hours, including a lunch stop.

Start and finish: The former station at Dufftown, now a Community Projects Agency workshop, ¾ mile (1.2km) to the north of the town, beyond the entrance to the Glenfiddich distillery. Aberlour station is in the Alice Littler Park, with an entrance off the town's square. Ballindalloch lies at the end of the B9137, approximately one mile (1.6km) from the Dalnashaugh Inn.

The simplest way to return is by using the bus service that operates from Aberlour to Dufftown (moderately frequent except on Sundays) or to Grantown (a few buses per day with no Sunday service).

Approach: Dufftown is located at the junction of roads from the towns of the Morayshire plain as well as two roads over the Grampian mountains to Tomintoul and Rhynie. The town has several cafés and hotels, toilets and ample car parking.

Attractions: The route follows the valleys of the Rivers Fiddich and Spey, forming an interesting walk through mixed agricultural land, interspersed by many distilleries to help raise flagging spirits. The former railway line has been converted into an official footpath, generally providing firm and dry conditions underfoot.

OS sheet: 28

There is a small car park and picnic place at the start of the walk, as well as an information board depicting the route. Leave the car park and head north towards the buildings of the Convalmore Distillery. The track is a sanded path on the ballast chippings of the original railway.

Having left the modern and more traditional buildings of the distillery behind, the walk enters mixed woodland that runs along the banks of the River Fiddich. Shortly after entering the wood, a set of steps leads down from the track to allow inspection of a culvert passing underneath the railway. Gradually the woods are left behind as the trackbed crosses over the Fiddich on a curving bridge resting on a series of stone pillars. The sand-covering on top of the original stone ballast stops for about a mile (1.6km), leaving the original ballast in situ, which needs to be walked with care.

The route passes through a series of rock cuttings as it follows the course of the Fiddich to reach the derelict house and distillery of Birchdean. The remains are worthy of inspection, revealing a derelict waterwheel in what appears to be traditional distillery buildings. Beyond Birchdean the route crosses the Fiddich to reach the site of Craigellachie station. Before the river, ¼ mile (.4km) south of the station, an access road crosses the railway on a

bridge which is now unsafe. The path therefore diverts up the cutting on the right and down again past the bridge. This is at grid reference 295447.

The former station (4 miles (6km) from Dufftown) has been converted into an attractive park, with ample parking and toilet facilities. Benches and tables are provided for those wishing to picnic, while the nearby village has a café and hotel. The route passes an imitation signal box, built out of logs in the former turntable pit, and curves gradually westwards to pass underneath the leftmost of a pair of bridges, to follow the Spey valley towards Aberlour. The track is now a firm earthen track, which is generally dry underfoot. Once past the typically Victorian buildings of Craigellachie Hotel, head underneath the new road from Craigellachie to Aberlour by means of a corrugated-iron subway. Emerging from its curvaceous interior, one can look back along the line of the road to view the original bridge over the Spey built by Thomas Telford.

The railway is regained where it enters a short tunnel, emerging onto a shelf above the Spey, where a large brick-built retaining wall separates the track from the road above. Wooden benches are provided at regular intervals along the way allowing one to rest and admire the view. By the junction of the A95 with a minor road signposted to Bluehill Quarry, an access point with limited parking space has been provided. A mile (1.6km) further on lies the small town of Aberlour (2¼ miles (3.6km) from Craigellachie), where the path passes by the side of the former goods yard with its mountains of coal, to emerge in the well-kept lawns of the Alice Littler Park. The former station buildings have been converted into a tea room run by the local community association. Aberlour (originally known as Charlestown) was built in 1812 by Charles Grant of Wester Elchies as a planned town for his estate workers.

Those wishing to end their walk at Aberlour may head up into the nearby town where the bus service back to Dufftown leaves from the Square, opposite the Lour Hotel. Alternatively return to Dufftown along the railway, making a round trip of some 13 miles (21 km) (allow 5–6 hours). The town has several hotels, cafés and shops. Toilet facilities are provided at the rear of the station building, while there are ample car-parking facilities.

To continue to Ballindalloch, head under the bridge at the end of the station and pass the nearby car park. Cross the Burn of Aberlour by means of a modern timber suspension bridge, built on the abutments of the original. Walking towards Carron, you will pass several mileposts and a faded 'Stop Look and Listen' notice – artefacts of the railway age. The route is generally a grassy track, and occasionally wet underfoot. Nearing the minor road from Carron to the A95, the trackbed is used as an access road for a nearby works. Where the track turns to head for the main road, continue straight on past the overgrown platform and the white-painted sign of Dailuaine platform; a short distance further on, a branch which served a nearby distillery passes underneath the minor road and joins the railway.

Tunnel on the Speyside Way, Craigellachie (Michael Ellison)

Spey viaduct, Ballindalloch (Michael Ellison)

Nearing Carron (3¼ miles (5.2km) from Aberlour), leave the railway and join the minor road in order to cross over the River Spey. This single-arched span once carried both road and railway, but one soon realises why the path uses the road and not the railway side. Once over the river, a Speyside Way signpost directs you back onto the railway along a path which wanders through the grounds of the Imperial Distillery.

However, if you miss the signpost, there is no real problem as the walk can be rejoined by turning left into the road leading to the distillery, opposite the village pub. There are limited parking facilities in the village. The small single-storeyed stone building to the left of the entrance to the distillery was once Carron station. Turning right by this entrance, the path is a grassy embankment passing between the distillery and a nearby lane leading to Dalmunach. At the edge of the well-kept grounds, continue straight on through a gate (with low stile) onto a grassy track that is again signposted as the Speyside Way.

Passing Dalmunach, there are traces of a wooden platform on the northern side of the trackbed. A short distance further on another bridge is crossed over the Ballintomb Burn – a bridge that was reconstructed by the army, as is indicated in the concrete capping of the bridge ends. The walk is very pleasant, a mixture of woodland and pasture, with a great profusion of wild flowers that support an assortment of butterflies and small mammals

The next access point is at the former station of Knockando (2½ miles (4km) from Carron), that has been converted into a visitor centre for the nearby Tamdhu Distillery. The station has been renamed 'Tamdhu' and retains its original wooden buildings and signal box. There is car parking nearby, and toilet facilities when the distillery is open to visitors. The latter is reached by means of a minor road from the B9102 which follows the northern bank of the River Spey. Once past the station, continue along the entrance road to the distillery and its various buildings (by means of a dirt track used by lorries to reach a nearby loading apparatus) to rejoin the grassy track of the railway.

The Allt Arder is crossed on wooden duckboards laid on top of the original stone-built railway bridge. A small viewing platform in the middle of the bridge allows one to rest and take in the view. The route then passes alongside a lengthy wood emerging at the site of Blacksboat station (2¼ miles (3.6km) from Knockando). There is a limited amount of car parking at the station which is reached by turning off the B9138, which links the A95 and B9102.

Having perhaps paused to view the well-restored station building and the nearby goods shed, embark on the final section of just over 2 miles (3km) to Ballindalloch. Many mileposts are passed as the grassy track heads over another suspension bridge, this time over the Allt Gheallaidh. Once the lonely cottage of Dalnapot has been passed you will obtain a first sighting of the lattice girder bridge that crosses the Spey. This bridge still proclaims that it was built in Dundee by the firm of C. McFarlane.

Across the bridge the track curves gently westwards to the single-storey stone station building, passing alongside the once extensive sidings for goods and cattle. The station buildings are now an outdoor pursuits centre and mark the end of the walk. There is a limited amount of car parking nearby, while those requiring public transport should head up the B9137 (turning left at the roadside by the station, passing the many derelict cattle pens on the right-hand side) to reach the A95 after ½ mile (.8km). At the A95 turn left to reach the Bridge of Avon (where there is a well-stocked shop) or Dalnashaugh Inn, ¼ mile (.4km) further on.

83 WICKHAM·TO·WEST·MEON

Time: Allow 5 hours.

Start and finish: The walk begins at Wickham, 11 miles from Southampton or Portsmouth at the junction of the A32 and A333 roads. The finish at West Meon is 2 miles before the A32/A272 crossroads. Stout shoes or boots are recommended.

Approach: From London and the north: M3 exit 5 and A32 to Wickham or West Meon. From the west: A333 from Southampton. From the east: A27/M27, exit 10 and A32.

Attractions: The 22 mile (35km) railway from Knowle Junction, Fareham, to Alton was something of a rarity in that the opening was in the twentieth century, on 1 June 1903, and its passenger service lasted only until 1955. Although the walk starts 2 miles (3km) further on, the town of Fareham should be mentioned for its quayside of boats and the Georgian High Street which is in stylish contrast to the relatively new shopping precinct. At Wickham, Georgian architecture is in evidence again in the superb market square where on 20 May the annual Wickham Fair is held. Chesapeake Mill is another attraction. It is a four-storey building mostly of brick, but partly in timber from *The Chesapeake*, a captured American frigate. Wickham was also the birthplace of the great Bishop of Winchester, William of Wykeham.

OS sheets: 185 and 196

Leaving Wickham along the platforms which are the only remains of the station, the walk passes a wood to the east and continues along the valley of the little River Meon through the attractive villages of Soberton and Droxford, where Isaac Walton spent his last years. For the railway enthusiast Droxford is the pièce de résistance as the station, including pink canopy, is intact, thanks to Portsmouth & District Transport Training Ltd who used the buildings and yard as a heavy goods vehicle training centre before the property was sold as a private residence. The station also has the distinction of being the venue for the final planning in 1944 of the D-Day Normandy landings. A section of trackbed near Droxford is still ballasted, hence the stout footwear recommendation, but the remainder of the walk is relatively easy on the feet.

The next stretch to West Meon is also delightful, with pleasant views across the South Downs. There are interesting churches at all three villages of Meonstoke, Exton and Warnford, the first being particularly attractive, built of stone with tiled roofs and unusual tower. The chalk downs contain a good deal of flint which is put to effective use in the local walls and buildings, many of which are roofed with handmade clay tiles and thatch.

At West Meon, as at Wickham, sadly only the railway platforms remain, but the village is very attractive and should be visited if possible. In the churchyard is the grave of one Thomas Lord, founder of Lord's Cricket Ground. There is also a public house named after him in the village.

As the whole of this walk is an official walkway, there are several access points along it, complete with steps, so that the walk can be started or finished at places other than Wickham or West Meon. Bits and pieces of the remaining half of the Meon Valley line can be walked, such as from East Tistel to Farringdon (almost), but most of the last section from Farringdon to Alton (main line) is not recognisable as a former railway track, having been obliterated by fields and modern road development.

Droxford Station

84 WOODHALL·SPA·TO· HORNCASTLE

Time: Allow 3 hours' walking.

Start and finish: Where the railway used to cross the Broadway in Woodhall Spa there is now a car park opposite Clarence Road Post Office and entrance to Eagle Lodge. The start of the trail is about 50yd (45m) beyond the car park at Iddesleigh Road and is marked by an information board. Finish at the crossing-keeper's cottage by the canal bridge 500yd (450m) from the A153 or continue along the canalside footpath to Horncastle.

Approach: The B1191 passes through Woodhall Spa from the direction of Lincoln or Horncastle. From the south and east the best approach is the A153.

Attractions: Woodhall became a spa following the discovery of minerals during drilling for coal in the early nineteenth century. The Bath House was erected in 1850, but the inland resort scheme failed after the Edwardian period. Many fine houses remain as a legacy of that time, but unfortunately little remains of the station. The single-track branch actually started at Woodhall Junction in the shadow of Kirkstead Bridge over the River Witham, and it is worth the 2 mile (3km) trip along the Witham Road (B1191) to see the station. The Horncastle Railway opened its 7 mile (11km) line on 11 August 1855, and although GNR trains operated, it remained an independent company for sixty-eight years, until the LNER arrived.

OS sheet: 122

The Spa Trail, which is the name given to the walk by the local council, starts through an avenue of trees and diverts to the left after ½ mile (.8km) to avoid the major part of a golf course. The path can easily be followed along the edge of a field with a glimpse of The Tower on the Moor to the right, past the eighteenth golf tee and through a tunnel of trees to a minor road. Marker posts bearing a Viking helmet show that the path is part of the Viking Way and at the road an arrow points to the right. By following the arrow, the Trail is found again at the former level crossing, one of sixteen on the branch. A crossing-keeper's house marks the spot – a functional building lacking the usual ornamentation. There are several like it along the Way.

The birch trees of Highall Wood are to the left and there is an abundance of bracken, wild flowers and butterflies, the area having been designated of special scientific interest. An information board here depicts the various birds which can be seen. A picnic area and car park are provided in a shaded cutting where the road turns to run parallel with the Trail for a short distance before crossing it on what was the only overbridge on the line, which curved at this point to a north-westerly direction.

Immediately past the bridge the scenery changes from woodland to the open countryside of the Bain valley where the little River Bain is companion to the Horncastle Canal abandoned a century ago. The canal, however, is not weed-choked as it is used to collect drainage water from farm land, and it is haven for a variety of waterfowl and fish.

At Thornton Lodge Farm a minor road crosses the Trail and another crossing-keeper's cottage still stands guard, this one painted white. It marks the end of the Spa Trail, the gate ahead bearing a 'Keep Out' notice; but the footpath to Horncastle is only a few steps away at the canal bridge and the last mile (1.6km) can be covered with footpath, canal and railway all running parallel within yards of each other. The station at Horncastle was on the Langton road near the point where the canal branched off eastwards. Much of it has gone but the coal yard remains with some attractive cottages and a handsome warehouse with scrolled-iron brackets supporting its canopy. Passenger traffic ended in 1954, but diminutive freight trains continued until 1970, a bad year for Lincolnshire railways for it saw the closure of the greater part of the rail system in the eastern part of the county.

The attractive little market town of Horncastle repays time spent there. Present-day markets are modest by comparison with the ten-day horse fairs which used to be held there every August, but the market square is in a pleasant setting and there are some very fine Georgian houses, old inns and warehouses. St Mary's Church has relics of the Civil War, gleaned from the battlefields at Winceby in which Oliver Cromwell fought. The town also has the distinction of being the home of Alfred Lord Tennyson's bride, Emily Sellwood, before their marriage. Tennyson was born in 1809 at the rectory in Somersby some 6 miles (9.6km) to the north-east in the Lincolnshire wolds.

The Tower

85 PENMAENPOOL·TO· BARMOUTH

Great Western Railway Signal

Time: Allow 3 hours.
Start and finish: Start at Penmaenpool toll bridge 6 miles (10km) east of Barmouth. The finish is at Morfa Mawddach station at the south end of Barmouth Bridge.
Approach: Take the A496 from Barmouth or the A493 from Dolgellau.
Attractions: On 3 July 1865 the Cambrian Railway opened its line from Penmaenpool to Barmouth Junction, and by the end of the decade it formed the beginning of a route from Barmouth right across Wales to Wrexham, eventually becoming wholly Great Western. A hundred years and many holiday trains later it closed, but travellers on foot can still enjoy the splendours of the journey along the beautiful River Mawddach to its estuary.
OS sheet: 124

There is a toll bridge at either end of the walk; the shorter of the two is at Penmaenpool where the river is narrower and this is where the walk starts. In close proximity to the bridge and the George Hotel, are several relics of the railway – the signal box now used as a nature information centre, the station, a gas lamp, a fine pair of Great Western Railway signals and a cast-iron notice boldly stating 'Beware of Trains'. A straight embankment leads across marsh-land, enabling the walker to keep his feet dry and cutting off a bend in the river. At the end of the embankment the marshes give way to a thickly wooded hillside to the left and the lapping water on the shore to the right. The retaining wall between path and river is topped with enormous slabs of local red slate. The height above sea level here is only 21ft (6.4m) as the route hugs the shoreline.

There are mountains on both sides, the range on the northern side being visible all along the estuary. On the other side, 2 miles (3km) away, are the foothills of Cader Idris, a mountain with its highest peak at 2,927ft (892m), overlooking the counties of Gwynedd and Powys on opposite sides. A tributary of the Mawddach flows from it through the woods, and the footpath crosses where the waters meet by a small bridge. The main river then narrows as the path curves to the south-west, where there is a sudden transformation with an expanse of water 1½ miles (2km) wide and a fine view of Barmouth railway bridge. The wildlife revels in its seclusion and at low tide there are flocks of sea birds, including cormorant, shag, oyster catcher and shelduck. Butterflies flit amongst the wild flowers, amongst which are varieties of orchid.

There are still gangers' huts along the way to provide refuge from a sudden shower. At Arthog a lane leads up the lower slopes of Cader Idris to water-falls, and lower down the railway walk continues, still well away from the road. Arthog station has gone, leaving only its nameboard on a timber garage. A small headland juts into the river and the path moves away from the water for a short distance, turning back again when it finally meets the road, to end at the car park next to the railway station at Barmouth Junction, renamed Morfa Mawddach in 1960.

An unusual and welcome provision is a continuous wooden handrail with inlaid bilingual (Welsh/English) Braille plaque, installed (as of 1984) for ⅓ mile (.5km) from the car park, as a guide for blind and partially sighted people and those with difficulty in walking. Seats are built into the hand-rail. The facility was provided by the Snowdonia National Park, of which the railway walk now forms a part.

If a train is due on arrival at the station it is only a few minutes' ride to Barmouth, but most walkers would prefer to cross the railway bridge on foot. A timber walkway runs alongside the track on the east side, and a toll is paid at the far end. British Rail has had problems with the ½ mile (.8km) bridge as the timber sections below water have been progressively attacked by marine worms. Closure of the line has been threatened several times because of this, but repairs have been carried out allowing lightweight trains to cross.

At the north end of the bridge are the Dinas Oleu cliffs which in 1895 became the National Trust's first acquisition. The railway cuts through the foot of the cliffs by a short tunnel to the station, the line terminating at Pwllheli.

86 WADEBRIDGE · TO · PADSTOW

Time: This walk can be completed comfortably in 3 hours. Note that there are no intermediate towns or villages, so ramblers who require refreshments en route should take their own.

Start and finish: The walk starts from Eddystone Road near the centre of Wadebridge and ends at the South Quay car park in Padstow. Boots or stout shoes are advisable as the surface of the path is knobbly in places, doubtless evidence of its railway origins.

Approach: Wadebridge lies at the junction of the A39 and A389, while Padstow is the terminus of the A389. In a countryside of villages, these compact Cornish towns are difficult to miss. Car parking is available in Wadebridge at the town's main car park off Molesworth Street and in Padstow at the South Quay car park – formerly the station yard and now the end of the railway path. A No 55 bus provides occasional but useful service for the return journey, but ramblers are advised to contact the operator – Cornwall Busways, Bus Station, St Austell (St Austell 2212) – for details.

Attractions: The path offers a level, easy walk along the south bank of the River Camel. The views are extensive and even in summer the salty air is invigorating. Here and there, an abandoned gradient or milepost plots the old railway's progress from Waterloo and a sturdy, three-span girder bridge carries the line over Little Petherick Creek. The station buildings survive at both Wadebridge and Padstow, a short distance beyond the respective ends of the railway path.

OS sheet: 200

The walk begins along the service road to a new sewage works, where only the remains of a railway fence on the riverside betray its origins. This unpromising introduction is soon forgotten as the rambler reaches the official start of the walk and enters the secluded world of the old railway with a succession of rocky cuttings and shallow embankments carrying it resolutely towards Padstow. It is worth noting that, until 1967, the fine forward views of the estuary which follow were the privilege of only the local train drivers; ordinary passengers had to be content with the restricted sideways view through their carriage window.

The path soon passes under Tregunna Bridge, a stout structure of brick and stone. The railway drainage, which still gives excellent service elsewhere, is evidently blocked here and it can be wet underfoot. The water channels on either side of the line are always full and in May positively teem with tadpoles – a rare sight these days. A mile (1.6km) further west, disused quarries above Carhart and Bodellick Farms are passed. This whole area is a cascade of aban-

Triple-span iron bridge over Little Petherick Creek (Jeff Vinter)

doned slate – a striking reminder in this age of leisure and tourism that Cornwall has an industrial, as well as an agricultural, past. On the riverside lie abandoned wharves; on the landward side, abandoned cottages. Under a cold grey sky, this is a bleak and eerie place.

Soon in the distance, Padstow hoves into view as a speckled cluster of white and grey cottages on a hillside. Lush cuttings by Oldtown Cove are passed as the rambler approaches the triple-span iron bridge over Little Petherick Creek. This is approached by a long embankment and deserves a proper examination, if time can be spared. The path is conveyed through a tunnel of girders and the imaginative photographer can find many striking patterns and views.

Leaving the bridge, the path threads its way through a deep cutting (the scene of several rockfalls) to reach the outskirts of Padstow at Dennis Cove. The atmosphere of this homely and attractive town invites the rambler to quicken his pace for the last ½ mile (.8km), until the narrow passage of the old line bursts into the wide expanse of the former station yard. How many summer holidays began at this point one can only conjecture, but this delightful and varied railway walk is a fine reminder of the days when travellers could wonder, like John Betjeman: 'Can it really be that this same carriage came from Waterloo?'

Woods·and·Forests

Down in the forest something is stirring. It might be the ponies crossing one of the New Forest lawns; or deer hidden in the bracken of Charnwood Forest; or perhaps even the ghost of the dragon of Haugh Wood in Hereford and Worcester. And therein lies the prime attraction of woodland walking – the feeling that there's life out there, that the forest or wood is home to an extraordinary variety of bird and animal life and that it is itself a living, developing entity.

Many will, nevertheless, approach a forest walk with trepidation, expecting serried ranks of conifers, miles of dull forest roads, and a gloomy enclosed trail without interest or surprise. Such fears are not entirely without foundation: the worst forest trails are appallingly unimaginative, laid out with the foresters' convenience more to the fore than the enjoyment of the walker. But the best (which are generally the most recent) are superb, linking an introduction to the trees of the forest with an appreciation of the bird and animal life and the wider landscape of the area.

Certainly there has been a very considerable change of attitude on the part of the Forestry Commission, the major woodland owners, from one of indifference (and, at times, outright hostility) towards recreation in forests to one where the needs of walkers are recognised as a legitimate concern of foresters. Hence the recent explosion in the provision of picnic sites, visitor centres and forest walks, and the increased imagination evident in the creation of longer walks such as the Coed Morgannwg Way in the West Glamorgan forests and extensive waymarking in the Forest of Dean.

Not all the walks traverse Forestry Commission land – the Charnwood walk, indeed, has only one heavily wooded section, and that is managed by a local trust – and, just as important, by no means all of them are planned to stay within the forest for the whole walk. This is especially relevant where the surrounding landscape is of the highest quality: so the Glen Trool walk quickly gains height in climbing the Merrick, the highest mountain in southern Scotland and one which commands a magnificent view of Glen Trool Forest. Similarly, the summit of Dodd is the objective of the Thornthwaite Forest walk because of its stupendous views (obstructed by the trees to some extent!) into the heart of the Lake District.

In the pursuit of excellence in woodland walking I have adopted a fairly

Fonthill Woods above Hindon, Wiltshire (Geoffrey N. Wright)

wide definition of the term 'forest' in order to include Charnwood, by far the best walking country, albeit on a small scale, in the English shires. I have also included a particularly wide variety of woodland environments, from the remote splendour of Glen Affric to the splendidly cosy atmosphere of the woodlands on the western slopes of the Woolhope Dome, a little known but highly rewarding segment of the Welsh border country.

Even amongst the classic Forestry Commission forests, there is scope for a good deal of variety. The Forest of Dean walk conforms more than most, on the surface, to the stereotype of a route march along forest roads, but has the totally unexpected Speech House Lake and remnants of the area's lively industrial past amongst its attractions. The New Forest, on the other hand, has a succession of different habitats: broadleaved forest, conifers, heath and lawn, the last of these environments being favoured by the eponymous ponies. Gwydyr, in contrast, is largely coniferous, but again there are large open areas with excellent views of the mountains of Snowdonia, and there is also an exhilarating walk through the Llugwy Gorge, with a succession of falls and rapids.

Inside a forest the environment is far from dull: where there is space and light under the trees the undergrowth can be spectacular and the bird and animal life particularly varied. And the trees can have another function too, as a protection against the elements – not so much the rain as the wind. On the windiest of days there is a surprising degree of peace and quiet in the forest, so much so that a sudden buffeting on leaving the trees can be quite unnerving.

The mountain forests arouse fierce controversy because of their effects on the landscape, but in the examples selected the trees have not encroached too far, either aesthetically or as a hindrance to walkers. Certainly Glen Trool Forest is too big and too dense, out of sympathy with its surroundings; but the Merrick and the views east across the little known lochs to the Rhinns of Kells are unimpaired. Equally, it can be argued that the attractiveness of Glen Affric has actually been enhanced by the forest, though doubtless many would dispute this view.

At lower altitudes over-planting (from a landscape point of view) is more prevalent, to the detriment of at least one of the walks which follow. Here I have in mind the Forest of Dean. One has only to climb to the New Fancy viewpoint – provided, ironically enough, by the Forestry Commission – to be overwhelmed by a vista which consists almost entirely of conifers. The other lowland forests suffer less in this respect.

In the broadleaved woodlands there is, in any case, more variety and an environment more conducive to walking. In Charnwood Forest, for example, Swithland Woods are exceptionally popular as a destination in their own right, and never more so than at bluebell time when the woods are thickly carpeted in delicate shades of blue. And in the New Forest, where conifers have been introduced but have not been allowed to dominate the broad-leaved trees, there is perhaps the ideal blend for woodland walking – part open countryside with heaths and grassy lawns allowing freedom from the trees and, just as important, views of rather than through the trees, and part woodland, with a succession of oak glades and conifer plantations to maintain the high quality of the walking.

87	Affric Forest, Highland	17 miles (27km) or less
88	Glen Trool Forest, Dumfries and Galloway	9 miles (14km)
89	Thornthwaite Forest, Cumbria	3 miles or 5½ miles (5 or 9km)
90	Gwydr Forest, Gwynedd	8 miles (13km)
91	Charnwood Forest, Leicestershire	6 miles (9.6km)
92	The Woolhope Dome, Hereford and Worcester	5 miles (8km)
93	Forest of Dean, Gloucestershire	3½ miles (5.6km)
94	Epping Forest, Essex	6 miles (9.6km)
95	New Forest, Hampshire	7 miles (11km)

87 Affric·Forest

Time: Allow 4 to 5 hours for a leisurely low-level circuit of Loch Affric, but up to 9 hours for the much more strenuous route including the ascent of Mam Sodhail, a 17 mile (27km) trek.
Start and finish: The car park near the western end of Loch Beinn à Mheadhoin (grid reference 217242).
Approach: From Inverness via Struy or Drumnadrochit and the A831 to Cannich, then via Fasnakyle and the Glen Affric road.
Attractions: Glen Affric, hemmed in by majestic mountains – the Carn Eighe range to the north reaches over 3,800ft (1,424m) – and with two lochs set amongst the trees, is widely regarded as one of the most beautiful glens in the Highlands.
OS sheet: 25

The walk begins along the northern shores of Loch Beinn à Mheadhoin, now a reservoir and hence remembered most vividly for its ugly 'tide-mark', the extent of which varies with demand from the power station at Fasnakyle, where water from this loch merges with a much greater supply from Loch Mullardoch to provide hydro-electric power. After a mile (1.6km) in which the Caledonian pine and birch woods clinging to the lower valley sides provide the chief interest, the track diverges to the left, crosses the wooded banks of the River Affric and keeps below the hidden Loch Pollan Buidhe, with Loch Affric now sparkling below.

To the south of Loch Beinn à Mheadhoin and Loch Affric the Forestry Commission are engaged in a long-term project to preserve one of the more important remnants of the Caledonian Forest. A reserve of some 2,000 acres (810ha) has been established to ensure the survival of the pine, which together with the birch – the commonest tree in the lower reaches of Glen Affric, and once used in the manufacture, at Drumnadrochit, of bobbins destined for the Indian jute mills – forms the classic woodland scenery of the Highlands.

Remnants of a Scots pine 3,900 years old, were discovered in the 1970s by Forestry Commission workers making a forest road, and it seems that it was not until the nineteenth century that the Affric woodlands – not just pine and birch, but also willow, alder, oak and mountain ash – were seriously threatened. Then much of Glen Affric was converted to a sheepwalk, with the consequence of depopulation for many of the valley's inhabitants, and the regeneration of the forest through the growth of young trees was brought to an end.

Affric Lodge, majestically situated on its promontory amongst a patchwork of green fields and pine woodlands, lies across the loch to the north, forming the foreground for a classic view of the Carn Eighe ridge, with Sgurr na Lapaich, the eastern shoulder of Mam Sodhail (pronounced mam soul), very prominent. The track continues westwards across the Allt Garbh and keeps well above Loch Affric and its Scots pines for nearly 3 miles (5km) to Athnamulloch, a place of some historical importance.

It was here at Athnamulloch, in its remote situation below towering mountains, that Prince Charlie stayed for a while in August 1746 after his defeat at Culloden, whilst waiting for news of a French ship at Poolewe – news which came only after a further six weeks during which he had abandoned the windswept bothy at Athnamulloch and sought refuge in nearby Glen Cannich and in Badenoch.

By Athnamulloch the forest has been left behind: to the west is a much bleaker landscape of bare, treeless moorland, much of it clothed with heather. After ¼ mile (.4km) a crucial decision has to be made: to tackle the demanding ascent of Mam Sodhail, or to return above the north shore of Loch Affric. Those short of time or mountain experience should turn right at Cnoc Fada, head across rough ground to the oddly shaped, isolated Loch Coulavie and follow the path above the woods past Affric Lodge to the pine forests and the car park.

Hardier souls can follow the Affric track, which leads in 3 miles (5km) to the Youth Hostel at Alltbeithe and, eventually, to Loch Duich via the Bealach an Sgàirne or the Falls of Glomach – both of them magnificent, demanding expeditions. The way to Mam Sodhail, however, leaves this track after a mile (1.6km), following the Allt Coire Ghàidheil steeply upwards and then heading more gradually for the bealach (col), which is reached after 2 hard miles (3km) and a climb of about 1,600ft (488m).

Mam Sodhail is now only a mile (1.6km) or so distant, though the route encounters more rough and steep ground north of the crags circling Coire Coulavie before reaching the summit (3,862ft, 1,177m), with its fine views over Kintail and Benula Forest. Peak-baggers will hurry north to 'collect' Carn Eighe, only 7ft (2m) higher and reached around the head of the deserted Gleann nam Fiadh. Others may be tempted by the east ridge, leading down to Sgurr na Lapaich; but the easiest descent starts some way south of the summit, into Coire Leachavie and to the east of the prominent cliffs of An Tudair Beag. Eventually the Affric track comes into view above the pines, and this leads back in 4 more miles (6km) to the car.

88 GLEN·TROOL·FOREST

Time: Allow 4 to 5 hours for this walk, which has some route-finding problems and a fairly strenuous ascent.

Start and finish: The car park at Loch Trool (grid reference 416804).

Approach: The Loch Trool car park lies 5 miles (8km) along the Glen Trool valley road, which leaves the A714 Newton Stewart to Girvan road some 8 miles (13km) north-west of Newton Stewart.

Attractions: Magnificent mountain and glen scenery in the unjustly neglected Galloway hills. Includes visits to several lochs and the summit of Merrick, the highest mountain in southern Scotland.

OS sheet: 77

The Glen Trool Forest Park has a total area of about 230sq miles (595km^2) and comprises all or part of seven individual forests: Glentrool, Carrick, Garraries, Kirroughtree, Bennan, Clatteringshaws and Dundeuch. Glentrool itself accounts for more than a third of the total area, and more than half of this has been planted (mainly with Sitka spruce), leaving only the hilltops and steep slopes bare.

The result of all this, on approach along the valleys, is to give a first impression of an impenetrable coniferous forest, and undoubtedly on the lower slopes this is a fair assessment. Once through the forest barrier, however, the magical character, almost Highland in nature, of the hills and glens asserts itself, and for this reason the walk chosen starts from Loch Trool and climbs Merrick, looking down on the forest rather than stumbling through it.

On a rocky knoll above Loch Trool is the Bruce Stone, commemorating the nearby victory of Robert the Bruce over the English in 1307. The English soldiers were apparently ambushed at a point on the lower slopes of Mulldonach where there was a sheer drop to Loch Trool below; the Scots created havoc by rolling boulders down from the mountain. The dead were buried on the alluvial flats east of Loch Trool, an area now known as Soldiers' Holm.

From the Bruce Stone the track to follow continues along the Glen Trool road eastward, across the Buchan Burn and then across the rather rough and quite steep slopes of Buchan Hill to follow the hanging valley of the Gairland Burn upstream to the outflow of Loch Valley, a fine trout loch about a mile (1.6km) long. Just above it, reached by a path around its western shores, is Loch Neldricken, almost separated into two lochs by a wedge-shaped promontory. Keep to the western fringes of Loch Neldricken, which are reed-choked and bouldery, to find the little hollow known as the Murder Hole. The murder, that of a pedlar, actually happened at Rowantree Toll, some 6 miles (9.6km) to the west, but the novelist S. R. Crockett transported it to the more dramatic shores of Loch Neldricken.

The way now lies along the Rig of Loch Enoch, above Helen's Stone, which marks the place where a woman died, and then, with fine views of Loch Enoch and its islands (one of them large enough to have its own lochan) to the east, quite steeply up the east ridge of Merrick, gaining the summit (2,764ft, 842m) after a scramble through a rocky, untamed landscape. Hidden on the slopes is an extraordinary rock outcrop resembling a human face, known as the Grey Man of the Merrick. Beyond Loch Enoch in its granite basin to the east is the wilderness of Dungeon Hill and Craignaw, with the Rhinns of Kells beyond.

The summit of Merrick – literally 'the Branched Finger', a reference to its prominent ridges – is marked by an OS pillar and a substantial cairn, and the summit plateau is ringed on three sides by crags. To the south, however, a broad ridge leads back towards Glen Trool, past the Neive of the Spit and over gentle, grassy slopes to the subsidiary summit of Benyellary (2,360ft, 719m). There are two possibilities now: a descent south-south-east towards the Buchan Burn, or a ridge-walk south-south-west to Bennan.

The valley route is perhaps slightly easier, following a dyke down into plantations and then to the ruined farmstead at Culsharg. Now the path, losing height gradually, meanders pleasantly through the forest, with the hanging valley of the Buchan Burn down to the right. There are fine views across Glen Trool and to the series of cascades through which the burn careers down to the floor of the main valley, close to the Loch Trool car park.

The ridge-route from Benyellary to Bennan is straightforward, though one small plantation forces a slight detour. Keep to the ridge, south-eastwards now, to gain the top of the Fell of Eschoncan and a stunning 'aerial' view of Loch Trool (the car park is now only a short walk to the east) and its circling hills. From here it is easy to appreciate Robert the Bruce's strategy in ambushing his opponents on the opposite shores of the loch. Away to the right, too, is the location of another and less creditable episode in Galloway history. This is Caldons, where the Glen Trool martyrs, six Covenanters, were murdered by Colonel James Douglas as they prayed, in 1685. A hundred years later, though, Glen Trool was on the tourist itinerary, and it has deservedly remained there ever since.

89 THORNTHWAITE·
FOREST

Forest Road

Time: Allow 2 hours or so for the short walk, and 4 hours for the longer walk, which includes a steep ascent of Skiddaw.

Start and finish: The car park at Mirehouse (grid reference 235281), on the eastern side of the A591, 4 miles (6km) north of Keswick.

Approach: The car park, which is not especially well signposted, is easily reached along the A591 from either Keswick or Castle Inn, at the northern end of Bassenthwaite Lake.

Attractions: A varied forest walk, with magnificent views across Bassenthwaite Lake and Derwentwater into the heart of the Lake District, with the optional addition of a stiff climb to the summit of Skiddaw, one of the four Lakeland 'Threethousanders'.

OS sheet: 90 (or Outdoor Leisure Series sheet 4, 'English Lakes – NW')

The forest walk, waymarked in green and described as the 'Long Walk', starts in common with two others at the Mirehouse car park, next to the former sawmill (now tea room) of the Mirehouse Estate, which began planting conifers on Dodd in 1790. The way lies across a wooden footbridge over the Skill Beck, then steeply up to join a tarmac forest road. This forest road continues ahead at a quite severe gradient for some time hemmed in by the conifers on both sides. It offers little enjoyment, though the cascading beck down to the right is noisily picturesque.

At last the Long Walk climbs the bank to the left of the forest road, almost doubling back on itself as it follows a much more level path through mature Douglas fir and then swings round to traverse an area which has recently been clear felled. Here, at last, is a view of the rounded and well-wooded summit of Dodd, almost directly ahead, with Bassenthwaite Lake down to the right. Abundant purple heather and occasional rocky outcrops form an attractive interlude here, before the path rises again through recently planted Sitka spruce to rejoin the forest road.

The road rises relentlessly, with the bulk of Carl Side – a supporting buttress of the Skiddaw massif – directly ahead. Eventually, as the col known as Long Doors is approached, another and much more recent forest road takes over the route (there are fine views over the northern reaches of Bassenthwaite Lake here) on the way to a clearing where there are clear signs of forestry operations.

At the col, a stile over the fence to the left marks the public footpath to Carl Side and Skiddaw. This is unquestionably a route for the energetic only, since from the stile the way lies over steeply inclined shaly scree and then over a rough, stony track to the craggy shoulder of Carl Side some 800ft (244m) above the col. The flat summit of Carl Side and a comparatively gentle stroll to the top of Skiddaw (3,054ft, 931m) are easy meat after the gruelling passage over the scree, which then has to be descended on the way back to Long Doors.

Despite the arduous ascent, those who accomplish it will – given a fine day – gain ample compensation, both in the satisfaction of conquering one of the four Lakeland 'Threethousanders' (the others are Scafell Pike, Scafell and Helvellyn) and also in the magnificent views of the spectacular mountain ridges which make up the Lakeland fells. Dodd's less lofty summit has a fine panorama, focusing on the interplay between mountain and lake, but from the southern slopes of Skiddaw's summit plateau the view is more uncompromising, with its concentration upon rocky summits and bare mountain ridges.

The route from the col to Dodd summit heads off into the forest on a pleasant slanting path, though the journey through the trees can be dark and eerily quiet. The path has a thick bed of pine needles overlying rather marshy ground as it circles around the south-eastern shoulder of Dodd, before beginning to climb again (take the left-hand path at a junction bereft of waymarks), quite steeply as it twists between rock outcrops and over tree roots.

The steepest part of the ascent entails a little mild rock scrambling, but the expected summit does not materialise: instead there is a descent, a less exacting climb and then a traverse of a particularly muddy section. The path eventually turns left and upwards to reach a slate monolith, a recently erected memorial stone, at the summit of Dodd (1,612ft, 507m).

The view is tremendous, though a good deal of dodging between the stunted mountain pines is necessary to take it all in: it's a shame that the little summit plateau could not have been left alone when planting took place. Prominent in the scene are Helvellyn, the central fells behind Derwentwater, the north-western fells around the Newlands Valley and Coledale, and the main part of Thornthwaite Forest around Whinlatter, beyond Bassenthwaite Lake.

It is now necessary to retrace one's steps from the summit back to the pine-needle path running around the southern and south-western sides of Dodd, eventually emerging at a junction of forest roads. Follow one (not in very good condition) down for a while before taking either of two gravelly paths. That to the left proceeds on a level course through plantations of Douglas fir, with Bassenthwaite Lake and Thornthwaite Forest prominent ahead, before dropping down the roughly stepped hillside to Mirehouse; the right-hand alternative descends more steeply to the Skill Beck valley and follows the beck back to the car park.

Bassenthwaite Lake from the summit of Dodd

90 GWYDYR·FOREST

Time: There is some rock scrambling in the Llugwy Gorge, and navigational problems elsewhere, so allow 3½ to 4 hours.

Start and finish: Pont-y-Pair car park, Betws-y-Coed (grid reference 792567).

Approach: Pont-y-Pair car park lies immediately to the north of the A5 in Betws-y-Coed and is well signposted.

Attractions: Varied forest walking, including a visit to the Swallow Falls and Llugwy Gorge, together with evidence of the area's industrial past and excellent views into Snowdonia, combine to produce a forest walk of exceptional quality.

OS sheet: 115 (or Outdoor Leisure Series sheet 16, 'Snowdonia National Park – Conwy Valley').

Gwydyr Forest, marvellously situated within the Snowdonia National Park, takes its name from Gwydyr Castle, the former home of the Wynn family, which is now open to the public and is well worth a visit. The forest area is some 20,000 acres (8,000ha), and the first Forestry Commission plantations took place in 1921. Sitka spruce is the predominant species, as a result of the elevation and poor soils, though there are also plantations of Scots pine, lodgepole pine and larch.

From the car park, which is located north of Pont-y-Pair Bridge (the five-arched 'bridge of the cauldron', named after cascades on the Afon Llugwy), head east for 100yd (90m), then north along a forest road until a path climbs up to the left into the Aberllyn ravine. This is quite a steep section of the walk, following a stony path to the head of the ravine, where there are the remains of the Aberllyn lead and zinc mine and old quarry workings. At the southern end of Llyn Parc, a narrow and surprisingly remote stretch of water, bear right along a forest road to Drws Gwyn ('the white gate').

There is no gate now at Drws Gwyn, which was one of the entrances to Gwydyr High Park, a former deer park whose wall was built by French prisoners during the Napoleonic Wars. The route, well waymarked, zigzags left and right and then descends slowly along the heavily wooded hillslope forming the western wall of the Conwy valley, with glorious views along the valley and across to the hills above Llanrwst.

The path quickly arrives at the picnic place next to Gwydyr Uchaf chapel, built in 1673, and best known for its striking decorated ceiling and surviving gallery and pews. The mansion of Gwydyr Uchaf, built by the Wynns in 1604, has not survived. The Forestry Commission exhibition marked on the Outdoor Leisure map is now closed, but compensation is close at hand in the form of Gwydyr Castle, superbly restored after a series of fires earlier this

The Llugwy gorge above Miners Bridge (M. Dunn)

century. Most of what remains is sixteenth century, though there was a fortified tower here early in the fourteenth.

So far the walk has traversed forest paths, but now the way lies to the west, heading for the more secluded parts of Gwydyr Forest. Follow forest trail signs uphill from Gwydyr Uchaf and above the spoil heaps of the Parc lead mine, but before reaching the head of Llyn Parc take a clear path on the right probably first used by lead miners. The path runs below Graig-y-Fuches-lâs, passing plantations of oak, beech and birch and an undergrowth of bilberries, and curves round to the left, avoiding the derelict chimney stack of the Llanrwst mine, to reach Llyn Sarnau, a very shallow lake which often disappears completely in summer.

Follow the minor road from Llyn Sarnau to Cyffty Mine. The forest draws back a little here and so there are excellent views across the Llugwy valley to Moel Siabod and its satellites. Then take the track on the left, dropping down quite sharply to Hafotypencraig and, almost ½ mile (.8km) further south, Diosgydd-isaf. Cut across the public road here to descend to the banks of the Afon Llugwy and follow the river upstream. This is a fine scramble over boulders, fallen trees and steep wooded slopes, but the reward, after only five minutes or so, is a view of the Swallow Falls. This series of cascades and crashing waterfalls is justly renowned and is said to attract well over half a million visitors annually – the vast majority of whom will have paid to see the falls from the opposite bank.

Return along the river bank (or, as a less energetic alternative, along the minor road which runs at a slightly higher level), passing more cascades and magnificent river and rock scenery and, in the forest above, a plantation of Western red cedar. Above to the left is Coed Diosgydd, the former nursery for the Gwydyr Forest. Between 1925 and 1948 some 15 million young trees were nurtured here and later transplanted elsewhere in the forest.

Less than a mile (1.6km) from Betws-y-Coed, the path passes above the Miners Bridge, now a strong wooden tourists' bridge (almost a ladder, in fact, since it is inclined at an angle of 30 degrees) but originally a vital link for workers at the mines on the Gwydyr plateau who lived in Pentre-Du. Keep to the north bank of the Llugwy, leaving the woodland over a stile and following the river quite closely back to the Pont-y-Pair car park and the finish of an exceptional walk.

91 CHARNWOOD·FOREST

Time: 3 hours.
Start and finish: The large car park at the entrance to the Bradgate Park country park in Newtown Linford (grid reference 523097).
Approach: Leave the M1 at Junction 22, take the A50 towards Leicester and turn north onto the B5327 to Newtown Linford. From Leicester, take the B5327 to Anstey and Newtown Linford.
Attractions: An outstanding walk in a surprisingly wild part of the East Midlands, with rocky hills, bluebell woods and the ruins of Bradgate House, home of Lady Jane Grey.
OS sheets: 129 (one very small section at the start of the walk lies on sheet 140)

Charnwood Forest is the one unforgettable piece of the Leicestershire country-side, a priceless contrast to the clay vales in the west of the county and a more dramatic landscape than the rolling uplands in the east. Like so many other areas bearing the name, it was never a true forest, but merely a piece of country reserved for hunting game. Bradgate had been enclosed as a deer park by 1247, following a twelfth-century agreement between the earls of Leicester and Chester which had seen Charnwood Forest divided between them. Now Charnwood, a rich mixture of heath, woodland and miniature rocky outcrops formed from ancient volcanic rocks, is an important recreational resource, with a wide variety of excellent walks.

The first stage of the walk, through the wooded gorge of the River Lyn, with small cliffs to the left and deer amongst the bracken to the right, is delightful, though it should be said that it is also extremely crowded at weekends. Immediately before the ruins are reached, a natural spring can be seen on the right. At the far end of the gorge the tower known as Old John can be seen to the left, whilst immediately ahead the ruins of Bradgate House come into view.

One of the first unfortified houses to be built in England, Bradgate House was erected by Thomas Grey, Marquis of Dorset, between 1490 and 1507. Mainly of brick, it was enlarged in the seventeenth century but abandoned by the Greys in the 1730s and became ruinous. Only the chapel with its tomb of the first Earl of Stamford, remains intact. Lady Jane Grey was born at Brad-gate in October 1537 – in 1550 she was discovered reading Greek by Roger Ascham – and following her execution in 1554, after nine days as Queen of England, the foresters reputedly beheaded all the oaks in the park: hence the pollarded oaks which are still a feature of Bradgate. Behind the ruins is a lake which provided water for the fishponds serving the great house, fulfilled drainage purposes, and supplied the mill attached to the south-east corner of the house.

Beyond the ruins is the site of the walled kitchen garden, with a mulberry tree, supposedly one of those brought to England by Sir Walter Raleigh, over-hanging the wall. Now Cropston Reservoir fills the view to the right (the village of Bradgate, deserted around 1500, lay on the far side of the water), whilst to the left Coppice Plantation, planted in 1953 to mark the Corona-tion of Queen Elizabeth II, keeps the road company as far as the Hallgates entrance to Bradgate. Turn left for a few yards along the B5330, then right to cross fields and enter Swithland Woods, a tract of mixed deciduous wood-land best known for its magnificent carpet of bluebells in spring.

Some 200yd (180m) into the woods is the first of the quarries, abandoned in the late nineteenth century, which produced the renowned blue-grey Swithland slates, used as roofing materials from Roman times onwards. From the thirteenth century onwards the slates were produced continuously until the advent of cheap Welsh slates destroyed the market. Now the flooded quarries, securely fenced, make a picturesque addition to the scenery.

At the Brand, close to the northern edge of Swithland Woods, where there are more disused slate pits, turn back to follow a bridleway, later a narrow path, to the B5330 and re-enter Bradgate Park, following a grassy path between bracken, making for Old John. The route leads past Sliding Stone Spinney, one of the many small plantations which originally served as pheasant coverts (there was a medieval pheasantry close to Bradgate House), and then quite sharply up to Old John. The tower was built as a folly in 1786 by the fifth Earl of Stamford; there are wide views over the Forest and south-east towards Leicester. Much of the 4½ mile (7km) long stone wall enclosing the park can be seen.

On the far side of Old John Spinney is a war memorial above a series of miniature crags offering easy rock scrambling, and then a well-worn path heading south past Elder Plantation and Tyburn Wood to the top of the Lyn Gorge (the deer sanctuary across the river, home for a herd of about 300 red and fallow deer, is well seen from here). Eventually, the prim village of Newtown Linford, now a dormitory settlement for Leicester but with some surviving cruck-framed cottages, is reached.

92 The·Woolhope·Dome

Time: Up to 3 hours should be reserved for a leisurely stroll including the Haugh Wood forest trail.

Start and finish: At the junction of minor road and bridleway east of Cherry Hill, near Fownhope (grid reference 581352), where there is limited parking space.

Approach: From Hereford or from the end of the M50 near Ross-on-Wye, follow the B4224 to Fownhope and turn into the minor road opposite Fownhope Forge. The start of the walk is ½ mile (.8km) along this road.

Attractions: A fascinating combination of old bridleways, forest roads and forgotten paths in the Woolhope Dome.

OS sheet: 149

Haugh Wood, a mixed woodland managed by the Forestry Commission, was once owned by the Canons of Hereford Cathedral but, so legend has it, was the home of a dragon (commemorated until Victorian times by a 12ft (3.6m) long green dragon which used to adorn the outside of Mordiford church tower). The dragon's reign of terror over the surrounding villages was finally ended when its heart was pierced by an arrow fired by a man concealed inside a cider barrel. The wood, high above the Wye valley south-east of Hereford, lies within the fascinating and surprisingly beautiful area known as the Woolhope Dome, a circular series of outcrops of Silurian shale and limestone resulting in a complex pattern of ridges and valleys.

Cherry Hill, its heavily wooded summit adorned by an Iron Age hillfort, lies to the left as the walk begins by passing through a five-barred gate and crossing a field as a rutted track which later becomes less distinct along the western edge of Haugh Wood, making for the farm complex at Littlehope. Close by is the Bronze Age barrow known as Bagpiper's Tump. At a junction north of Littlehope the right-hand track, lined with trees, leads to the minor road running between Mordiford and Woolhope: turn right along this for some 300yd (270m), then left along a muddy lane unofficially signposted to Pound.

The lane passes outbuildings, a caravan and a cottage before leading through a gate into Haugh Wood, then past a newly constructed house into – disconcertingly – a large shed. Closer inspection reveals that the true line of the path is immediately to the left, through (or over) a half-submerged gate and into 50yd (45m) of desperate scrambling through conifers and over fallen branches. The path here, a sunken trackway, is in danger of disappearing (all the more reason for walking this way and ensuring its survival), but in 50yd (45m) it merges with a forest track, waterlogged in places, and then joins a

The Tom Spring Memorial (M. Dunn)

much newer forest road. Turn right here, swing left and climb steadily, with increasingly fine retrospective views over the Wye valley to the Black Mountains.

At the crest of the hill there is a junction of forest roads, and by turning left the bulk of the Forestry Commission's Haugh Wood forest trail can be incorporated into the walk. At first the trail runs between stands of Western hemlock and beech, with gorse and purple heather fringing the forest road. The view to the left opens out considerably after a few hundred yards, however, where a plantation of Douglas fir has recently been clear felled. Now the trail (poorly waymarked for once) enters the forest along a damp, grassy path which winds between the trees – mature larch given plenty of space to develop. This is easily the best part of the trail, with bracken and blackberries amongst the trees.

The trail joins another forest road, drops down to cross a deeply incised stream on Dingle Bridge, with ninety-year-old oak standards on the left, and then climbs quite steeply on a good track to a junction of grassy forest rides (point 7 on the forest trail, as indicated on a post). Turn left here, leaving the trail, and pass between young fir trees on a well-defined path which loses height gradually as it approaches the hamlet of Broadmoor Common. Turn right along the road here, then left after 100yd (90m) onto a forest road (barred to private cars) heading through the southerly part of Haugh Wood.

Keep to the gravelly forest road, ignoring side-turnings, as it crosses a plateau – there are wide views south to the Forest of Dean – before falling fairly rapidly and becoming quite overgrown. The road swings left, down to a timber storage point, then right, close to the edge of Haugh Wood for a while, before meeting a more heavily used forest road. Turn left along the road, with the Rudge End Quarry nature reserve on the right, to join the Cherry Hill–Woolhope road at Hill View Cottage.

Head along the road towards Cherry Hill, but follow the signpost after 200yd (180m) towards the Tom Spring Memorial, which is only one field away. The monument, which consists of a millstone and memorial slab set on a round base, commemorates the pugilistic feats of Thomas Winter, alias Tom Spring, who was born in Rudge End, Fownhope, and became English champion in 1821. Return across the field and follow the road back to the start of the walk near Cherry Hill.

93 FOREST·OF·DEAN

Time: 1 ½ hours should be sufficient for the New Fancy forest trail itself, with additional time for visits to Speech House Arboretum and the Speech House itself.

Start and finish: New Fancy View picnic site and car park, near The Barracks (grid reference 628095).

Approach: From the A48 at Blakeney, past the exposed section of Roman road at Blackpool Bridge to The Barracks and the car park.

Attractions: An easy walk in the heart of the Forest of Dean. Unquestionably the highlight is Speech House Lake, an outstanding Forestry Commission contribution to the Dean landscape.

OS sheet: 162 (or Outdoor Leisure Series sheet 14, 'Wye Valley and Forest of Dean')

Save the climb to the New Fancy viewpoint until last, and walk past the massive, squat boulder which commemorates the planting by the Forestry Commission of 2 million acres (809,371ha) in Great Britain between 1919 and 1976, to reach the start of the trail. Its initial stage follows the course of an abandoned branch line to New Fancy Colliery, which closed in 1944. At first it is prone to waterlogging, as far as a gate, but the going improves and the trail then reaches a surfaced forest road, turning left.

The road, degenerating into a rough track, runs beneath tall lime trees before crossing the course of the mineral loop-line of the former Severn & Wye Railway Company. This is now a quite well-used grassy footpath (and indeed the forest trail utilises its route later on). The line was opened in 1872 to serve local collieries, but traffic declined from thirteen trains a day in 1912 to a single train twenty years later, and it was finally closed in 1953.

The forest road, a delightfully wide break in the trees, is followed for about 300yd (274m), past a recently felled stand of Scots pine, until at a crossroads it becomes a grassy ride. The trail veers left, along a rough track, and then there is an excellent grassy break between the trees. This, too, was intended as a railway (the Forest of Dean Central Railway), but the money ran out before this section of the line was laid. Although the trees deny even a glimpse of distant views, this is the best part of the walk so far.

The trail climbs slowly, over slightly marshy ground, then turns right alongside Scots pines and left into another ride, this time flanked on both sides by a miniature bank and ditch, and with a bridge carrying the former mineral loop-line framing the view ahead. The trail passes under the bridge (later it follows the former railway on the bridge itself), turns right onto another surfaced road fringed with bracken, and climbs quite steeply amongst young trees to meet and bear left along the Spruce Drive near a rotted water tank.

The trees along the Spruce Drive stand back some 20yd (18m) from the track, allowing bracken, thistles and even blackberries to colonise the wild intervening area. The result is to diminish the oppressive effect of the towering, ninety-year-old Norway spruce and create the right conditions for an excellent walk, as far as the head of Speech House Lake. The lake, created as recently as 1975 as a wildlife habitat at the head of the Blackpool Brook valley, is a marvellously situated and very attractive addition to the landscape, with little islets and fringing bracken, gorse and young conifers.

From the head of the lake the Spruce Drive leads in about ¼ mile (.4km) to the arboretum, where more than 200 different species have been planted over the last half-century. A further 200yd (180m) to the north is the Speech House itself. It was built in 1676 for the 'Court of Speech' of the verderers of the Forest of Dean – one of the few surviving Royal Forests, later exploited for its considerable mineral wealth, and later still, in 1938, designated as the first National Forest Park in England and Wales. The Speech House is now an hotel, but the court room is still preserved.

Return along the Spruce Drive to the forest trail, which becomes a pleasant narrow path winding between Scots pine, larch and beech. The path crosses little streams on makeshift wooden bridges, curving through the pine plantation, then crossing a forest road and plunging into a dark, closely packed beech plantation. Soon the path emerges into the old Acorn Patch sidings, built in 1943 by the Severn & Wye Railway to serve a US Army ammunition depot. Random areas of concrete hard-standing remain amongst the trees, and the trail uses some in proceeding south to join the course of the mineral loop-line and follow it back towards New Fancy.

The straight, grassy, bracken-fringed track of the loop-line is utilised for about ½ mile (.8km), passing over the bridge seen earlier in the walk and then, where a bridge has been dismantled, over the culverted Blackpool Brook and steeply up again onto the embankment, much of which has been colonised by shrubs and young trees. The trail eventually bears right, across a forest road and along a grassy ride, finally zigzagging through a plantation to the site of the Gravitation Shunting Sidings of New Fancy Colliery. A few yards away is the car park and the short climb to New Fancy View, with the reward of an extraordinarily wide view over the Forest of Dean, still more than half broadleaved (mainly oak) but with major conifer plantations dominating much of the scene.

94 EPPING·FOREST

Time: 2½ hours should be ample.
Start and finish: Start at Epping station (grid reference 462016). Finish at Loughton station (423957).
Approach: From London, Epping is best approached via the M11 to Junction 5, then the A1168, A121 and B1393. Train travellers can travel direct from central London to Loughton and Epping on the Central Line.
Attractions: Less than an hour from Oxford Circus, Epping Forest is one of London's vital green lungs, and this walk penetrates the heart of the forest on clear paths.
OS sheet: 167

The 6,000 acres (2,428ha) of Epping Forest, administered by the Conservators under the Epping Forest Act 1878, were purchased by the City of London to protect them from the threat of development. The threat was a very real one; the vicar of Loughton had enclosed some 1,300 acres (525ha) to sell for building plots, erecting a fence to keep out his parishioners; whose commoners' rights included the right to lop wood. One of the villagers, Thomas Willingale, was jailed for doing just that, and it took the Commons Preservation Society and, ultimately, the City to preserve the open space.

Now the forest, still under pressure – the M25 passes under its northern extremity and other busy roads bisect the beech woods – has to cope with ever-increasing numbers of walkers, horse riders and weekend motorists with their picnics. Despite this, the heart of the forest remains quiet and relatively little frequented, and away from the roads and car parks there are plenty of opportunities for excellent walking.

Our walk begins by turning right out of Epping station, left at the main road and left again through suburban Epping. At a T-junction bear right, through the hamlet of Ivy Chimneys (the M25 is close at hand and aurally very intrusive) and past the Forest Gate pub, very popular for its real ale and food. Just before the B1393 turn left along a forest path, at first running pleasantly through woodland but later rather unpromisingly as it skirts a cricket field and enters the forest close to the main road, and above the new tunnel which carries the M25 under the forest.

The path, though well-defined in most places, is nevertheless marshy at times, especially where over-use by horses has churned up the surface, and would benefit from waymarking. It passes close to one of Epping Forest's many ponds (some 150 are accounted for, though this shallow and stagnant expanse close to the B1393 is not one of the best) and then skirts Ambresbury Banks, an Iron Age fort covering 12 acres (5ha) enclosed by a ditch and rampart. Overgrown by trees and with its banks covered by a layer of fallen leaves, the fort considerably enhances the Epping landscape.

Make for a wide, gravelly track running south of the earthworks and turn right along it as it curves left and runs through pleasantly mature woodland to the Theydon Bois road (B172), where there is a parking place. On the way up to Jack's Hill, beech is the predominant tree, despite fatalities caused by droughts in the mid-1970s and old age. The path is still wide and gravelly, with widely spaced trees and a luxuriant undergrowth of bracken and blackberries. On either side of the track, which traverses a wide, flat-topped ridge and then descends to cross a substantial stream, is a low ditch.

Perhaps the most attractive route hugs the eastern edge of the forest, reaching its boundary at Debden Green; turn right here to arrive at the A121 opposite a milestone. The main gravelly path running southwards through the forest can then be rejoined in five minutes or so by using a pleasant, narrow path winding through the trees beyond the A121. The main route then crosses two streams, the second fairly substantial, before rising sharply to a junction of paths.

The ramparts of Ambresbury Banks (M. Dunn)

The main forest path near Debden Green (M. Dunn)

A right turn here leads in about ½ mile (.8km) to the Epping Forest Con-servation Centre at High Beach, a scattered village with pubs and a youth hostel. The main path, however, keeps southwards past the inconspicuous earthworks of Loughton Camp, buried in the trees, and then descends steadily into Woodbury Hollow and crosses the stream on a brick bridge with wooden ramparts. On the left are the extraordinary deep-cut meanders of the stream as it winds through the forest.

The path crosses the minor road from Loughton to High Beach and then returns to the forest, skirting another small pond which, picturesque as it is, would benefit from the clearance of the rubbish which has accumulated around its shores; but the way to Loughton station now lies down the road to the left, which quickly reaches the edge of the village. There is then quite a walk down the hill into the centre of Loughton, across the main road and along Station Road (the Lopping Hall, built in the late nineteenth century and with a panel depicting villagers exercising their right of lopping, is on the right) to the instantly recognisable façade of the station.

95 NEW·FOREST

Time: Since this is a very easy walk with no real climbing involved, a maximum of 3 hours should be sufficient.

Start and finish: Start at Brockenhurst station (grid reference 301019) and finish at Lyndhurst Road station (334103); an hourly train service connects the two.

Approach: Brockenhurst lies on the A337 about 4 miles (6km) south of Lyndhurst and the A35.

Attractions: An introduction to the magnificent variations of scenery in the forest – a mixture of woods, heath, 'lawns' and lush river valleys.

OS sheet: 196 (or Outdoor Leisure Series sheet 22, 'New Forest')

The New Forest, a royal forest since the time of William the Conqueror, has in places changed only marginally since then despite the increasing importance of timber, at first for charcoal-burning and shipbuilding. Now about two-fifths of the forest is actually wooded, the remainder forming the open heaths and lawns which give the New Forest so much of its character, and which are also the main habitat of the deer and the New Forest ponies, descendants of the original wild horses of ancient Britain but 'improved' since the nineteenth century so that they have gained stature but lost their toughness.

The quickest way out of the commuter village of Brockenhurst is to walk along the busy A337 towards Lyndhurst for some 300yd (275m), then to cut across Waters Green on the northern edge of the village – the first New Forest ponies of the day may well be grazing here – to a minor road. After only a few yards, just before a right-angled bend in the road, turn off to the right, crossing a footbridge over a surprisingly wide stream and then traversing Butts Lawn, one of the open forest lawns, known as such because they are kept so close-cropped by the ponies. The track across Butts Lawn is not at all obvious, though since the objective is eventually to join the path alongside the edge of the woods forming Water Copse enclosure, which frames the view to the right, the way forward is not in doubt. A brackish drainage channel can be followed for a while, but eventually it has to be crossed and a way found through the gorse (which New Forest ponies, possessed of a soft palate as a result of interbreeding with Arabian stock, cannot now eat) to find the wide track near to the woodland edge.

The route continues along the edge of the lawn with its heather, gorse and occasional clumps of small trees, through a barrier to join a gravelly track, and turns down to Bolderford Bridge where the Highland Water, gently meandering through the trees, is crossed on a substantial wooden bridge. Fifty yards (45m) beyond the bridge bear left, between the Highland Water and a boundary bank, to reach the Queen Bower, named after Queen Phillippa, the

A rider approaching Bolderford Bridge (M. Dunn)

wife of Edward III. With its magnificent oaks in a fine, open valley setting, this is a real highlight of the walk.

After about ¼ mile (.4km), just before a footbridge, bear right along a narrow path running along the western boundary of New Park plantation. To the left are marshy streams and luxuriant undergrowth, with a good deal of bird and animal life. The path widens and becomes a muddy track, churned by horses, running between ditches for almost a mile (1.6km), latterly as a gravel track, to the much more open landscape around a second Butts Lawn.

Fork right through an open heather moor to Butts Lawn cross where bracken, small oak trees and grassland combine to offer a rich landscape which attracts New Forest ponies. A grassy ride leads up a short hill, almost as a hollow way, and past High Coxlease to the A337. Cross the road and, after only 20yd (18m), turn onto a track which quickly curves left, behind forestry houses, and becomes a narrow path leading towards Clayhill and the edge of Lyndhurst. Cross a tarmac road at Clayhill and follow the edge of the wood along a forest road, bearing left at a junction just after the road turns into the woodland.

The road leaves the wood, passes some cottages and reaches the B3056.

Cross this, climb The Ridge – an ascent of only a few feet – and turn right along a very obvious, sandy track running just north of the Park Pale, a low bracken-covered bank which indicates the boundary of a deer park created by Charles II in the seventeenth century to protect a specific breed of red deer imported from France.

After ¼ mile (.4km), an equally obvious track diverges to the left, crossing Matley Heath on its way to Lyndhurst Road station. At first this is a rutted track running through a flat landscape of heather with a little gorse, but after ½ mile (.8km) there is another miniature ridge to be surmounted, with the trees around Row Hill close by on the left.

Now the way lies along a more grassy path, descending very gently to Long-water Lawn, another favourite spot for New Forest ponies. The Beaulieu river is crossed on a footbridge; although this is close to its source, the river has already become quite a substantial stream in an eroded channel. The path is now very clear as a grassy strip, fringed by heather, making for woodland.

Within the oak and holly wood the wide path meanders gently and then bifurcates; take the right-hand path, back onto the heath, and cross several small streams and then the Ashurst Lodge access road. Keep straight ahead, parallel to the A35 (now very audible), past a caravan site and over a stile to walk alongside the main road for 100yd (90m) to the New Forest Hotel (real ale), Lyndhurst Road station and the end of a gentle but wonderfully scenic walk.

MYTHS·AND·LEGENDS

A myth is a fictitious story, whilst a legend may contain elements of historical fact. The tale of the witch cooking pancakes beneath a hill at Toddington in Bedfordshire must be a myth whilst the story of Robin Hood is a legend because, in spite of part of its traditions being disproved, the man is known to have existed. Other stories cannot be so easily categorised. New scientific research fails to resolve the mystery of the Loch Ness monster who continues to clock up more and more 'appearances'. Is the celebrated monster a myth or a legend?

The greatest mysteries are probably posed by haunted Britain. Traumatic events in our history only add to the ghostly presence – Cavaliers and Roundheads are still spotted 300 years after the Civil War. Even the more minor Monmouth Rebellion has left a trail of haunted buildings to keep the story alive in the West Country. It seems that Henry VIII never really managed to shut down the monasteries, for ever since the 1540s there have been glimpses of monks gliding through ruined abbeys. At Beaulieu and St Albans they can even be heard chanting, whilst Bayham, on the Kent and Sussex border, boasts not just unexplained plainsong but even whiffs of incense. At the repossessed Buckfast Abbey in Devon, it is said by some that the monks never really left.

Another much reported sighting is the coach and four. Stories invariably involve headless horses, as at Penryn and Penzance, but occasionally the driver is headless, and at Great Melton in Norfolk the usually headless passengers sometimes appear with their heads to foretell good fortune. More recently there have been reports of ghostly horsepower taking the form of phantom cars. A driver in goggles is believed to haunt the partly destroyed race track at Brooklands.

Featured in this chapter is Pluckley, the most haunted village in Britain, where new ghosts often appear and cause local controversy. It has been said that residents born in this hill-top Kent Weald village are untroubled by the spirits, who only bother the newcomers. The Ghostly Priest and Hounds and Rufus Stone walks illustrate three popular themes associated with outdoor ghost stories – horses, dogs and hunting.

The Prince and the Maiden story (inspiring the walk near Narberth in Dyfed), being part of The Mabinogion, the Welsh medieval romances, may not be a ghost story; but whether a myth or legend is debatable. The witches of Pendle did exist even if they should not have been branded as witches, but

on the Witch's Boulder walk it is mere speculation as to whether there really is a body beneath the stone in the churchyard.

Clearly those who gather on Conger Hill behind Toddington's church ostensibly to hear the witch's bubbling cauldron, should not be encouraged to believe the story. But how did such a tradition start and why was this man-made hill thrown up? There is plenty of mystery in the countryside and much to debate on these walks, which should also be enjoyed by those who care nothing for myths or legends.

96	Ghostly Priest and Hounds, Devon	8½ miles (14km)
97	Little John and Robin Hood, Derbyshire	4½ or 6 miles (7 or 9.6km)
98	Rufus Stone, Hampshire	5½ miles (9km)
99	Witch's Boulder, Lancashire	3½ miles (5.6km)
100	Pluckley Ghosts, Kent	5 miles (8km)
101	Prince and the Maiden, Dyfed	5 miles (8km)
102	Witch's Cauldron, Bedfordshire	2¼ miles (3.6km)
103	Loch Ness Monster, Highlands	4 miles (6km)
104	Dick Whittington, London	4½ miles (7km)

View of Cotehele Quay on the banks of the River Tamar which is said to be haunted by a renegade hunting priest and his pack of hounds (Leigh Hatts) (*see* overleaf)

96 Ghostly·Priest·and·Hounds

Time: 5 hours to allow for enjoying the views and picnicking. There are no shops or pubs on the route although it passes tantalisingly near Calstock across the water.

Start and finish: Bere Ferrers station is the starting point; the finish is Bere Alston station where there are trains running to Bere Ferrers.

Approach: The Bere peninsula lies at the end of a minor road 3 miles (5km) south of Tavistock; or it is reached by British Rail from Plymouth. Note that trains do not run on winter Sundays (details can be checked on Plymouth 21300).

Attractions: The banks of the River Tamar are said to be haunted on Sunday mornings by Dando, a renegade hunting priest, and his pack of hounds. Claims are also made that during morning service in nearby St Germans he can be heard calling the hounds. The walk is on the little known Bere peninsula with views across to the Tamar's west bank which must have been more favoured by Dando. This remote area, with no southern road access, relies heavily on the railway link. Indeed, a scenic rail trip is an important part of this walk and motorists may well wish to leave the car in Plymouth in order to experience the longer ride under the Tamar Bridge and across the Tamerton and Tavy bridges each side of the wooded Warleigh Point.

OS sheet: 201

On leaving Bere Ferrers station approach, bear right and at the junction go right again. Beyond the railway bridge keep ahead up a rough, fenced track and follow gates through fields. Over the brow of the hill there is the first magnificent view – down to the Tamar Bridge and over to Cargreen on the far bank. Walk down the hill, but do not go through the gate. Turn right to follow the wire fence along the bottom of the field and then cut the corner to go over a stile. Walk towards the building and cross the sets of stepping stones. Pass between the two farm buildings and across a field to a gate in the far left corner. Walk ahead with a view of the river through the trees before the way runs down onto the beach below a cottage.

Turn up a grass slipway and make a double bend to pass through a gateway. At once turn left off the drive to pass under apple trees and up to a stile. Keep along the bottom of the sloping fields with first the Tamar, and then a stream, below the trees. At the far end cross the stream and climb the steps to a lane. Go left along the narrow road, which bends and rises giving another view of the Tamar and of the Tamar Bridge. At Clamoak Quay the road stays by the water for about a mile (1.6km).

Where the road rises and turns inland (by a permanently moored wooden ship) turn left down a slope to an enclosed path which quickly rises with the wooded cliff. Take care to stay on the path, which can be slippery in wet weather. Keep ahead where the path divides, go over the stile and along the side of a field. Remember to look back at the view. Cross a lane and go over the left-hand gate to continue north. Suddenly the Tamar appears below and there is a panoramic view down the river to the west and ahead to Cotehele Quay. The path drops rapidly and very steeply to a stream at the bottom.

Cross the plank bridge and find a stile ahead in the corner of the small over-grown area. Bear left and right up a short wide enclosed way and go forward to find the start of a sunken path which runs gently to the right. Still keep ahead to the start of a tunnel of trees and turn left to find a (sometimes hardly discernible) gap in the reeds indicating the short path to a plank spanning a stream. Bear left up a wooded bank, then turn right to walk up the side of a curving field. Behind is another view down the Tamar. At the far end of a second field turn left, back towards the river. Turn right through a gap, along the left side of a pond and up through the trees to a field. Keep along the bottom of the field, by the trees overhanging the river. At the far end a good path leads to South Ward Farm and then bends to the end of a metalled lane. Go up the drive of the stone cottage (Ward Mine) and bear down through a wood to the water's edge opposite the preserved eighteenth-century Cotehele Quay. After crossing the grass, go through an iron gate (next to a gap) and along a narrow enclosed path. Cross a road and follow the path ahead giving views of Calstock and its famous railway bridge. At another road turn left to follow it under the great bridge and into a farmyard.

The ferry stopped working in the 1970s so the way is to the right past the farmhouse (once The Ferry Boat Inn). In the wood take the steep right-hand path giving views down through the trees to the water. At the top do not be tempted through the gate, but go downhill on the covered path which eventually reaches a stile at the edge of the wood. Bear round to the left to ascend a slope to a gate below a house. Go through the kissing-gate and turn right onto a lane which passes under the railway bridges, to Bere Alston station.

97 LITTLE·JOHN·AND· ROBIN·HOOD

Time: 2½ hours, or 3 hours if not returning directly to the village.
Start and finish: The car park in Oddfellows Road at Hathersage. Boots should be worn.
Approach: Hathersage is on the A625, just south-west of Sheffield. Once in the village turn left at the George Hotel to pass the Little John pub and go left again into Oddfellows Road and the car park.
Attractions: Hathersage has strong claims to be the Morton in Charlotte Brontë's *Jane Eyre*, but the village is better known as the possible resting place of Robin Hood's lieutenant Little John who died at a cottage near the church. The long tomb is between two yews opposite the church porch; there are various stories suggesting that the spot was chosen by the firing of an arrow by Little John or even Robin Hood. When the grave was opened in the eighteenth century a 32in (812mm) thigh bone was found indicating a very tall person; but the bone was soon replaced after bringing bad luck to all who had it in their care. This hilly area abounds with more Robin Hood tales than Nottingham cares to admit. The walk goes south across the valley to the mysterious Robin Hood Stoop.
OS sheet: 110

From the car park go north into the main street and take the signposted turning at the east end to the church on the hill. Walk through the lich-gate to the Little John tomb on the left. The church has plenty of Robin Hood literature and the important Éyre brasses inspected by Charlotte Brontë.

Keep ahead past the church on a path which runs downhill to a lane. Turn left, but before the main road bear off down Besom Lane to join the main street at the Post Office. Just past the George Hotel leave the main road to go up Jaggers Lane and enjoy the local buildings. Just past the last one on the left, bear down a field with a splendid view of the walk to come, and go over the railway line and main road. Go forward down a field to the River Derwent and turn right to walk upstream along Hope Valley. After just over ¼ mile (.4km) cross the water by the stepping stones. (If the stones are below water do not attempt to cross but return to Hathersage and Leadmill Bridge to follow the river's south bank.)

Once across the river, follow the slightly hollowed path up the hill ahead. Remember to use the stone stiles at the side of the gates and to look back at the view of Hathersage in the valley. Just before the buildings at Offerton go through a gate and turn left. Keep right at the divide to follow a metalled lane which, after a treble bend, runs east along the side of Offerton Moor. Although surfaced the road is, apart from farm vehicles, traffic free and offers a magnificent view. After ¼ mile (.4km) the fenced road passes a lonely stone known as Robin Hood's Stoop. From here the walker looks down directly onto Hathersage and its church. Over the hill behind the village is Robin Hood's Cave.

Stay on the lane as it turns sharply south-west to run downhill and over the Dunge Brook waterfall at the head of a dramatic valley. On approaching Highlow Hall bear left to join another road – with traffic – on the east side of the valley. This road runs downhill, but just before passing the end of a wood on the right go over a stone stile on the left into a field. Take the hollowed path which turns a corner to another stile at the top of a surprise garden. The occupants of the house are used to seeing walkers, so keep straight ahead down the lawn and over the stile by the house. Still keep forward to another stile by a junction of driveways. The way is now half-right along the edge of a wood. Having climbed the stile by the gate at the end, find a narrow path which runs down the high bank to a stile below. The river is ahead.

Except for those who want to return to Hathersage more quickly or have already discovered the water to be above the stepping stones, the way is now upstream along the riverside path below the wood for 1¼ miles (2km) to the stepping stones.

The quicker way back to Hathersage is downstream to Leadmill Bridge from the north side of which a footpath runs north-west up to the Nether Hall lodge. Go left onto a lane which passes under the railway viaduct and enter the village from behind the Little John pub.

Little John's grave at Hathersage (Leigh Hatts)

98 RUFUS·STONE

Rufus Stone

Time: 2½ hours.
Start and finish: The Forestry Commission car park at Ocknell Pond in the New Forest. Boots should be worn.
Approach: The Ocknell Pond car park is north of the A31 and can be reached by turning north at Stoney Cross and then left after a mile (1.6km).
Attractions: The New Forest is not only trees but also heathland with shallow valleys and streams. The route includes all these features and, in summer, a camping area. The 2,000 ponies and 1,000 deer wandering at will are best seen in the quiet of autumn and spring; but to catch the ghost of William II the walk should be undertaken in summer, for the king was mysteriously shot with an arrow on 2 August (22 July by the Old Calendar) 1100, and on the anniversary he is said to follow the route of his coffin procession to Winchester Cathedral. This walk starts at Ocknell Pond which sometimes appears to be red, giving rise to the suggestion that Sir Walter Tyrrell, the alleged assassin, washed his hands in the pond whilst making his getaway to Poole where he boarded a boat sailing to France. Near Rufus Stone is the Sir Walter Tyrrell pub, the halfway point on the walk.
OS sheet: 195

Leave the car park by the way in, but before reaching the road turn right through a wooden barrier gate to follow a wide and partly concreted path. Ocknell Pond, often rather shallow in summer, can be seen to the left (beyond the wooden posts) after 400yd (365m).

Just after the path turns sharply right, bear half-left towards a wooden gate in the Ocknell Inclosure trees. Beyond the gate keep forward into the inclosure to cross a shallow ditch and turn right onto a cross-path. The wide way runs into the darkness of the mature trees before falling gently downhill into lighter foliage and passing over a stream. A path then bears uphill to the left; keep to the main path which levels out between trees and holly bushes.

After a small clearing, the path runs down to cross another stream. Soon the way becomes narrow and wooded again as it climbs, and here there is sometimes a gully of running water down the centre of the path. At the top, below a bank (left), step over a low barrier to go forward and turn left onto a gravel path leading away from a picnic area (used by caravanners).

On reaching a wide concrete area (part of a wartime airfield) walk half-right over the concrete to a path. Keep to the right, following a path which curves to the left. On approaching a concrete path at a bend, turn right over a shallow ditch to follow first the short side, then the long side, of an enclosure. Before the end take a surprise grass path running half-right through the heather. Traffic can normally be seen on the main A31 ahead. The grass way widens when joined by another path from the right.

Walk across a forest road to find the hidden entrance to a path which curves in a south-easterly direction. After 300yd (275m) the narrow way joins a wide green ride and runs ahead for ½ mile (.8km) beyond two lonely buildings (right). When the path narrows and then divides, take the less firm left-hand path ahead. At a junction of paths still keep ahead (whilst avoiding a stream emerging from a pipe). The way soon runs downhill and across sometimes boggy open ground before reaching a gap in the trees and the sheltered Rufus Stone marking the spot where William II died.

Turn left at the nearby road which leads to the Sir Walter Tyrrell pub. (But to avoid any seasonal traffic go ahead where the road bends, follow a rough lane and turn left by a cottage to rejoin the road at the inn.) At the end of the Sir Walter Tyrrell frontage go left off the road, turning your back on the pub. Keep to the right side of the open space (except for the small indentation) which is bounded by the Blackthorn Copse boundary. Pass under the oak trees on the gently curving (to the right) path. After ½ mile (.8km) the way runs into more trees and through the Coalmeer Gutter stream, where there is usually the odd stepping stone.

The path then climbs in a gentle curve to cross often damp ground, where there is usually a helpful plank thrown down. Bear slightly left – and not up to the King's Coalmeer Gutter Inclosure gate. Soon the way narrows and suddenly becomes concreted. Being near (summer) camping sites there are occasional camouflaged toilet blocks. To the right is the Inclosure.

Keep uphill with the concrete way and ignore all turnings. After passing a water tower, the way bends to reach a road. Cross this road and bear half-right across the open grass. Fritham, where Virginia Woolf stayed, can be seen a mile (1.6km) away to the north. On approaching another open forest road bear half-left to follow the side of the road where there is wide open ground. Just over ½ mile (.8km) ahead is Ocknell Pond car park.

99 WITCH'S·BOULDER

Time: 2 hours.

Start and finish: Outside Woodplumpton Post Office, but some motorists may prefer to turn into Plumpton Field at the side or ask the landlord at the Wheatsheaf if the car can stay in his car park outside opening hours.

Approach: Woodplumpton Post Office is in the middle of the single-street village on the B5411 north of Preston.

Attractions: Lancashire is rich in tales of witches and at Hallowe'en many people gather on Pendle Hill at midnight. Although the ten Witches of Pendle were executed in 1612, witch legends persisted in such places as Woodplumpton where a large boulder in the churchyard marks the grave of the witch Meg Shelton, whose body was said to keep rising until secured by the stone. She was alleged to live on haggis and to walk with a limp after being caught at the heel by a dog when she had temporarily turned herself into a hare. This walk circles the countryside she may have roamed in the late seventeenth century.

OS sheet: 102

Walk south to the church at the bend near the Wheatsheaf and go through the kissing-gate by the stocks and lich-gate. Walk past the partly fourteenth-century church to the witch's stone at the side of the path. Leave the church-yard by the gap in the wall to the north of the witch's tomb. Turn left for a few yards before following the curving hedge on the right through two fields to a gateway leading to a lane. Do not go through the gate; instead turn left across the field and go over a stile at a corner. Keep by the hedge (right) for a short distance and then bear left past a sometimes empty pond (left). Veer half-right down the sloping land towards a wooden footbridge – known locally as Sergeant Bridge – spanning the Woodplumpton Brook.

Beyond the stream go up right to a stile. The footpath continues ahead near the brook but, well before the end of the field, look out for a telegraph pole, then turn away from the stream and walk uphill to find a gateway over the brow. Once in the next field follow a depression on the left to the far side, then turn to keep the hedge on the left. On approaching a gateway look for a stile on the left by a water trough. Once over the stile, go over the nearby footbridge. Beyond a stile keep ahead whilst the hedge curves away to rejoin the path on the far side of the field where a large gate leads onto Rosemary Lane.

From here Stone Chimney Bridge can be seen over the fields. Go ahead down Old Rosemary Lane – a through road before the nearby Blackpool motorway was built. At the bend keep forward up an unmetalled lane

Mounting block and stocks in Woodplumpton (Leigh Hatts)

signposted 'Blackleach ½m'. After a few yards fork left onto a green way which is soon raised to give views over the hedges. When the left-hand hedge falls away and the path turns, get ready to cross an easily missed stile on the right. Walk across the centre of the field to the far top where another stile leads onto a lane. Go right for ¼ mile (.4km) to round a bend and find, usually, a sudden view of moored boats on the Lancaster Canal cut in the 1790s.

The road climbs steeply over Stone Chimney Bridge. On the far side follow the wall round to the right to find the way down to the towpath. Turn left along the towpath past a row of back gardens (where Pam and Peter's has sold teas for many years). Round the corner is Swillbrook Bridge, where the canal widens at the old changeover point for the horses on the Preston–Lancaster canal trip. Part of the stables is now a café (often open even on a winter's day when there is little navigation). The towpath runs straight on for ½ mile (.8km) and, on crossing an aqueduct over the Woodplumpton Brook, there is a view of the distant Forest of Bowland fells rising above Whinnyfield Bridge. Surprisingly, the view is less good from the bridge, especially in summer when the fully leaved trees hang over the water.

Cross the bridge and keep ahead in a south-easterly direction towards Whinnyfield Farm. At the pond go left through the farmyard and bear right to exit through a gateway onto the beginning of a metalled lane. After two bends and just over ¼ mile (.4km) there is Whinnyfield Cottage Farm and then a gate where the outward route touches the lane. Either go through the gate and over the fields back to Woodplumpton church, or continue on the lane to emerge in the village near the school. Turn left from the church or school to reach the Post Office.

Further reading:
Spiby, Cyril. *Walking in Central Lancashire* (Dalesman, 1980)

100 PLUCKLEY·GHOSTS

Time: 2½ hours including time to enjoy the view and call at a pub.

Start and finish: The Dering Arms near Pluckley station where parking is possible on the road. (Or park at the top of Forge Hill in the village to follow the same route from the top of the hill.)

Approach: The Dering Arms is reached by turning off the A28 at Bethersden, just east of Ashford, and taking the second turning on the left. Or take the B2077 south of Charing.

Attractions: The hilltop village of Pluckley is said to be Britain's most haunted village with at least twelve known ghosts. One of the three pubs, a seventeenth-century building with the ghost of a horse in the stable, is even called Ghosts. Most of the cottages on this walk have rounded windows, known as 'Dering windows', in memory of the occasion when a member of the local Dering family escaped through a rounded window from the Round-heads. The route up to the village is a gentle climb through typical 'Garden of England' orchards, whilst the downward path offers splendid views.

OS sheet: 189

Walk up the side of the Dering Arms on an enclosed track serving a row of houses with varying styles of Dering window, to enter a field and find a stile in the far left-hand corner. Go over the stile and footbridge and turn right into a vast field. Walk half-left (between telegraph poles) towards a point just to the right of an iron barn. On the far side go over a stile in the hedge and continue half-left to another stile at the end of a line of trees.

Turn right up the road which at once bends and, on reaching Dowle Cottage (before Dowle Street Farm), go left through a collapsible wire gate. Walk forward down the field, keeping to the left side of the telegraph poles, and go over a stile. Bear half-right to the top of the triangular field where the path joins the Gore Court driveway which runs downhill to join a road at a bend. Keep ahead on the road which climbs Millpond Hill to a row of cottages.

At the cottages turn right through a wooden gate to enter a field. Follow the hedge on the right and go over the low wooden fence ahead. Avoid the iron-gate entrance to Malmains by keeping towards the field corner where there is a wooden stile by a gate. Follow a wide path up the side of an orchard; the wire fence soon gives way to a line of poplars. The climb uphill is gentle but suddenly the curving path turns sharply to follow a very tall hedge to a cross-path. The metalled way to the right leads to Surrenden Dering – once home of the Dering family and still haunted by a white Lady Dering – but the walk continues ahead on another metalled drive. Just before reaching Sheer-land Farm turn left off the drive. Soon there is a view of the farmhouse and

its formal garden. The way is now straight ahead to a road – keep to the right side of a line of trees; across an open field; through a hedge gap and over a recreation ground. Turn left along the road for a few yards to the top of Forge Hill. Pluckley village square and church (haunted by a red Lady Dering) are to the left.

The walk continues down Forge Hill. Keep to the pavement on the right side to pass the newsagent's, and at Coopers Cottage go right down a narrow metalled path. Cross the stile by the wooden gate and keep ahead up a narrow field to another wooden stile by a narrow wooden gate. Here there is a magnificent view over typical Kent countryside.

Bear half-left through another narrow gate to continue in the same direction down a sloping field and reach another gate on the far side. Keep forward (towards the oasthouses in the distance) to where the field narrows to a wooden gate. Keep by the ditch (right) to cross the wide bridge, and turn left to follow the far side of the ditch. Ahead, beyond a bend, is Honey Farm, complete with the local rounded windows.

Do not go over the stile in the hedge ahead, but turn left to follow the ditch (right) for a few yards to a corner. Now bear slightly left to the far side of the field where a post can be seen in front of a house in the trees. Cross a plank bridge and go through the gap into another large field. Do not continue in the direction of the house ahead but bear quarter-right towards the left end of a line of trees where the path can be seen rising up a hill. On the far side the path crosses a ditch and climbs the hill to run along the side of a garden before meeting a road at Pluckley Thorne.

Turn right to pass the Ghosts pub and, on reaching the blue gate of Thorne House, turn left into another road. After 100yd (90m) the road runs gently downhill. Just before the bottom, turn right over a stile and walk half-left across the centre of a field to the far corner, over a footbridge and another stile. Climb half-right up a steep field with, soon, a view of three houses to the left. Cross a stile and bear half-left down another field towards the left side of the trees at Chambers' Green.

Cross a stile in the field corner and turn right along the road (ignoring any turnings) to reach the Dering Arms at the end of Dering Terrace opposite the brick church.

101 THE·PRINCE·AND· THE·MAIDEN

Time: 2½ hours.

Start and finish: Car park at the end of High Street in Narberth. Boots should be worn.

Approach: The car park at Narberth is at the north end of High Street which is reached by turning north off the A478 as it passes through Market Square.

Attractions: It was when the Normans were building a castle at Narberth that the tales from earlier times were probably first written down. One tells of Prince Pwyll and his court sitting on the castle mound, the Gorsedd Arberth, and seeing a beautiful girl ride past on a white horse. No matter how much the Prince of Dyfed pursued her around the lanes, she could never be caught. Narberth means 'a slope clothed in bushes' and today the high walls of the ruined castle are still hidden behind trees in both summer and winter. This walk follows the bridleways where the prince may have chased the apparition.

OS sheet: 158

Turn south down High Street towards the medieval centre of Narberth. Keep to the left of the tiny Town Hall, pass through sloping Market Square and into Market Street. At the castle entrance bear left round Castle Terrace to a narrow footpath running down the castle's east side. When the path turns to cross a stream (from the spring which supplied the castle), remember to look back at the ramparts. (The best view of the walls is from the churchyard which is also on high ground.)

Beyond the footbridge bear half-right to the corner and go over a fence, then a stile. Walk over the centre of the sloping field to a gateway and keep in the same direction to two farm gates near a barn. Go through the higher (and more hidden) of the two, at the start of an enclosed path which avoids the farmyard. At the end follow a downhill track along the side of the valley to join another wide track and reach the bottom. Here turn left, but where the way becomes metalled do not go ahead up to Forest Farm but veer slightly towards the parallel stream to a bridleway which continues along the valley.

After a ¼ mile (.4km), when the path bends slightly, turn sharply right up a steep curving hollowed-out bridlepath (which can become a stream in bad weather but usually dries out quickly). After another track joins from the right, the surface improves to rise and fall each side of the farm on Myrtle Hill. On reaching a row of houses there is a fine view down onto Narberth – the castle, as always, being less visible than the church.

Cross the road, leading up to Cold Blow, and leave the hamlet behind to

The Castle ruins

enter a tunnel of trees. Beyond a tiny ford by a house, the way becomes firmer. At a main road turn left and right to another bridleway. Beyond a farm there is a junction of good paths known as Pitch Cross; here turn right onto a mainly tree-lined path which, for much of its ¾ mile (1.2km) gives views through the trees to Narberth. On passing a turning there is a view across the 2 mile (3km) long Canaston Wood which lies to the west of Narberth and offers good walking opportunities. The path then becomes snug in a belt of trees until reaching a crossroads by a cottage known as Captain Style.

Do not go up the lane ahead; the tempting footpaths on the OS sheet are not as good on the ground as the bridleways. Instead turn right down the road to a white cottage at Peter's Lake Bridge. Go carefully at the bend to turn into the hidden entrance to a 'tunnel' bridleway on the left. Soon the way drops steeply to a minor metalled road; turn left past farm buildings and, further on, Valley Farm.

On reaching a house called Valley Gate turn right onto a bridlepath running below a bank. Bear left where the path divides (to avoid the ford ahead) and find, beyond the bridge, the path rising and curving eastwards. The wooded way now runs for 1½ miles (2km) to a picnic area below the car park in Narberth.

102 WITCH'S·CAULDRON

Time: 1 hour.
Start and finish: The Green at Toddington.
Approach: Toddington village is a mile (1.6km) west of Junction 12 on the M1.
Attractions: Every Shrove Tuesday morning the Toddington schoolchildren gather on Conger Hill, a 92ft (28m) diameter earthwork behind the church, and press their ears to the ground in the hope of hearing a witch cooking pancakes over her bubbling cauldron. The thirteenth-century church of St George of England overlooks a typical English green which still has every facility from a library to a fish and chip shop. Toddington is famous for its nearby M1 service station and this short walk offers a peep at the countryside around the original Toddington. Although footpaths in this part of Bedfordshire are in a notoriously bad state, those radiating from the mysterious witch's mound are still in use.
OS sheet: 166

The landmark on this walk is the church which has the finest central church tower in Bedfordshire. Inside there is a noted Perpendicular roof, a unique fifteenth-century priest's lodging and the tombs of Lady Henrietta Wentworth, the Duke of Monmouth's mistress, and Lord Wentworth who founded the Grenadier Guards.

Walk down Conger Lane at the side of the Oddfellows Arms and just beyond the entrance to Griffin Farm turn left through an iron kissing-gate to see Conger Hill. Bear half-right to pass the earthwork and go through another kissing-gate in the far corner of the field. A cart track passes a corner of Toddington cemetery before running over open ground with a view of the famous M1 service station below and the trees of Sharpenhoe in the distance. Near the bottom of the hill, the path loses its width and follows a ditch. Where the left-hand boundary becomes fenced, the public footpath leaves the side of the field to continue ahead to a stile by a road (although locals tend to stick to the fence which also leads to a roadside stile).

Opposite is the white-painted gateway of Cowbridge Farm where a footpath runs near the right side of the driveway. Just beyond the buildings (left) turn right to follow a field boundary (right). A wire fence soon gives way to a hedge as a lonely waterworks building is passed. At the end of the field go over a stream and continue in the same direction along the side of the next field to the next corner. Go over the wooden fence and turn right through double wooden gates. Follow a hedge (right) along the side of a field which is usually used as a paddock. Over to the left is the back of the Fancott Arms. At the end of the field go over a stile next to an old gate, to reach the road again.

Conger Hill at Toddington (Leigh Hatts)

Turn left to the T-junction and cross the road onto the safety of a pavement. (Turn left now only to visit the Fancott Arms.) The walk continues to the right up the gentle hill. About 100yd (90m) beyond White Hart Farm turn right by a signpost and go over a stile by a gate.

Bear half-left up the ridged field. On the way there is a view (north-east) of the fourteenth-century church tower at Harlington beyond the M1. Go through the wooden gate in the hedge on the left and walk ahead in the direction of Toddington's church tower. The way is through a gap on the far side of the field and then downhill through another gap, before climbing up to go over a high wooden stile in a hedge. Still keep in the direction of the church along the sloping field, with a long hill on the right. In the far right-hand corner go over a stile by a gate. The path then becomes enclosed as it climbs uphill to run into the end of Conger Lane at Toddington.

103 Loch·Ness·Monster

Time: 2 hours.
Start and finish: Dores Post Office. There are no parking restrictions in the village.
Approach: Dores is on B862, 6 miles (9.6km) south of Inverness and at the end of B852 which follows the east side of Loch Ness. The Post Office – a cottage – is just south of the junction on the B852.
Attractions: The very first reference to the Loch Ness Monster is in the sixth-century writings of St Columba. More recently, alleged sightings have been followed by extensive but fruitless searches. Although there are several recommended walks near or overlooking the loch, few afford a view of the water from a traffic-free path. This route, probably the best 'Nessie' walk, offers a view down most of the 24 mile (38km) loch from Dores Bay where there have been five monster sightings. The path goes behind Tor Point where there have been seven sightings, including one on the beach.
OS sheet: 26

Look for the gateway set back from the road just north of Dores inn and the phone box. Go through the small wooden gate and across a recreation ground to join a path running ahead near the north end of Loch Ness. Beyond a gate the way is open, with access to the beach. Ahead is a tip of Torr Wood, with mountains behind.

Near a holly tree the ground begins to rise, and behind there is a view of Dores nestling at the corner of the loch. Go through the wooden gate into the fir wood. Ignore the first turning to the right (the return path) and keep forward. There is no clear view of the water as the wide path bears round to the right gently getting higher, but suddenly the way is close to the loch side. For the next ¾ mile (1.2km) there are fine views through thin trees to the water and up to the (sometimes snow-capped) mountains. Lochend, at the far north-west corner of Loch Ness, comes into view as the path gradually loses height and approaches the gate to Aldourie Pier, which has been unsafe for some time. It is usually very quiet here with nearby Pier Cottage the sole building and maybe a couple of yachts anchored off the beach. Traffic can just be discerned on the main road below the mountains. In the trees behind the pier there is a large pond.

Continue on the now quite straight path, passing Pier Cottage on the left. After another ¼ mile (.4km) the path reaches a gateway. Ahead, round a corner, is Aldourie Castle, but the walk begins its return to Dores just before this gateway on the right-hand path.

The woodland path makes its way to the east side of Torr Wood with occasional views down fire gaps to the mountains and, at one point, over Loch Ness. Keep to the main track, but at a junction of three ways turn left to leave the trees on a path which is soon lined with high rhododendrons. Soon there is a view over to the mountains behind Dores, and later Dores and the loch can both be seen.

At a divide, still keep left along the top to follow the path downhill back into the wood. After a short distance turn sharply left to descend again and join the outgoing path near the gate at the edge of the trees.

Tor Point at the end of Dores Bay in Loch Ness (Leigh Hatts)

104 Dick·Whittington

Time: Allow 3 hours for looking at the shops and having lunch.
Start: The bottom of Highgate Hill near Archway Underground Station.
Finish: St Paul's Cathedral in the City where there are Underground trains running back to Archway Station.
Approach: The Whittington Stone is outside the Whittington Stone pub at the bottom of Highgate Hill and a few yards north of Archway Underground Station. Cars may be parked at the far end of Macdonald Road, just below the Stone, and almost anywhere in the street at weekends. Walkers can easily return to Highgate Hill from the City by Underground (Northern Line from Bank).
Attractions: This is the route said to have been taken by Dick Whittington and his cat when they heard the bells of London calling them back. Being in the Thames valley the walk is downhill all the way and follows the old drovers' roads leading to London. Highgate was the last overnight stop for the cattle being driven to the live meat market at Smithfield.
OS sheet: 176 (or a London street map)

The Whittington Stone, surmounted by Dick's famous cat, marks the spot where Dick Whittington is said to have heard the bells calling him to 'Turn again Whittington, thrice Lord Mayor of London'. Doubt has long been cast on this story since the hill road may not have existed in the 1360s and by the fact that as Whittington came from Gloucestershire he was on the wrong road. However, anyone who questions the legend will be shown the shrivelled cat displayed in the Whittington & Cat pub a few yards uphill from the Stone.

Walkers should turn their backs on the Stone, compare the picture on the Whittington & Stone pub sign with the view in front and then head south for the City of London. Cross the end of Junction Road (where there is a cockles, mussels and whelks fish shop) and continue ahead down Holloway Road. After a short distance there is the Church of St John the Evangelist, designed by Sir Charles Barry (of Houses of Parliament fame), and, beyond Upper Holloway (BR) Station, Whittington Park. Mercers Road, opposite the Royal Northern Hospital, reminds us that Whittington became a member of the Mercers Company.

At the major road junction ahead is the entrance to Seven Sisters Road (left) where, on its northern corner, once stood Bowman's Lodge which was the birthplace of Edward Lear who wrote the nonsense rhymes and recalled looking out towards London when the capital was lit up for the Waterloo victory celebrations.

Stay on the Holloway Road to pass Jones Bros, founded in 1867, and walk under the King's Cross–Scotland railway line by Holloway Road Underground Station. Just beyond Georges Road (right) is the noted organic butchers. Opposite the public library (left and just beyond an old cottage similar to Bowman's Lodge) is St Mary Magdalene's, built in 1814 and standing in its large churchyard. A few yards further on is the splendidly unmodernised Hope Coffee & Dining Room (right).

Bear round Highbury Corner (by Highbury Underground Station) into Upper Street – famous for its interesting shops. At the end of Compton Terrace, behind the gardens over to the left, is Canonbury Lane which leads to Canonbury Tower, the former hunting lodge of the priors of St Bartholomew's, Smithfield.

The walk continues down Upper Street passing St Mary's where there was a church in Whittington's time. The right-hand pavement leads onto The Long Causeway – a raised path which avoided the muddy road often made worse by the cattle being walked to Smithfield. At The Angel crossroads keep forward into St John Street and pass the Old Red Lion (left) dating from 1415. The road bends for ½ mile (0.75km) until there is a sudden view of St Paul's Cathedral.

Beyond the Clerkenwell Road crossroads is the easily missed Passing Alley leading to the only remaining gated street in London. The walk continues ahead as St John Street widens (to accommodate waiting cattle) and through the Smithfield Market buildings to reach St Bartholomew's Priory and St Bart's Hospital which Whittington helped to rebuild with his fortune.

Walk ahead along Little Britain, which also pre-dates Whittington, to reach St Paul's Cathedral. St Paul's Underground Station is at the north-east corner of St Paul's Churchyard. (Change at Bank for the Northern Line and Archway.)

Further reading:
Freeman, Danny. *Hughie's Hikes* (London Borough of Islington, 1984)

THE·CONTRIBUTORS

BOB BRASH *Writers and Artists*
Bob Brash was born at Bolton, Lancashire, in 1924 and did his first real walking with his father in the Lake District. He served with 14th Army Signals during the war and, back at Trinity College, Cambridge, he achieved a First in History and passed into the Foreign Service. He married Barbara Clarke during his first posting, to Jakarta, Indonesia and they have four children. He served at various posts at home, in Europe and South-east Asia, ending his career as British Ambassador at Jakarta. Walking was always a particular pleasure and he managed to fit in three treks to the Himalayas. On his retirement back in Woking, Surrey, in 1984 he became a member of the Guildford Ramblers and an active explorer of the national long-distance footpaths.

MIKE DUNN *Moorlands and Hills, Woods and Forests*
Mike Dunn is a planning researcher who has specialised in landscape, recreation and rural housing. He is married, has two daughters, and lives in Penarth. He is a former director of the Campaign for Real Ale, and his interest in the brewing industry is reflected by two books, *The Penguin Guide to Real Draught Beer* (1979) and *Local Brew* (1986), and his continuing membership of CAMRA's Economics, Industry and Government committee. He has a particular interest in the landscape and rural economy of the Lake District and has walked the Lakeland fells extensively, producing *Walking through the Lake District* in 1984. His most recent book on walking, describing a selection of prehistoric ridgeways, Roman roads, Saxon herepaths and medieval drove routes and saltways, is *Walking Ancient Trackways* (1986).

LEIGH HATTS *Myths and Legends, Coasts*
Leigh Hatts, the South-east correspondent for *The Great Outdoors* magazine, compiled several editions of the London Transport *Country Walks* book before writing *Country Walks Around London*, featuring both inner London and the Home Counties. His first walks book was devoted to the New Forest near his home town of Bournemouth where he pioneered the twenty-mile Bournemouth Coast Path which closes the gap between the South-west Way and the Solent Way.

RONALD RUSSELL *Rivers and Valleys, Canal Walks*
Ronald Russell, following wartime service in the Royal Air Force and a degree in English at Oxford, entered the teaching profession from which he has recently retired. He has been involved with waterways for more than twenty years, having been founder chairman of the Cambridge branch of the Inland

Waterways Association and chairman of the 1973 National Rally of Boats. His first book, *Lost Canals of England and Wales*, a descriptive study of eighty derelict and abandoned navigations, was published in 1971, and an expanded and updated version appeared in 1982 under the title *Lost Canals and Waterways of Britain*. Among his other books are *Waterside Pubs*, *Rivers*, *Discovering Lost Canals*, and he is co-author of *Canals of Eastern England* in the 'Canals of the British Isles' series. He edited *Walking Canals*, a collection of sixteen towing-path walks which was published in 1984. He also lectures on waterway subjects and is a member of the Railway and Canal Historical Society.

NIGEL WILLIS *Walking Old Railway Lines*
Nigel Willis spent much of his childhood in the countryside of Essex and Leicestershire. The magic of railways was discovered by him more than 30 years ago, shortly before the modernisation plan when there was still a network of branch lines. He has a particular interest in closed railways and their history. He was a founder member of the Railway Ramblers and is vice-chairman and magazine editor. He was assisted by other members of the Railway Ramblers: Jeff Vinter, Stephen Gray, Michael Ellison, Maurice Blencowe, Rhona White, Chris Wright and team and Geoffrey Sargeant.

JOHN WHATMORE *Downlands*
John Whatmore, the General Editor of this book, is a professional journalist working as a sub-editor on the Foreign Desk of the Guardian. He was born in Birmingham but has lived and walked in many parts of England, and spent eight years in Rhodesia, now Zimbabwe. Outside England his favourite country for walking is France, but he has also trekked in remote parts of Turkey and has walked part of the Appalachian Trail in Virginia. Among his other interests is cycling and he is the author of *The CTC Book of Cycling* and *The CTC Book of Cycletouring*.

GEOFFREY WRIGHT *Mountains, City Heritage, Lowlands*
Geoffrey Wright was born and spent the first twenty-five years of his life in North-east England. After service in the Royal Air Force he trained as a teacher at Durham University and later taught for twenty-six years at Bradford-on-Avon, Wiltshire. He retired early, in 1976, to concentrate on his first love, writing and photography. Having earlier bought and restored an eighteenth-century farmhouse in Wensleydale, he moved there with his wife in 1976. His recent books include *Roads and Trackways in the Yorkshire Dales*, *Stone Villages of Britain*, *View of Northumbria*, *View of Wessex*, *The Yorkshire Dales*, *Yorkshire, the East Riding*, as well as *Discovering Avon*, *Discovering Epitaphs* and *Discovering Abbeys and Priories*. He has recently moved to Shropshire where he plans to continue walking and lecturing. His eldest son, Peter, contributed the Scottish mountains to the chapter on Mountain Walks together with the Somerset Levels in the Lowland Walks. Peter, who is the author of *Mendip Rambles*, now has a croft in the north of Scotland.